PRAISE FOR *ARMSTRONG'S H*
OF LEARNING AND DEVELO

This book is both thought-provoking and academically astute; it explores various emerging areas within learning and development concisely and clearly. Armstrong is able to bring theory to life, helping readers to develop their own understanding of critical HR practice.
Rebecca Huws, Human Resources Lecture and CIPD Programme Lead, Cardiff and
Vale College

Armstrong's Handbook of Learning and Development offers an excellent overview of topics related to learning, knowledge and skills formation in the context of organizational behaviour. A valuable resource for management students and practitioners.
Giorgos Gouzoulis, Assistant Professor in HRM and Future of Work, School of
Management, University of Bristol

This new book on Learning and Development is ideal for my module on this topic. I am delighted to see that Armstrong's book includes a whole chapter on Individual learning, including self-directed and lifelong learning. I particularly liked the link of chapters to each other, and their relevance to current organizational learning and practices. I will certainly add it to my reading list.
Dr Angela Mansi, Senior Lecturer, MA in Human Resource Management, Westminster
Business School, University of Westminster

Armstrong's Handbook of Learning and Development

A guide to the theory and practice of L&D

Michael Armstrong

KoganPage

First published in Great Britain and the United States in 2022 by Kogan Page Limited

2nd Floor, 45 Gee Street	8 W 38th Street, Suite 902	4737/23 Ansari Road
London	New York, NY 10018	Daryaganj
EC1V 3RS	USA	New Delhi 110002
United Kingdom		India

www.koganpage.com

Kogan Page books are printed on paper from sustainable forests.

© Michael Armstrong, 2022

The right of Michael Armstrong to be identified as the author of this work has been asserted by him in accordance with the Copyright, Designs and Patents Act 1988.

ISBNs

Hardback	978 1 3986 0190 1
Paperback	978 1 3986 0188 8
Ebook	978 1 3986 0189 5

British Library Cataloguing-in-Publication Data

A CIP record for this book is available from the British Library.

Library of Congress Cataloging-in-Publication Data
Names: Armstrong, Michael, 1928-author.
Title: Armstrong's handbook of learning and development: a guide to the
   theory and practice of L&D / Michael Armstrong.
Description: London; New York, NY: Kogan Page Inc, 2022. | Includes
   bibliographical references and index.
Identifiers: LCCN 2021041927 (print) | LCCN 2021041928 (ebook) | ISBN
   9781398601888 (paperback) | ISBN 9781398601901 (hardback) | ISBN
   9781398601895 (ebook)
Subjects: LCSH: Personnel management–Study and teaching. |
   Management–Study and teaching. | Leadership–Study and teaching.
Classification: LCC HF5549.15. A75 2022 (print) | LCC HF5549.15 (ebook) |
   DDC 658.30076–dc23
LC record available at https://lccn.loc.gov/2021041927
LC ebook record available at https://lccn.loc.gov/2021041928

Typeset by Integra Software Services, Pondicherry
Print production managed by Jellyfish
Printed and bound by CPI Group (UK) Ltd, Croydon CR0 4YY

To Clarissa Rose Adie Slade
with love

CONTENTS

Introduction

Learning and development is concerned with ensuring that the organization has the people with the capabilities (knowledge, skills and behaviours) it needs. To do this it:

- creates and maintains a learning culture, one in which learning is recognized by top management, line managers and employees generally as an essential organizational process to which they are committed and in which they engage continuously;

- formulates and implements a learning and development strategy that supports the achievement of the organization's strategic goals, defines the priorities that should be attached to different aspects of learning and development and spells out how these should be aligned with the corporate or business strategy and integrated with each other;

- ensures that L&D plans and outputs are underpinned by evidence, not just good ideas, and are informed by metrics not guesses;

- facilitates 'learning in-the-flow of work', that is, the learning acquired when actually carrying out work;

- adopts a learner-centric perspective – the belief that development activities should concentrate on the needs of the learner and that learners should be the given the maximum amount of opportunity and support to manage their own learning;

- provides learning and development opportunities as required in the shape of formal learning events and programmes and digital learning.

The aim of this book is to explore and describe how each of these purposes can be realized. A route map of the book is provided in Figure 0.1. The logic underpinning this plan is described below.

FIGURE 0.1   Handbook of learning and development route map

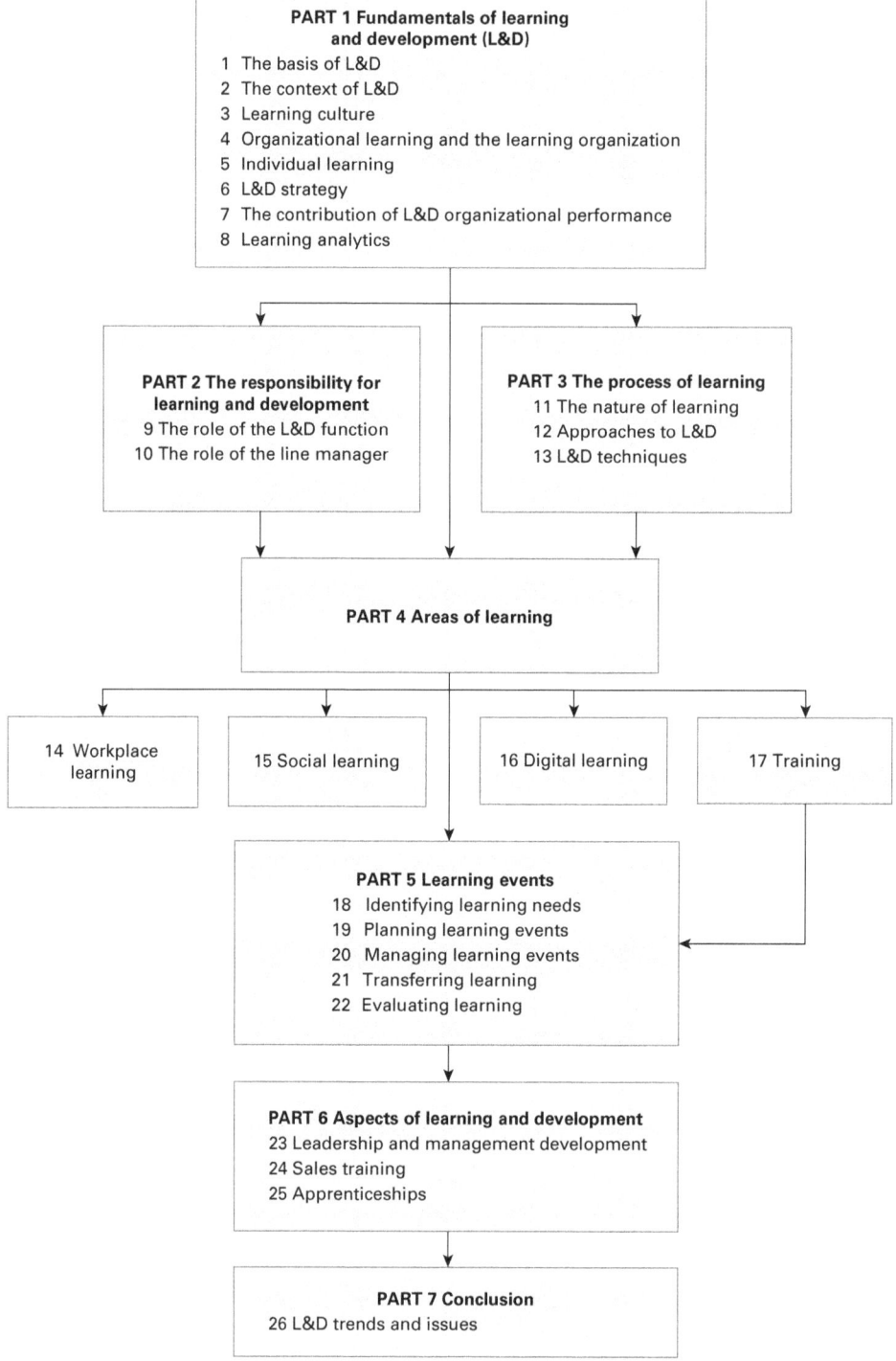

- **Part One** The starting point should be an understanding of the fundamentals of learning and development (L&D) – its meaning, the context in which it operates, the importance of learning culture and the practice of organizational and individual learning. These aspects are considered in the first five chapters of this part. Two recurring themes in the book are the need to align L&D strategy with business and corporate strategy and the role of L&D in enhancing organizational performance. A third theme is the need for evidence-based L&D which uses learning analytics to provide the data required. These themes are explored in the last three chapters of Part One.

- **Part Two** Learning and development policy and practice is the responsibility of the learning and development function and its L&D professionals, individual learners, and line managers. To paraphrase Professor Purcell and his colleagues (2003), it is the latter who bring L&D policy to life. It is necessary to understand these roles before embarking on the more detailed consideration of the policies and process of L&D covered in the rest of the book. The roles of the learning function and line managers are described in Chapters 9 and 10 respectively. That of individual learners was dealt with in Part One (Chapter 5).

- **Part Three** Learning is a complex process and there are many theories explaining what it means and many ways of making it happen. To put these into effect it is necessary to understand the nature of learning – how people learn (Chapter 11). This provides the basis for applying the approaches to learning covered in Chapter 12. 'Approaches' to learning are defined as general ways in which learning and development activities happen, for example through formal or informal learning, as distinct from specific techniques such as coaching or instruction that are dealt with in Chapter 13.

- **Part Four** There are four areas in which learning takes place by putting into practice the approaches and techniques described in Part Three. These are: the workplace, social learning, digital learning, and training (Chapters 14–17).

- **Part Five** Training was treated in Part Four as one aspect of learning amongst others. But formal learning events still loom large as a major L&D activity. The CIPD (2020) noted that training in the shape of face-to-face delivery in courses or 'interventions' is still dominant in L&D practice, contributing to the majority of learning provided (60–100 per cent) in 44 per cent of organizations. This is in spite of the increased emphasis on workplace and digital learning. The sequence of training for the delivery of such events was defined at the end of Chapter 17 as consisting of five activities: identifying learning needs, planning learning events, managing learning events, ensuring the transfer of learning and the evaluation of learning. These activities are covered in this part (Chapters 18–22).

- **Part Six**   This part (Chapters 23–25) deals with a group of important L&D activities not covered earlier, namely: leadership and management development, sales training and apprenticeships.
- **Part Seven**   Chapter 26 in this part sums up the L&D trends, issues and themes that have been explored in earlier parts of the book.

Online resources

The online resources provided with this book consist of:

- manuals for lecturers and students including session notes, questions and case studies;
- an L&D bibliography;
- an L&D glossary;
- information on how the text is aligned with the provisions of the professional standards for learning and development issued by the Chartered Institute of Personnel and Development in 2018.

References

Chartered Institute of Personnel and Development (2020) *Learning and Skills at Work 2020*, CIPD, London

Purcell, J, Kinnie, K, Hutchinson, Rayton, B and Swart, J (2003) *Understanding the People and Performance Link: Unlocking the black box*, CIPD, London

PART ONE

Fundamentals of learning and development

01

The basis of learning and development

Introduction

This chapter covers:

- the nature, history, elements and components of learning and development (L&D);
- the relationships of L&D with other aspects of people management (human resource management);
- the ethical dimension of learning and development; and
- the state of L&D as revealed by four recent surveys.

Learning and development defined

The purpose of learning and development (L&D) is to ensure that organizations have the knowledgeable, skilled and engaged people they need to achieve their goals, now and in the future. It means developing the capabilities of employees so that they can carry out their work effectively and progress in their careers. Capability is defined as a combination of knowledge, skills and behaviours – what people know, understand and do.

This purpose is achieved by learning through experience and by social contacts, coaching, mentoring, guidance from line managers, self-directed learning and formal training. It was stated by Flanagan (2015: 34) that: 'The ultimate aim of L&D is to lead people to personal growth.' This is true, but its fundamental aim is to improve individual, group and organizational effectiveness by developing the organization's skills base which consists of the people in the organization who have the capabilities it requires.

To achieve this aim L&D is concerned with organizational learning (see Chapter 4). But it is mainly about individual learning (Chapter 5) as described by Birdi *et al* (2007: 266):

> Individual learning can be facilitated by a number of practices within organizations. The two most common types of activities are: (1) on-the-job training, where employees new to a job are paired up with more experienced employees for observation, practice and feedback on tasks as they are carried out in the job; and (2) off-the-job, classroom-based training, where combinations of lecturing, discussion and practical exercises are used. Both of these types of training tend to be task-specific and tied to the incumbent's current job requirements. Broader educational opportunities can also be used to widen individuals' understanding. These include more knowledge-based activities, such as provision of open learning centres, e-learning, funding of college courses or employee development schemes.

Learning and development is also concerned with fostering and managing the learning environment – the surroundings in an organization in which learning takes place. This can be described as a learning ecosystem which consists of interconnected individuals and communities of people who work and learn together, bearing in mind the guidance provided by a learning philosophy and within the context of a learning culture.

Learning and development philosophy

A learning and development philosophy consists of the overarching beliefs, values and guiding principles adopted by an organization to ensure that learning takes place in the interests of all the organization's stakeholders – top management, line managers, employees and learning and development professionals. This philosophy may be implicit or, preferably, explicit. It will emphasize the importance attached to learning as a significant part of the organization's strategies for development and growth, even survival. It will govern the development of a learning culture by expressing the organization's commitment to the continuous development of employees in order to maximize their contribution and to give them the opportunity to enhance their knowledge and skills, realize their potential, advance their careers and increase their employability, both within and outside the organization. It will stress the significance of organizational learning and knowledge management while recognizing the benefits of learner-centric policies that focus on individual learning needs and on self-directed learning, the process by which individuals identify and satisfy their own learning needs with help and guidance from managers or learning and development professionals as required.

Learning culture

A learning culture embeds learning into the way organizations do things. It will be based on a learning philosophy and is the environment in which that philosophy will be put into effect. The difference between a learning philosophy and a learning culture is that the former is about beliefs while the latter is about behaviours. A learning culture provides the framework for learning and development policy and practice and its creation is a priority for strategic L&D

Learning and development: A brief history

In the past, and to a degree, still in the present, learning and development was all about face-to-face (F2F) training, usually in formal learning events or training centres. The advent of e-learning in the 1990s and its rapid development since then has meant that computer-assisted or online learning is playing a more important part although this often means supplementing rather than replacing F2F training. Since then, the move has been to extend the use of digital learning and the opportunities it provides for remote (distance) learning. Increasing use is being made of smartphones and social media. These have changed the way people interact with learning content and made it relatively easy to use video, short-form content (brief and single subject) and mobile apps to provide learning opportunities and support.

'Training' became 'human resource development' and this changed to 'learning and development', partly in revulsion to the term human resources but also to emphasise that it is learning that counts,

Perhaps the most significant development has been the attention paid to learning through experience and to social learning. This has been prompted by the 70:20:10 concept which suggests that 70 per cent of learning happens through workplace experience, 20 per cent from social interaction (social or collaborative learning) and only 10 per cent from training in the shape of formal instruction. These proportions need not be taken too literally but the message is clear: experience is what matters most, followed by working with other people. Formal training provided by the organization has its uses but is no longer all-important.

The 'learning in-the-flow of work' notion has recently come to the fore as an important aspect of experiential learning in the workplace. The phrase was coined by Josh Bersin and refers to the learning that happens while people are actually working – 'learning as you go'. He wrote (2018: 10) that: 'What we ultimately want to do is embed learning into the platform in which people work'. The concept is discussed more fully in Chapter 12.

The elements of learning and development

The elements of learning and development are:

- *Learning* – the process by which a person acquires and develops capabilities in the shape of knowledge, skills and behaviours. It involves the modification of behaviour through experience as well as more formal methods of providing people with learning opportunities within or outside the workplace. A learning experience can be structured (eg formal events, e-learning, coaching) or unstructured (eg experiential and self-directed learning).

- *Development* – the realization or growth of a person's capabilities and potential through the provision of learning and educational experiences.

- *Training* – the systematic application of formal processes to help people to acquire the knowledge and skills necessary for them to perform their jobs satisfactorily. A training event or intervention is a course in which face-to-face learning takes place, ie by direct training or teaching from a trainer or lecturer, usually in locations outside the workplace (off-the-job training). A training programme is a planned sequence of training events or learning experiences or a combined sequence of both events and experience.

- *Education* – the expansion of the knowledge, values and understanding required for all aspects of life rather than a knowledge or skill in only a limited area of activity.

The components of learning and development

With two exceptions, these components are described in later chapters of this book. The exceptions are L&D policies and L&D processes which are considered below.

FIGURE 1.1   The components of learning and development

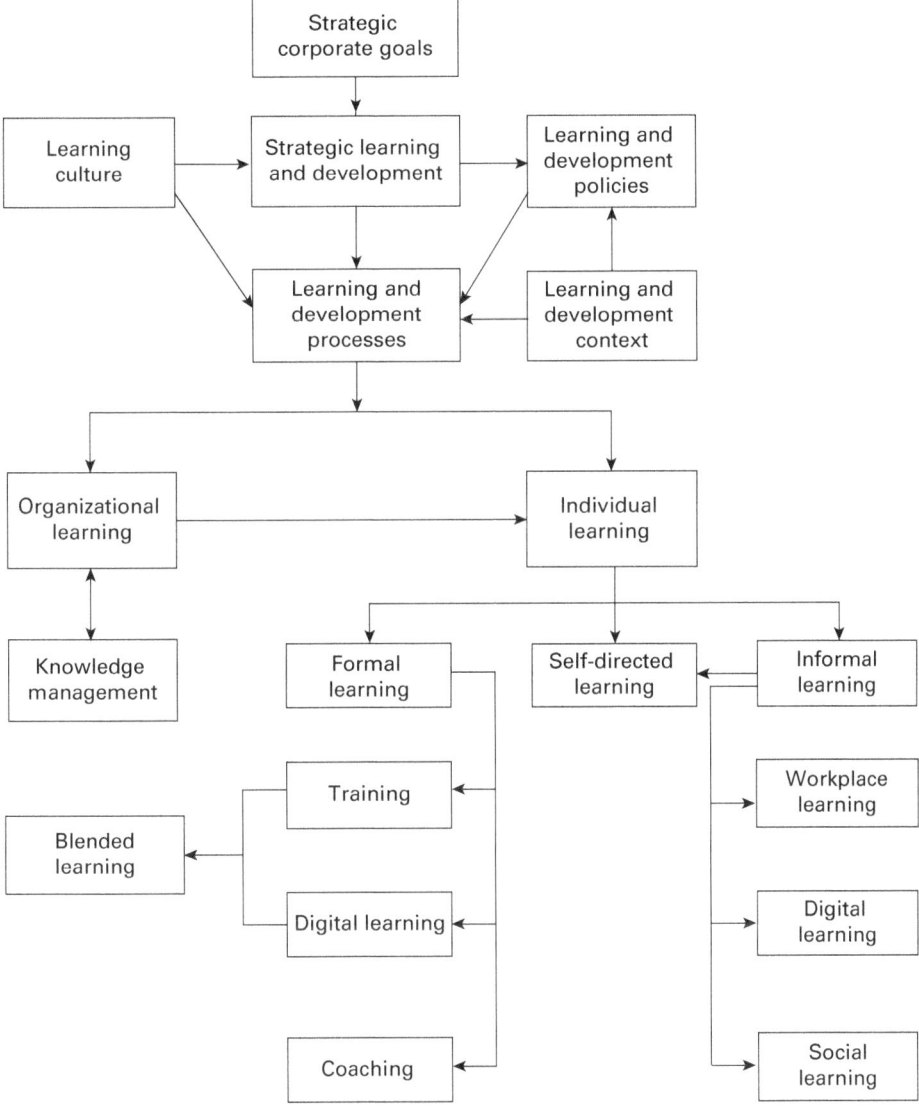

Learning and development policies

Learning and development policies provide guidelines on planning and conducting L&D activities. They cover how, where and when learning takes place, who is involved – as learners or providers of learning, and what factors should be taken into account when designing and delivering learning events and programmes. The policies should reflect a concern with ethical considerations by stating that gender, ethnicity, sexual orientation or age should not be a barrier to learning opportunities from which everyone can benefit. They should emphasize the importance of dealing with diversity and inclusion issues.

Learning and development processes

Learning and development processes are the activities and behaviours which contribute to the enhancement of the knowledge, skills and abilities (KSAs) required to carry out work effectively and develop potential for future success. They are determined by the learning and development strategy adopted in order to further the achievement of the organization's objectives and are influenced by its learning and development philosophy and policies, its learning culture and its context.

The basic processes are organizational learning and individual learning. Organizational learning is the development and acquisition in organizations of knowledge, understanding, insights, techniques and practices in order to improve organizational effectiveness. Individual learning is concerned with the capabilities that individuals need to do their jobs and advance their careers. It takes place formally and informally. Formal learning is carried out by means of face-to-face training and coaching or digital technology in the form of e-learning or a virtual learning environment. These approaches can be blended to maximize their impact. Informal learning occurs mainly in the workplace while people actually carry out their work ('learning in-the-flow of work') and get help from other workers (social learning). It can be supplemented by some varieties of digital learning, for example the use of social media, enterprise social networks and smartphones. Most learning happens as a result of these processes and by self-directed activities rather than by formal training.

Relationships between L&D and other people management activities

Learning and development take place within the framework of the people management policies and practices of an organization. These provide advice and services on all aspects of the employment relationship to ensure that the organization has the skilled, engaged and productive people it needs. L&D activities are closely linked to the people management activities of resourcing, organization design and development, knowledge management, talent management and performance management. This underlines the importance of aligning L&D strategy with people management strategy and provides some support to the contention that L&D should be regarded as an aspect, albeit a key aspect, of people management. One of the important aims of strategic L&D is to integrate its activities with these related people management activities and so achieve what is called 'horizontal fit'.

People management

People management is about how people are employed, managed and developed in organizations. People management philosophy is underpinned by the resource-based-view (Barney, 1991, 1995) that it is the range of resources in an organization, including its human resources, that produces its unique character and creates competitive advantage. People (HR) management delivers added value and helps to achieve sustainable competitive advantage through the strategic development of the organization's rare, hard to imitate and hard to substitute human resources. Learning and development plays a major part in this.

The philosophy of people management is based on two interrelated principles. The first is that a multi-stakeholder approach should be adopted, one that aims to achieve a balance between the needs of employees and those of the other stakeholders, ie people who have a legitimate interest in an organization and what it does. The stake that employees have in their organization is just as important as the stake held by owners and senior management. The attention given to the interests of employees has to be commensurate with the attention given to the interests of the business. In their seminal book on HRM, Beer *et al* (1984: 15) observed that:

> HRM policies are and indeed should be influenced by the interests of various stakeholders: shareholders, management, employees, community and government. Unless these policies are influenced by all stakeholders, the enterprise will fail to meet the needs of these stakeholders in the long run and it will fail as an institution.

In 2015, Michael Beer and colleagues reviewed the state of this neglected perspective after 31 years. They stated that 'we need to take a wider, more contextual, more multi-layered approach founded on the long-term needs of all relevant stakeholders' (page 427). They also argued that: 'Fundamental to a multi-stakeholder approach must be the creation, maintenance, and development of a culture of trust among the different stakeholders. Considering HRM as a social system, in contrast to the dominant individual perspective, puts the relationships between stakeholders at the centre of our studies' (page 432). The second principle is that employees should be treated ethically as discussed later in this chapter.

People resourcing

People resourcing, often called 'employee resourcing' or simply 'resourcing', is the term used to describe the employment activities of workforce planning, recruitment and selection and talent management. Resourcing is a vital organizational activity that recognizes that the strategic capability of a firm depends on its resource capability in the shape of people (the resource-based view).

People resourcing is not just about recruitment and selection. It deals with any means available to meet the firm's need for certain skills and behaviours. Learning and development has an important part to play in this. Recruitment activities bring in people from outside the organization when they are not available within in spite of L&D efforts. A strategy to ensure the organization has the talented people it needs (a talent management strategy) may start with recruitment and selection but would extend into learning and development to enhance abilities and skills and modify behaviours. It also extends into succession planning. 'Make or buy' policies may be formulated to determine the extent to which people should be developed within the organization or brought in from outside. Performance management processes can be used to identify development needs (skills and behaviours) and motivate people to make the most effective use of their abilities. Competency frameworks and profiles are prepared to define the skills and behaviours required and are used in selection, employee development and employee reward processes. Efforts can be made to develop an attractive employer brand (the image of the organization as an employer) so as to enhance the employee experience. The aim should be to develop a reinforcing bundle of practices along these lines.

Organization and job design

Organization design decides on the shape and operation of the structure of an enterprise – the framework for getting things done. It considers how the responsibility for carrying out the overall task should be allocated to individuals and groups of people and how the relationships between them function. It will influence job design – the process of specifying the content of jobs in terms of what job holders are expected to do and how they are expected to do it. Organization design and job design determine the type of skills an organization needs and are therefore important considerations when formulating L&D strategies and planning L&D activities.

Organization design is not, as is sometimes assumed, an approach based on absolute principles that produces an inevitable 'best' result. As Charles Handy (1985: 13) observed: 'The multiplicity of variables impinging on any one organizational situation is so great that data on all of them sufficient to predict the precise outcome of that multiple relationship would never in practice be forthcoming.' And Henry Minzberg (1991: 332) pointed out that: 'A great many problems in organizational design stem from the assumption that organizations are all alike; mere collections of component parts to which elements of structure can be added and deleted at will, a sort of organizational bazaar.'

There is never one best way of organizing anything. There is always a choice. It is necessary to bear in mind that structural requirements in organizations or organizational units will vary widely according to what they are there to do and the activities they have to carry out. That is why there are no fixed principles. It all depends. Burns and Stalker (1961) established in their study of electronic companies in Scotland that in stable conditions a highly structured or 'mechanistic' organization will emerge that has specialized functions, clearly defined jobs, strict administrative routines and a hierarchical system of exercising control. However, when the environment is volatile, a rigid system of ranks and routine will inhibit the organization's speed and sensitivity of response. In these circumstances the structure is, or should be, 'organic' in the sense that, in accordance with contingency theory, it is a function of the situation in which the enterprise finds itself rather than conforming to any predetermined and rigid view of how it should operate. These sort of differences will make a significant impact on learning and development requirements and need to be taken into account.

L&D professionals should be aware of the importance of the associated process of job design which should aim to create good quality jobs. The CIPD (2018a: 18) stated that: 'Good-quality jobs allow individuals to develop and deploy their skills and offer some degree of challenge commensurate to the demands of the job and the capabilities of the individual.' Advice on how that should be done can be provided by L&D.

Organization development

Organization development (OD) is a systematic approach to improving organizational capability, which is concerned with process – how things get done. The original purpose of OD programmes was to increase the effectiveness of the various processes that take place in organizations relating to the ways in which people work together. Its philosophy was that of humanism – the belief that human factors are paramount in the study of organizational behaviour. Increasingly, however, the focus of organization development is on any means available to increase organizational capability – the capacity of an organization to function effectively in order to achieve its purpose.

The CIPD (2018b) described the aims and characteristics of organization development as follows:

1 It focuses on maximising the value gained from the organization's resources.

2 It is concerned with an organization's strategy, goals and core purpose.

3 It involves applying behavioural science knowledge and practice, such as leadership, group dynamics and work design to enable the organization to achieve competitive advantage through its people.

4 It is related to change management in the sense that many developments are implemented using change management practices, but also, because it is a planned, ongoing, systematic change activity that aims to institutionalise continual improvement within organizations.

In its earlier days, organization development focused almost entirely on social interactions such as team building. It tended to be the preserve of external process consultants with behavioural science backgrounds. It is now more concerned with any aspect of how enterprises function and has become a territory largely inhabited by business-oriented people based in the organization. They include L&D professionals who are there not just because they know about learning and development but because they have business acumen, are familiar with how businesses operate and where L&D fits in, and understand the factors that influence the effectiveness of an organization, especially the capabilities of the people working there. They function as performance consultants and can play a major part in helping to plan and deliver what are called in OD speak 'interventions' (a term that has entered the L&D vocabulary) such as those listed in Table 1.1.

TABLE 1.1   Organization development interventions

Organization development intervention	Description	Objective
Business model innovation	The process followed by an organization to develop a new business model or change an existing one.	To obtain insight into the business issues facing the organization, leading to plans for practical interventions that address those issues.
Change management	The process of planning and introducing change systematically.	To achieve the smooth implementation of change.
Culture change	The process of changing the organization's culture with regard to its values, norms and beliefs.	To improve the ability of an organization to achieve its goals by making effective use of the resources available to it.
High-performance working	Developing work systems, processes, practices and policies to enable employees to perform to their full potential.	To impact on the performance of the organization through its people in such areas as productivity, quality, levels of customer service, growth and profits.
Lean manufacturing	A process improvement methodology that focuses on continuous improvement, reducing waste and ensuring the flow of production.	To deliver value to customers.
Smart working	An approach to organizing work that through a combination of flexibility, autonomy and collaboration, in parallel with optimizing tools and working environments for employees.	To drive greater efficiency and effectiveness in achieving job outcomes.
Agile working	Providing for flexibility in management practices and in the use of resources and for adaptability to change.	To support rapid decision-making and execution
Team building	Using interactive skills training techniques to improve the ways in which people in teams work together.	To increase group cohesion, mutual support and cooperation.

Knowledge management

Knowledge management is concerned with storing and sharing the wisdom, understanding and expertise accumulated in an organization about its processes, techniques and operations. It gets knowledge from those who have it to those who need it. Knowledge management plays a key role in organizational learning by identifying, storing and disseminating relevant information. It promotes individual learning by sharing organization-specific knowledge – linking people with people and then linking them to information so that they learn from recorded experiences. This involves curation – informing learners, especially those managing their own learning, of the internal sources of relevant information available in databanks, manuals, policy documents, the proceedings of communities of interest and learning material such as handouts, PowerPoint slides and videos used in training events. Knowledge management deals with both stocks and flows of knowledge. Stocks include expertise and encoded knowledge in databanks. Flows represent the ways in which knowledge is transferred from people to people or from people to a knowledge databank.

Talent management

Talent management aims to ensure that the organization has the capable and well-qualified people it needs to attain its goals. It involves the systematic attraction, retention, identification and, importantly, development of individuals who are of particular value to a business. A model of talent management is shown in Figure 1.2.

The development of talent is clearly a major concern of L&D. But talent identification is equally important. This is mainly the responsibility of line managers and many of them will need guidance on how to do this which can be provided by L&D.

FIGURE 1.2   The process of talent management

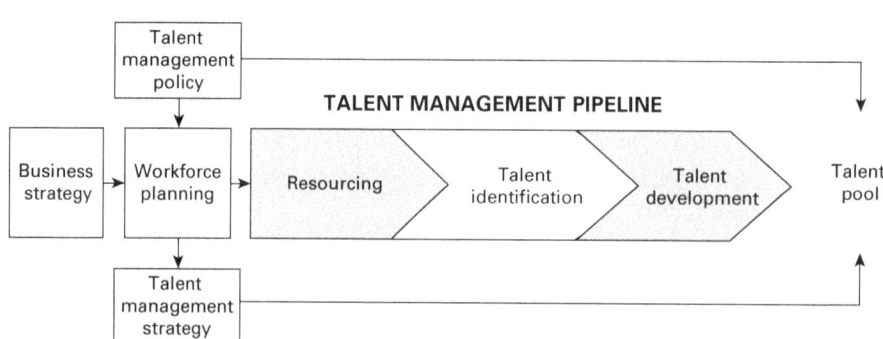

Performance management

Performance management is a systematic and continuous process for improving organizational performance by developing the performance of individuals and teams. It operates as a cycle as shown in Figure 1.3.

The focus in current approaches to performance management is on development rather than simply appraising performance. It provides the means to identify learning and development needs on the basis of a joint analysis of performance in terms of outcomes and behaviour. Planning how to satisfy those needs is an important part of performance management. And performance management provides the opportunity to review how well the plans have been implemented. It is often treated as a formal system but the recent trend is to see it as a natural process of management that takes place as part of everyday working life rather than in the artificial setting of an annual appraisal.

Some managers are naturally good at managing performance because they are effective managers and have learned to be so over the years from experience, observing other successful managers and taking part in more formal

FIGURE 1.3 The performance management cycle

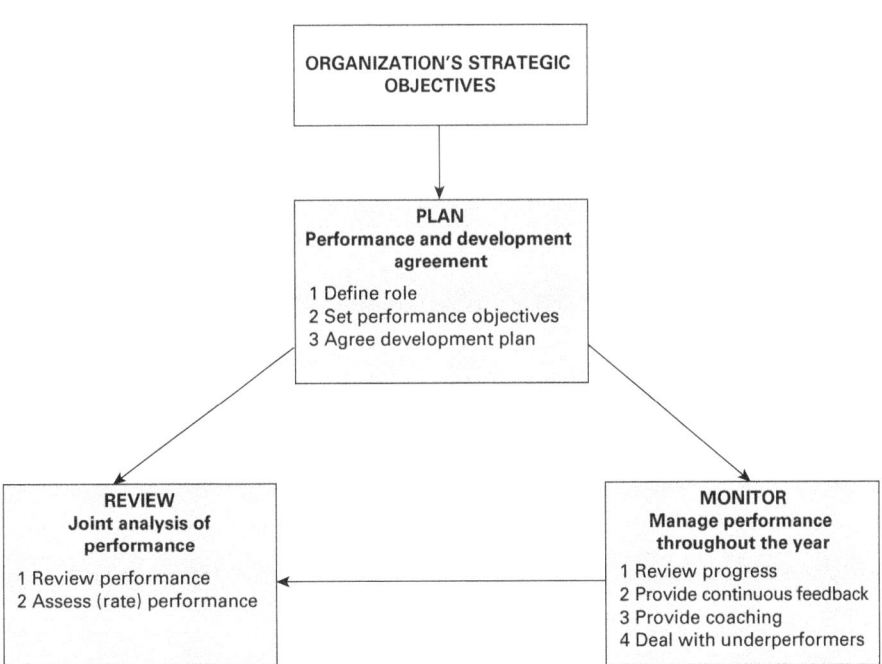

coaching and mentoring procedures. However, these skills are not shared amongst all managers and steps need to be taken by L&D to develop the essential skills, namely:

- defining roles and setting objectives;
- conducting performance and development discussions;
- giving feedback;
- handling challenging conversations.

The learning required will not be achieved by a 'sheep-dip' process of half-day training sessions for all concerned. It is far better to cater for it by an extended leadership development programme, an important part of which should be conducted through mentoring and coaching. Experienced managers who have demonstrated that they have the skills required and are keen to help can usefully act as mentors.

The Institute for Employment Studies published in 2013 the results of interesting research by Dilys Robinson on how managers who had achieved high levels of engagement in their teams went about it. Here is what four of those managers told her about how they managed performance:

- 'So, the key for me is just one-to-one time, and they know what they're aiming for, and we talk about it regularly. So it never really gets to the situation where there's like a really great big formal sit-down to say let's review everything you've done.'

- 'I think it's regular dialogue… at least once a fortnight for an extended period of time, just one to one and just about them and the work they're doing and what's going on… just so that I understand what they're doing and so I can give a bit of a steer or give them a bit of coaching if they need some coaching; help them if they want some help and support.'

- 'Every week I have a one-to-one session with people who work for me. And it's half an hour; it's the opportunity to talk things over with people. I say to people it's your time with me. But, to be honest, it's not just that; it's me getting to talk to them.'

- 'This organization has a very structured performance management framework, as you would imagine from a big company. I try and avoid using it unless I have to, I would rather try and develop the personal relationship with someone, to understand their issue and try and improve their performance by working with them, rather than going through procedural ways of managing performance.'

FIGURE 1.4   The Halifax Bank performance management model

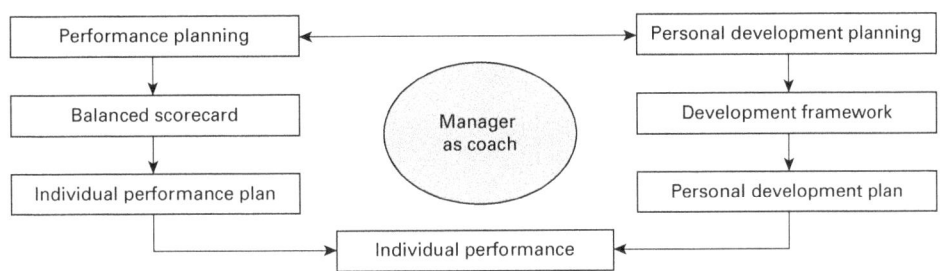

L&D has the important responsibility of helping to develop managers who manage performance like these.

The emphasis placed by Halifax Bank on development as a key aspect of performance management and the role of the manager as a coach is demonstrated in the model of their performance management system shown in Figure 1.4.

The ethical dimension

Ethics is concerned with making decisions and judgements about what is the right course of action to take. It embraces concepts in the shape of equity, justice and fair dealing that affect and guide behaviour. An ethical approach to learning and development is required in order to ensure that everyone involved in learning activities is treated in accordance with these concepts. John Rawls (1973: 183) wrote that: 'We must treat persons solely as ends and not in any way as means.' This means that while learning and development practices are expected to further the aims of the organization they should also take account of the needs of employees for fulfilment at work and for the opportunity to develop their knowledge, skills and abilities (this is an aspect of the learner-centric approach).

Winstanley and Woodall (2000: 7) commented that: 'HR professionals have to raise awareness of ethical issues, promote ethical behaviour, disseminate ethical practices widely among line managers, communicate codes of ethical conduct, ensure people learn about what constitutes ethical behaviours, manage compliance and monitor arrangements.' This applies equally to L&D professionals.

The following guidelines provide a basis for an ethical (learner-centric) approach to learning and development.

- Respect individual rights for dignity, self-esteem, privacy and autonomy.
- Recognize that it is necessary and legitimate to provide individuals with learning opportunities that enable them to gain the knowledge and skills required to perform well in their jobs and develop their potential. But note that individuals should still be allowed the freedom to choose the extent to which they pursue learning and development programmes beyond the basic requirement to be capable in their jobs.
- Ensure that learning opportunities are equally available to all, irrespective of gender, ethnicity, sexual orientation or age. Particular attention needs to be taken to supporting the management of diversity and inclusion.
- Accept that while the organization has the right to conduct learning and development activities that enhance performance, individuals also have the right to be provided with opportunities to develop their own knowledge, skills and employability.
- Ensure that people taking part in learning events feel 'psychologically safe' in accordance with the view expressed by Schein (1993: 91) that: 'To make people feel safe in learning, they must have a motive, a sense of direction, and the opportunity to try out new things without the fear of punishment.'
- Avoid manipulating people to accept imposed organizational values.

The state of L&D

Four recent surveys as summarized below have provided a picture of the current state of learning and development.

CIPD (2018c) Over-skilled and underused: investigating the untapped potential of UK skills

This survey of 3,700 employees found that of those who had received training, the most commonly reported types of training they got were on-the-job training (38 per cent), online learning (32 per cent) and learning from peers (30 per cent). The least commonly reported forms of training were mobile-device-based learning (5 per cent), job rotation, secondment or shadowing (6 per cent), and blended learning (7 per cent). A quarter (24 per cent) of respondents indicated that they had not received any type of training in the past 12 months. Employees get time away from their day-to-day jobs and take responsibility for learning in only 40 per cent of organizations.

Respondents were asked to indicate how useful they felt the training they received was. The majority of participants reported that the training they received had been useful to some extent. Learning through peers was perceived to be the most helpful (94 per cent of respondents). Job rotation, secondment and shadowing were also regarded as valuable. Online learning, mobile learning and induction and health and safety training were less positively viewed, although over six in ten still felt that they were useful.

CIPD (2020) Learning and skills at work survey

This survey (CIPD 2020a: 2) with 1,217 respondents found that high performing organizations were:

- using learning as a driver of business value and revenue – moving away from learning as a cost;
- investing in strategic learning to drive the skills needed in future work and using learning as an enabler of agility;
- nurturing a learning culture where learning is valued and supported by leaders – and people help each other to learn constantly;
- personalising learning for individuals, providing learning that's just enough and just for me;
- weaving learning into the flow of work and performance, where people learn as they work and work as they learn; the CIPD (2020b) commented on the move from less instruction to greater interaction with the job and with colleagues; enabled by digital technology and increased awareness of a broader range of learning sources;
- tapping into the value of powerful digital learning – from apps, to advanced simulations, to virtual reality;
- investing in learning platforms – to enable a better learning experience and also to prompt organizational insight through data and analytics.

The most commonly reported learning and development method was face-to-face training, contributing to between 60 and 100 per cent of the learning provided in 44 per cent of the respondents' organizations. However, it is much more prevalent in smaller organizations. The use of digital learning was limited, delivering less than 20 per cent of learning. As the CIPD (2020a: 19) commented: 'With the desire to facilitate accessible, personalised learning in the flow of work and to support remote working, this is a concern, highlighting the pressing need for digital transformation.' The CIPD (2020a) also noted that only 29 per cent of organizations had clear learning and development plans for their employees.

Back to the future

This survey by Emerald Works (Daly and Ahmetaj, 2020) involved the 'learning leaders' (heads of L&D functions) of 1,123 organizations. The 10 major problems identified by those leaders in order of significance were:

1　Learning responsibility not shared across the organization.
2　Shifting mindsets from classroom to beyond.
3　Lack of data-driven decision-making.
4　Value of learning not recognised by organization.
5　Lack of investment time and tools.
6　Traditional expectations.
7　Inconsistent learning approach.
8　Immature culture and approach to learning.
9　Lack of mandate and learning or people change capability.
10　Lack of alignment, buy-in and engagement from business.

Training Journal survey 2020

This survey asked 2,200 L&D specialists what they thought were the most important L&D trends in 2020. The answers in declining order of popularity were:

1　Learning analytics
2　Personalization/adaptive delivery
3　Collaborative/social learning
4　Learning experience platforms
5　Artificial intelligence
6　Micro-learning

7 Consulting more closely with the business

8 Coaching/mentoring

9 Showing value

10 Visual and augmented reality

11 Mobile delivery

12 Neuroscience/cognitive science

13 Curation

14 Video

KEY LEARNING POINTS

Learning and development defined

Learning and development (L&D) is concerned with ensuring that organizations have the knowledgeable, skilled and engaged people they need to achieve their goals. Its aim is to improve individual, group and organizational effectiveness.

This involves enabling employees to acquire knowledge and skills and develop their potential through experience and social contacts, coaching, mentoring, guidance provided by line managers, self-managed learning and training provided by the organization.

The elements of learning and development

The elements of L&D are:

- *Learning* – the process by which a person acquires and develops knowledge, skills, capabilities, behaviours and attitudes. It involves the modification of behaviour through experience as well as more formal methods of helping people to learn within or outside the workplace.

- *Development* – the growth or realization of a person's ability and potential through the provision of learning and educational experiences.

- *Training* – the systematic application of formal processes to help people to acquire the knowledge and skills necessary for them to perform their jobs satisfactorily.

- *Education* – the development of the knowledge, values and understanding required in all aspects of life rather those relating to particular areas of activity.

The components of learning and development

These were shown in Figure 1.1

Relationships between L&D and other people management activities

People management philosophy is underpinned by the resource-based-view (Barney (1991, 1995) that it is the range of resources in an organization, including its human resources, that produces its unique character and creates competitive advantage.

People (HR) management delivers added value and helps to achieve sustainable competitive advantage through the strategic development of the organization's rare, hard to imitate and hard to substitute human resources. Learning and development plays a major part in this.

This means that the people management activities of organization design and development, knowledge management, talent management and performance management are closely associated with L&D.

One of the important aims of strategic L&D is to integrate its activities with related people management activities such as these and so achieve what is called 'horizontal fit'.

The ethical dimension

Ethics is concerned with making decisions and judgements about what is the right course of action to take. It embraces concepts that affect and guide ethical behaviour, namely equity, justice and fair dealing. An ethical approach to learning and development is required.

Bibliography

Barney J B (1991) Firm resources and sustained competitive advantage, *Journal of Management* **17** (1), pp 99–120

Barney, J B (1995) Looking inside for competitive advantage, *Academy of Management Executive,* **9** (4), pp 49–61

Beer M *et al* (1984) *Managing Human Assets,* The Free Press, New York

Beer, M, Boselie, P and Brewster, C (2015) Back to the future: implications for the field of HRM of the multi-stakeholder perspective proposed 30 years ago, *Human Resource Management,* **54** (3), pp 427–38

Bersin, J (2018) *A New Paradigm For Corporate Training: Learning on the flow of work* [Online] https://joshbersin.com/2018/06/a-new-paradigm-for-corporate-training-learning-in-the-flow-of-work/ (archived at https://perma.cc/DEE2-UZKV)

Bersin, J and Zao-Sanders, M (2019) *Developing Employees: Making learning a part of everyday work* [Online] https://hbr.org/2019/02/making-learning-a-part-of-everyday-work (archived at https://perma.cc/VSB8-CCX6)

Birdi, K S, Patterson, M G and Wood, S J (2007) Learning to perform? A comparison of learning practices in profit- and non-profit-making sectors in the UK, *International Journal of Training and Development*, **11** (4), pp 265–81

Burns, T and Stalker, G (1961) *The Management of Innovation*, Tavistock, London,

Chartered Institute of Personnel and Development (CIPD) (2018a) *Understanding and measuring job quality*, CIPD, London

CIPD (2018b) *Organization Development*, CIPD, London

CIPD (2018c) *Over-skilled and underused: investigating the untapped potential of UK skills*, CIPD, London

CIPD (2020a) *Learning and Skills at Work 2020*, CIPD, London

CIPD (2020b) *Learning in the Flow of Work*, CIPD, London

Daly, J and Ahmetaj, G (2020) *Back to the Future: Why tomorrow's workforce needs a learning culture*, Emerald Works, London,

Flanagan, J (2015) Transformational L&D, *Training Journal*, January, pp 34–36

Handy, C (1985) *Understanding Organizations*, 3rd edn, Penguin Books, Harmondsworth

Minzberg, H (1991) Organization design: Fashion or fit?, in *Managing People and Organizations*, ed J J Gabarro, pp 332–51, Harvard Business School Publications, Boston, MA

Rawls, J (1973) *A Theory of Justice*, Oxford University Press, Oxford,

Robinson, D (2013) *The engaging manager and sticky situations* [Online] http://www.employment-tudies.co.uk/system/files/resources/files/493.pdf

Schein, E (1993) How can organizations learn faster? The challenge of entering the green room, *Sloan Management Review*, **34** (2), pp 85–92

Training Journal (2020) *Annual Global Sentiment Survey*, March

Winstanley, D and Woodall, J (2000) The ethical dimension of human resource management, *Human Resource Management Journal*, **10** (2), pp 5–20

02

The context of learning and development

Introduction

Typical approaches to learning and development (L&D) and typical organizations don't exist. Organizations function in many different ways depending on their contexts. And so does L&D. Contingency theory tells us that definitions of aims, policies and strategies, learning programmes, lists of activities and analyses of the role of the L&D function are only valid if they are related to the context or circumstances of the organization. A learning and development leader quoted by Daly and Ahmetaj (2020: 34) said that 'I don't think that it is possible to separate 'learning' from the context within which it takes place.' Descriptions in books like this can be no more than generalizations that suggest possible approaches: they cannot be prescriptive in the sense of laying down what should be done in all circumstances.

As covered in this chapter, L&D strategies and practices are affected by the needs and views of the main stakeholders. They are also very much influenced by the internal and external environment, the changing nature of work and major events such as the COVID-19 pandemic.

Stakeholders

The stakeholders in L&D are the people who have a legitimate interest in the organization's approach to learning and development. Stakeholders have been described by Stanford Research Institute (Freeman, 1984: 11) as 'those groups without whose support the organization would cease to exist.' They consist of:

- **Senior managers:** Who are or should be concerned about the skills base of the organization (the reservoir of skilled people it needs) and developing the capability of its employees so that it performs well and has the agility to manage challenges and change effectively.
- **Line managers:** Who need knowledgeable and skilled people in their team who will behave in ways that support the achievement of the purpose of their department.
- **Employees:** Who want to gain the knowledge and skills required to perform their job and advance their career and need to have the opportunities and help to do so.
- **The L&D function:** The members of which are there to help develop and implement the organization's L&D strategies.

The internal environment

The internal environment of an organization consists of its social system (the ways in which work groups are organized and the interactions that take place) and its technical system (the ways in which the work is organized and carried out to deliver products or services to customers or clients). The internal contextual factors that affect L&D include the sector in which the organization operates (eg public, private, voluntary, manufacturing, service) and its size, complexity, technology, culture and financial circumstances. Perhaps the most important factor is the type of people the organization employs. L&D activities in a firm mainly employing knowledge workers will clearly be different from those in one where the majority of workers are employed in activities such as manufacturing, delivery or customer service (call centres).

The financial situation of the organization is another factor affecting L&D activities. Some chief executive officers and many chief financial officers regard expenditure on training as a cost rather than an investment. When costs have to be cut it is often the training budget that suffers.

The external environment

The external environment impacts on organizations through the forces of national and international competition, the state of the financial and labour markets, economic and societal trends, the deregulation of markets and the impact of globalization. Another major influence is the constant state of change in the external environment which may be turbulent, even chaotic as a result of such events as COVID-19 and, in the UK, Brexit. This is about the impact of 'VUCA' (volatility, uncertainty, complexity and ambiguity). Organizations are also influenced by changes in the nature of work, developments in new technology, government interventions and initiatives in the shape of support for skills development, legislation and regulations and the availability of skills.

What's happening to work?

The nature of work is altering in many organizations and, clearly, L&D strategy has to take account of this. Some organizations are operating more flexibly and some, for example, high technology firms, are being organized organically, ie they are relatively informal with the emphasis on lateral processes and interaction (networking). As suggested by Green and Young (2020: 1):

> Businesses need new skills and more highly skilled people, as the world of work is disrupted. ... So learning is an essential part of any organisation's future – and learning and development teams are the custodians of that precious resource, but they're struggling.

There have been significant shifts in the demographics of the workforce in the shape of an increased proportion of women, greater ethnic diversity, more educated employees, more part-time employees and an ageing population. More people are engaged in 'knowledge work' (technology and professional services) and fewer in factory jobs following the decline of manufacturing in the UK. Work intensification is increasing. The pressure for flexibility has meant that traditional office or factory-based working is declining and the 'gig economy' and zero hours contracts are flourishing. COVID-19 has resulted in a considerable increase in homeworking, making it difficult to conduct face-to-face training but increasing the usefulness of digital learning.

Attitudes to work

Attitudes to work vary. Some people just see work as a means to an end while others see it as a source of fulfillment. Galbraith (2004: 75), argued for a distinction between 'people for whom work is exhausting, fastidious and disagreeable and...

those who manifestly take pleasure from it and feel no stress from it, with a gratifying sense of their personal importance, perhaps.' These are the people who are more likely to be fully engaged with the learning opportunities available to them.

Impact of the COVID-19 pandemic

The CIPD (2020) noted that:

> The COVID-19 pandemic has had an unprecedented impact on the way businesses operate, leading organisations to change where they work and also consider how they work and the services they offer. Many organisations have had to upskill or reskill staff quickly, owing to redeployment, or to support staff needing to work remotely. The ability to learn, adapt and continuously improve is vital in the face of such a challenge. A large number of employees worked from home during the 2020/21 lockdowns and many continued to do so when the lockdowns ended. This has made a considerable impact on learning provision with much more use being made of online (digital) learning.

A survey by Southampton University and the Institute for Employment Studies (Parry *et al*, 2021) revealed that:

> self-investment in training, learning and skill development was low. 33% of employees said they had engaged in extra training or learning during lockdown to enhance their skills. This compares to a national figure of 43% who had taken part in some form of lockdown learning, rising to 54% of those full-time workers not furloughed. Employers are going to need their workforce to be agile and ready to learn new skills as working practices change and restrictions are eased. This is an area that employers may want to focus on and increase their investment in content and innovative modes of delivery to suit new work patterns.

Research conducted by Pugh *et al* (2021) for the CIPD on the impact of COVID-19 on L&D identified the problems of the reduced visibility of learning needs, inadequate technology to support digital learning and the difficulty some people have of adjusting their learning to an online environment.

Impact of emerging technologies

The impact of emerging technologies and work intensification accompanied by major changes in the labour market has led some commentators to predict large-scale job losses. However, the Taylor Review (2017) noted that, technological advancements and the automation of individual tasks result in job creation as well as substitution of labour. This is the concept of the augmentation of human work rather than its replacement.

There is also evidence from research conducted by the CIPD (2017) in conjunction with Loughborough University that new technology can improve the quality of work by removing mundane tasks and allowing for some degree of role expansion. Examples identified by the research included:

- An automated dispensing system in a UK hospital reduced the amount of time pharmacists spent in the dispensary, which was better used to care for patients on wards.
- An automated decision support system for air traffic controllers, advising them on optimal solution in a real-time setting, increased their performance and accuracy without increasing their workload.
- A comparison of a realistic rail-signalling automation model and experienced human rail signal operators found that as automation increased, the perceived workload of human operators, both mentally and physically, decreased and the consistency of performance increased.

Skills

A context of underutilized skills affects L&D policies on skills development. According to OECD data (2015) the UK ranked fourth from the top of developed nations in terms of the proportion of workers who are either over- or under-qualified for their jobs. Alongside this challenge, international comparisons reveal a higher proportion of jobs with a low demand for skills in the UK than elsewhere. In a CIPD (2018) survey of 3,700 UK employees, 37 per cent of respondents thought that their skills were not being fully used in their jobs and that they could cope with more demanding job roles. By contrast only 12 per cent believed that they lacked the skills to carry out their jobs effectively. This skills mismatch was more marked among younger people, those working part-time and people working in the retailing and hospitality sectors. The CIPD concluded that the existence of such a significant skills mismatch is damaging both for employers and employees.

Working in a role which under-utilizes skills has the effect of reducing job satisfaction as well as earning potential and future career prospects. It is associated with low levels of engagement, poor wellbeing, higher reported levels of job-related stress and high levels of staff turnover. The result is inadequate performance.

Government support and interventions

In the UK the National Skills Fund helps adults to train and acquire the skills they need to improve their job prospects. It aims to support economic recovery by boosting the supply of skills that employers require. The level 3 adult offer enables any adult aged 24 and over who wants to achieve their first full level 3 qualification, which is equivalent to a technical certificate or diploma, or 2 full A levels, to access almost 400 fully funded courses. Complementing the level 3 adult offer, skills bootcamps offer free, flexible courses of just 12 to 16 weeks. They give people the opportunity to build up sector-specific skills and fast-track to an interview with a local employer.

The 'Lifetime Skills Guarantee' announced by the Government in January 2021 will offer adults the opportunity to retrain in later life, helping them to gain in-demand skills and open up further job opportunities. This includes the chance for those without a full level 3 qualification (A level equivalent) to gain one for free in a range of sectors including engineering, health and accountancy. A Lifelong Loan Entitlement will also make it easier for adults and young people to study more flexibly; this can be used over their lifetime and for modules of a course.

The Government also supports apprenticeships (eg the apprenticeship levy) and traineeships.

KEY LEARNING POINTS

The importance of context

Typical approaches to learning and development (L&D) and typical organizations don't exist. Organizations function in many different ways depending on their contexts. And so does L&D. Contingency theory tells us that definitions of aims, policies and strategies, lists of activities and analyses of the role of the L&D function are only valid if they are related to the context or circumstances of the organization.

Stakeholders

L&D strategies and practices are affected by the needs and views of the main stakeholders. They are also very much influenced by the internal and external environment, the changing nature of work and major events such as the COVID-19 pandemic.

The stakeholders in L&D are the people who have a legitimate interest in the organization's approach to learning and development. They consist of:

- senior managers;
- line managers;
- employees;
- members of the L&D function.

The views of all these stakeholders need to be taken into account when developing L&D strategy.

The internal environment

The internal environment of an organization consists of its social system (the ways in which work groups are organized and the interactions that take place) and its technical system (the ways in which the work is organized and carried out to deliver products or services to customers or clients). Other contextual factors include the sector in which the organization operates (eg public, private, voluntary, manufacturing, service) and its size, complexity, technology, culture and financial circumstances. Perhaps the most important factor affecting L&D is the type of people it employs and the presence or absence of trade unions.

The external environment

The external environment impacts on organizations through the forces of national and πinternational competition, the deregulation of markets and the impact of globalization (the process by which businesses or other organizations develop international influence or start operating on an international scale).

Organizations are also influenced by the state of the financial and labour markets, economic and societal trends, developments in new technology and government interventions in the shape of legislation and regulations.

What's happening to work?

The nature of work is altering in many organizations.

There have been significant shifts in the demographics of the workforce in the shape of an increased proportion of women, greater ethnic diversity, more educated employees and an ageing population. More people are engaged in 'knowledge work' (technology and professional services) and fewer in factory jobs following the decline of manufacturing in the UK. Work intensification is increasing.

References

Chartered Institute of Learning and Development (CIPD) (2017) *The impact of emerging technologies on work* [Online] https://www.cipd.co.uk/knowledge/work/technology/artificial-intelligence-workplace-impact (archived at https://perma.cc/4BEV-43HZ)

CIPD (2018) *Over-skilled and underused: investigating the untapped potential of UK skills*, CIPD, London

CIPD (2020) *Learning and Skills at Work 2020*, CIPD, London

Daly, J and Ahmetaj, G (2020) *Back to the Future: Why tomorrow's workforce needs a learning culture*, Emerald Works, London,

Freeman, R E (1984) *Strategic Management: A stakeholder perspective*, Prentice-Hall, New Jersey

Galbraith, J K (2004) *Les Mensonges de L'économie. Vérité Pour Notre Temps*, Grasset, Paris

Green, M and Young, J (2020) *Coronavirus and the workforce: Learning in a COVID world*, London, CIPD

OECD (2015) *Skill mismatch and public policy in OECD countries*, OECD, Paris

Parry, J, *et al* (2021) *Working from Home under COVID-19 lockdown: Transitions and tensions* [Online] https://www.employment-studies.co.uk/system/files/resources/files/Working%20from%20Home%20under%20Covid-19%20Lockdown%20-Transitions%20and%20Tensions.pdf (archived at https://perma.cc/23TL-D3QM)

Pugh, C, *et al* (2021) *Impact of COVID-19 on the L&D Profession: Perspectives from independent learning practitioners*, CIPD, London

Taylor, M, *et al* (2017) *Good Work: The Taylor review of modern working practices* [Online] https://assets.publishing.service.gov.uk/government/uploads/system/uploads/attachment_data/file/627671/good-work-taylor-review-modern-working-practices-rg.pdf (archived at https://perma.cc/L9JU-A69Z)

03

Learning culture

Introduction

A learning culture is an environment that embeds learning into the way organizations do things. It provides the foundation for learning and development policy and practice and its creation is a priority for strategic L&D and will be strongly affected by the organization's L&D philosophy. It supports learning at an individual and organizational level. In a learning culture, the importance of learning is recognized by top management. Line managers and employees regard it generally as an essential organizational process to which they are committed and in which they engage continuously. Research by the CIPD (2018) identified the key role that workplace culture supported by high-quality line management plays in enabling workers to use and develop their skills and progress at work.

Characteristics of a learning culture

Reynolds (2004: 9) described a learning culture as a 'growth medium', in which 'employees will commit to a range of positive discretionary behaviours, including learning.' He suggested that to create a learning culture it is necessary to develop organizational practices that 'give employees a sense of purpose in the workplace, grant employees opportunities to act upon their commitment, and offer practical support to learning.' He also advocated the provision by organizations of a supportive learning environment in which people's learning capabilities can be discovered and applied. Employees should be able to learn through their work challenges and should be provided with time, resources and, crucially, feedback. The importance of managers acting as coaches, mentors and role models should be recognized and learning networks (communities of practice consisting of groups of people with shared expertise who work together) should be encouraged.

As described by Marsick and Watkins (2003), a learning culture consists of seven dimensions: continuous learning, inquiry and dialogue, team learning, embedded system, empowerment, system connection and strategic leadership. The CIPD (2020: 7–8) defined a learning culture as one in which an organization 'embeds learning into its way of doing things, at an individual, team and organisational level. Strong leadership and organisation-wide buy-in are required to create a collective vision for learning. Learning also needs to be built into organisational strategy and ensure working practices allow for dialogue, reflection and continuous improvement.'

FIGURE 3.1   Model of learning culture

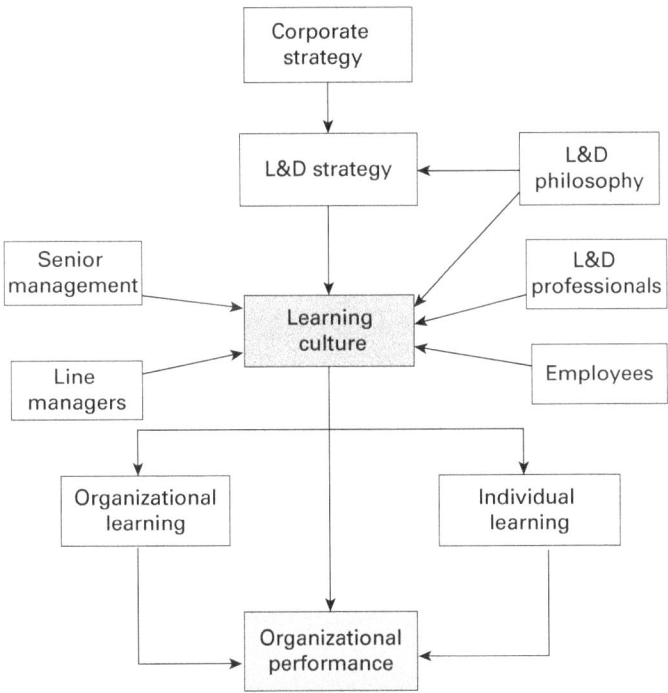

A model of how a learning culture functions is given in Figure 3.1. This illustrates the influence of L&D strategy and philosophy but also shows that the culture is affected by the behaviour of the different stakeholders.

Impact of a learning culture

As Paine (2019: 20) pointed out: 'A learning culture enables an organisation to learn fast, rapidly adjust to changes in the outside environment and constantly evolve as its staff continues to grow and accept new challenges.' And the CIPD (2020: 7) noted that: 'Recent research identifies that organisations in which learning has a deep impact on key behaviours and is supported by learning interventions and programmes experience better growth, transformation, productivity and profitability.' The key behaviours on the part of managers consist of active support and involvement in induction training, the subsequent development of the capabilities of individuals through experience, social learning and training and support to learners following a learning event to ensure that the learning achieved there is transferred to the workplace. The key behaviours for individuals are the motivation and levels of engagement required to make the most of learning opportunities whether these occur during their work or are provided by their manager or the organization.

In their study of learning cultures for Emerald Works, Daly and Ahmetaj, (2020) classed the top-performing 10 per cent of their data sample as high-impact learning cultures (HILCs). These environments typically see learning as having a deep impact on behaviour in that the ability of people to adapt is improved. This compares with organizations at lower levels of learning maturity, who have in place learning interventions and programmes, but are not business-aligned and thus fail to have more than a surface-level impact. HILCs have greater growth, profitability, transformation (ability to solve problems and respond quickly to change) and productivity.

Developing a learning culture

Perhaps the best way to develop a learning culture is to integrate learning into the flow of work at all levels. It will not happen overnight. But it is only when learning becomes embedded in day-to-day activities and is owned by individual employees and their managers that a true learning culture will be achieved instead of learning being seen simply as an event.

Guidance on creating a learning culture was provided by Marsick and Watkins (2003). Their *Dimensions of Learning Organization Questionnaire (DLOQ)* consists of the following seven dimensions, the first four of which operate at the people level, while the final three relate to the structural level of an organization.

1 Create continuous on-the-job learning opportunities for all members.

2 Promote inquiry and dialogue, creating a culture in which feedback and experimentation are encouraged.

3 Encourage and reward collaboration and team learning.

4 Empower people toward a collective goal, using feedback from members to bridge the gap between the current status and the new vision.

5 Connect the organization to the environment by helping people see the impact of their work on the entire business.

6 Create systems to capture and share learning, ensuring these are integrated with work and are accessible.

7 Enable leaders to think strategically about how to use learning to create change and move the organization in new directions.

But there are no easy ways of developing a learning culture. Daly and Ahmetaj, (2020: 69) warned that: 'Learning cultures are contextualized: there isn't an off-the-shelf version. In such contexts, people are rewarded and recognized for learning: it's integrated and not an afterthought.' Their development requires the concerted efforts of four parties: senior management, line managers, workers and L&D professionals.

Senior management

The senior management of an organization provides encouragement and support. It leads by example by promoting and getting involved in learning activities. It recognises that a good learning environment can make a significant impact on the organization's performance and will enhance its reputation.

Line managers

Line managers are facilitators of learning within their departments and as such play a major role in developing and maintaining a learning culture. They do this every time they help an employee to learn something, encourage them to pursue a self-development programme (self-directed learning) or support them after a learning event to transfer the learning to their work. Once a learning culture has been established at the top, managers at every other level can ensure that it takes root throughout the organization. They can be encouraged to fulfil this role by senior management and guided in doing so by L&D professionals.

Workers

Individual workers play their part by learning how to learn and managing their own learning with the guidance and help of the L&D function. An environment in which they can learn from each other (social learning) is promoted by the way in which work is organized in departments and the establishment of communities of interest – groups of people who meet to discuss work issues and learn thereby. Thus learning becomes a way of life.

L&D professionals

Clearly, L&D professionals have a major part to play in the creation and maintenance of a learning culture. They should base their initial contribution on an understanding of the state of learning in the organization and an analysis of its learning needs. They should update this regularly when the learning environment has been established.

The following recommendations on how L&D professionals should foster learning culture were made by the CIPD (2020:14).

- communicate learning opportunities across the organization;
- highlight everyone's role in organizational and team learning – consider how continuous learning can benefit individuals, their team and the wider organization;
- consider how opportunities to reflect on and share learning can be used to follow up formal training, or be encouraged as part of individual development;
- provide different types of learning that appeal to a range of learners and allow employees to build their own learning pathway within an organizational framework.

Importantly, L&D professionals also need to convince senior managers that a learning culture is desirable and provide advice on the role they can play.

KEY LEARNING POINTS

Learning culture defined

A learning culture is an environment that embeds learning into the way organizations do things. It provides the foundation for learning and development policy and practice and its creation is a priority for strategic L&D.

It provides the foundation for learning and development policy and practice and its creation is a priority for strategic L&D.

In a learning culture learning is recognized by top management, line managers and employees generally as an essential organizational process to which they are committed and in which they engage continuously.

Characteristics of a learning culture

Reynolds (2004: 9) described a learning culture as a 'growth medium', in which 'employees will commit to a range of positive discretionary behaviours, including learning.'

Organizations should provide a supportive learning environment where people's learning capabilities can be discovered and applied.

Impact of a learning culture

Paine (2019: 20) pointed out: 'A learning culture enables an organisation to learn fast, rapidly adjust to changes in the outside environment and constantly evolve as its staff continues to grow and accept new challenges. '

The CIPD (2020: 7) noted: that 'Recent research identifies that organisations in which learning has a deep impact on key behaviours and is supported by learning interventions and programmes experience better growth, transformation, productivity and profitability.'

Developing a learning culture

Learning cultures do not emerge overnight. They take time and trouble to create. Their development requires the concerted efforts of four parties: senior management, line managers, employees and L&D professionals. And that is not easy.

References

Chartered Institute of Personnel and Development (CIPD) (2018) *Over-skilled and Underused: Investigating the untapped potential of UK skills*, CIPD, London

CIPD (2020) *Creating Learning Cultures*, CIPD, London

Daly, J and Ahmetaj, G (2020) *Back to the Future: Why tomorrow's workforce needs a learning culture*, Emerald Works, London

Marsick, V J and Watkins, K E (2003) Demonstrating the Value of an Organization's Learning Culture: The dimensions of the learning organization questionnaire, *Advances in Developing Human Resources*, 5 (2), pp 132–51

Paine, N (2019) How do you build a learning culture? *Training & Development*, 46 (2), pp 20–23

Reynolds, J (2004) *Helping People Learn*, CIPD, London

04

Organizational learning and the learning organization

Introduction

Learning and development strategies and policies need to take account of how learning takes place at the levels of the organization and, within that context, that of the individual worker as discussed in Chapter 5. There are two approaches to the analysis of learning at the organizational level: the concept of organizational learning and that of the learning organization. At first sight these look the same but they are different.

The initial section of this chapter deals with organizational learning and the next one with the learning organization. The third section compares the two.

Organizational learning

Organizational learning is a somewhat elusive notion. It was suggested by Tsang (1997: 75) that: 'It is commonly agreed that the concept of organizational learning is complex and multidimensional.' It has been defined in many different ways and there are a number of theories on how organizational learning takes place.

Organizational learning defined

Organizational learning is defined as the development and acquisition in organizations of knowledge, understanding, insights, techniques and practices in order to improve organizational effectiveness. It is concerned with the methods adopted by organizations to promote learning; it is not simply the sum of individual learning, although the role of individuals as active agents is important. It was argued by Kim (1993: 37) that 'Organizations can learn independent of any single individual but not independent of all individuals.'

Organizational learning focuses on collective learning but takes into account the proposition made by Argyris (1992) that organizations do not perform the actions that produce the learning; it is individual members of the organization who behave in ways that lead to it, although organizations can and should create the conditions that facilitate such learning. The concept of organizational learning recognizes that the way in which it takes place is affected by the context of the organization and its culture.

There have been many other definitions of organizational learning. Examples are given below:

- Organizational learning is the process by which organizational members detect errors or anomalies and reconstruct them by theories-in-use. (Argyris and Schön, 1978)
- Organizational learning is adaptive behaviour of organizations over time. (Cyert and March, 1963)
- Organizational learning means the process of improving actions through better knowledge and understanding. (Fiol and Lyles, 1985)
- Organizational learning is an organizational capacity for growth, change and transformation. (Marsick, 1994: 16)
- Organizational learning is an academic field of research that seeks to understand how learning processes occurs within organizational settings. (Easterby-Smith, 1997)
- Organizational learning 'is the transference of learning from individuals and groups through to the learning that becomes embedded—or institutionalized—in the form of systems, structures, strategies and procedures'. (Crossan et al, 1999: 524)

The purpose of organizational learning

As Crossan et al (1999: 522) maintained: 'Organizational learning can be conceived of as a principal means of achieving the strategic renewal of an enterprise.' And Tsang (1997: 79) claimed that:

Learning usually, but not always increases an organization's capacity to perform better. An organization which is quick to correct its errors and reacts fast to environmental change should, on average, outperform one which seldom learns from its past mistakes. In addition, lessons learnt from the past, if properly stored in the organizational memory, are an important source of knowledge for members of the organization to draw upon.

The process of organizational learning

Organizational learning is an intricate, three-factor process consisting of the acquisition, dissemination and shared implementation of knowledge. As such it is closely related to knowledge management. Knowledge may be acquired from direct experience, the experience of others or organizational memory. There have been many explanations of what this involves. Five of the leading ones are summarized below. Each of them highlights significant features of organizational learning but perhaps the most persuasive one is the 4I theory of Crossan *et al* (1999).

THE 4I THEORY: CROSSAN *ET AL* (1999)

The main proposition of Mary Crossan and her colleagues is that organizational learning is a multi-level process: individual, group and organization. These three levels are linked by four social and psychological processes (the 4Is) which are defined as follows:

- *Intuiting* is the recognition of the pattern and/or possibilities inherent in a personal stream of experience. This process can affect the actions of individuals and of others when they interact with the individual.
- *Interpreting* is the explanation, through words and/or actions, of an insight or idea to one's self and to others.
- *Integrating* is the process of developing shared understanding among individuals and of taking coordinated action through mutual adjustment. This process will initially be ad hoc and informal, but if the coordinated action taking is recurring and significant, it will be institutionalized.
- *Institutionalizing* is the process of ensuring that routinized actions occur. Tasks are defined, actions specified and organizational mechanisms are put in place. Institutionalizing sets organizational learning apart from individual or ad hoc group learning. As Crossan *et al* (1999: 529) observe:

The underlying assumption is that organizations are more than simply a collection of individuals; organizational learning is different from the simple sum of the learning of its members. Although individuals may come and go, what they have learned as individuals or in groups does not necessarily leave with them. Some learning is embedded in the systems, structures, strategy, routines, prescribed practices of the organization, and investments in information systems and infrastructure... This institutionalization is a means for organizations to leverage the learning of the individual members. Structures, systems, and procedures provide a context for interactions. Over time, spontaneous individual and group learning become less prevalent, as the prior learning becomes embedded in the organization and begins to guide the actions and learning of organizational members.

ORGANIZATIONAL LEARNING AS A SOCIAL PROCESS

This perspective sees organizational learning as socially constructed. Brown and Duguid (1991) pointed out that learning is best understood (and best achieved) in the context of the community in which the work and therefore the learning takes place (social learning). Huysman (1999: 66) stated that when individual knowledge is shared among individuals the result is organizational knowledge. Learning can be regarded as the inevitable result of participating in social life. Organizations make use of the social capital that develops as people share ideas and knowledge.

ORGANIZATIONAL LEARNING AS A PROCESS OF KNOWLEDGE MANAGEMENT

As Huber (191: 89) explained: 'An entity learns if, through its processing of information, the range of its potential behaviours is changed... an organization learns if any of its units acquires knowledge that it recognizes as potentially useful to the organization.' Thus, organizational learning is about knowledge management.

ORGANIZATIONAL LEARNING AS A CYCLICAL PROCESS

The cyclical model of organizational learning as constructed by Easterby-Smith and Araujo (1999: 10) describes the enhancement of organizational learning as a continuous process which is helped by working through a series of stages comprising the generation of information, the interpretation of information and the development of action on the basis of these interpretations.

SINGLE AND DOUBLE LOOP LEARNING (ARGYRIS, 1992)

Chris Argyris believed that organizational learning occurs under two conditions: first, when an organization achieves what is intended and, second, when a mismatch between intentions and outcomes is identified and corrected. He called them single-loop and double-loop learning. These two types of learning have been described as adaptive or generative learning.

Single-loop or adaptive learning is incremental learning that simply corrects deviations from the norm by making small changes and improvements without challenging assumptions, beliefs or decisions. Organizations where single-loop learning is practised define what Argyris calls the 'governing variables', ie what they expect to achieve in terms of targets and standards and then monitor and review achievements and take corrective action as necessary, thus completing the loop.

Double-loop or generative learning involves challenging assumptions, beliefs, norms and decisions rather than accepting them. On this basis, learning takes place through the examination of the root causes of problems so that a new learning loop is established that goes far deeper than the traditional learning loop provided by single-loop or adaptive learning. Learning occurs when the monitoring process initiates action to redefine the governing variables to meet the new situation, which may be imposed by the external environment. The organization has learnt something new about what has to be achieved in the light of changed circumstances and can then decide how this should be done. This learning is converted into action. The process is illustrated in Figure 4.1.

As Easterby-Smith and Araujo (1999) commented, single-loop learning could be linked to incremental change. In contrast, double-loop learning is associated with radical change, which may involve a major change in strategic

FIGURE 4.1 Single and double-loop learning

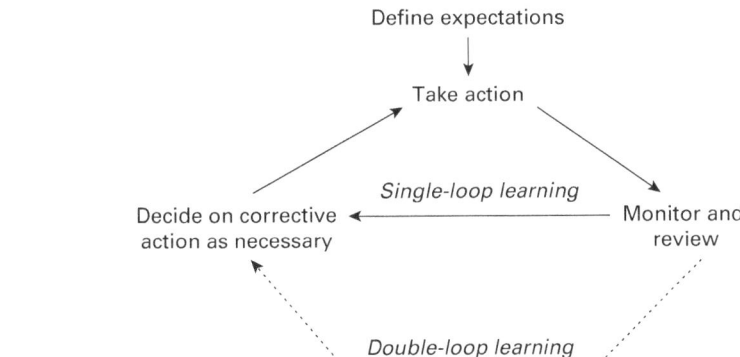

direction. It is generally assumed that double-loop learning is superior, but there are situations when single-loop learning is more appropriate.

Developing organizational learning

To develop organizational learning:

- Build into the learning culture the belief that organizational learning as a means of improving performance is important.
- Get top management to set the lead.
- Use knowledge management processes to capture and disseminate knowledge and learning. Learning and knowledge can be recorded in databanks, manuals and the intranet but the knowledge gained from experience should be exchanged and shared by creating networks and encouraging face-to-face communication between individuals and teams by means of informal conferences, workshops and communities of practice (groups of people bound together by shared expertise who meet together to share knowledge).

Get L&D to provide support by constantly emphasizing the importance of organizational learning and encouraging it by such means as conferences, workshops, seminars and the development of communities of practice.

The learning organization

A learning organization was described by Senge (1990: 3), who originated the idea, as one 'where people continually expand their capacity to create the results they truly desire, where new and expansive patterns of thinking are nurtured, where collective aspiration is set free, and where people are continually learning how to learn together.' He also observed (1990: 4) that:

> Learning organizations are possible because, deep down, we are all learners…
> Learning organizations are possible because it is not only our nature to learn but
> we love to learn.

Further definitions of a learning organization have been provided by Wick and Leon (1995: 299), who stated that it was one that 'continually improves by rapidly creating and refining the capabilities required for future success'; and by Pedler et al (1997: 3), who referred to it as an organization that 'facilitates the learning of all its members and continually transforms itself.'

Garvin (1993) suggested that learning organizations are good at doing five things:

1 Systematic problem solving – which rests heavily on the philosophy and methods of the quality movement. Its underlying ideas include relying on scientific method rather than guesswork for diagnosing problems – what Deming (1986) called the 'plan-do-check-act' cycle and others refer to as 'hypothesis-generating, hypothesis-testing' techniques. Data rather than assumptions are required as the background to decision-making – what quality practitioners call 'fact-based management' and what is generally referred to now as 'evidence-based management'. Simple statistical tools such as histograms, Pareto charts and cause-and-effect diagrams are used to organize data and draw inferences.

2 Experimentation – this activity involves the systematic search for and testing of new knowledge. Continuous improvement programmes – 'kaizen' – are an important feature in a learning organization.

3 Learning from past experience – learning organizations review their successes and failures, assess them systematically and record the lessons learnt in a way that employees find open and accessible. This process has been called the 'Santayana principle', quoting the philosopher George Santayana who coined the phrase: 'Those who cannot remember the past are condemned to repeat it.'

4 Learning from others – sometimes the most powerful insights come from looking outside one's immediate environment to gain a new perspective. This process has been called SIS, for 'steal ideas shamelessly.' Another more acceptable word for it is 'benchmarking' – a disciplined process of identifying good practice organizations and analysing the extent to which what they are doing can be transferred, with suitable modifications, to one's own environment.

5 Transferring knowledge quickly and efficiently throughout the organization – by seconding people with new expertise, or by education and training programmes, as long as the latter are linked explicitly with implementation.

Critical evaluation of the learning organization notion

The notion of the learning organization is persuasive because it incorporates many 'good practice' ideas as set out by Garvin and provides a rationale for comprehensive learning and development programmes. However, Scarborough *et al* (1999) argued that the learning organization concept is over-concerned with organization systems and design. Little attention seems to be paid to what individuals want to learn or how they learn. The idea that individuals should be enabled to invest in their own development seems to have escaped learning organization theorists, who are more inclined to focus on the imposition of learning by the organization rather than creating a climate conducive to learning.

Viewing organizations as learning systems is a limited notion. Argyris and Schon (1996) explained that organizations are products of visions, ideas, norms and beliefs, so that their shape is much more fragile than the organization's material structure. People act as learning agents for the organization in ways that cannot easily be systematized. They are not only individual learners but also have the capacity to learn collaboratively. This is described by organization learning theory and leads to the belief that it is the learning culture and environment that are important, not the systems approach implied by the concept of the learning organization.

The notion of a learning organization incorporates miscellaneous ideas about human resource development, systematic training, action learning, organizational development and knowledge management, with an infusion of the precepts of total quality management. But they do not add up to a convincing whole. Easterby-Smith (1997) contended that attempts to create a single best-practice framework for understanding the learning organization are fundamentally flawed. There are other problems with the concept: it is idealistic; knowledge management models are beginning to supersede it; few organizations can meet the criteria; and there is little evidence of successful learning organizations.

Burgoyne (1999), one of the earlier exponents of the learning organization, has admitted that there has been some confusion about it and that there have been substantial naiveties in most of the early thinking. He believes that the concept should be integrated with knowledge management initiatives so that different forms of knowledge can be linked, fed by organizational learning and used in adding value. More recently, Pedler and Hsiu S-W (2019: 98) conceded that: 'Whilst the early learning organization ideas retain attraction and relevance their practice has been disappointing and has produced unintended consequences.'

The CIPD as reported by Lancaster (2020) attempted to redefine the concept as 'the new learning organization' the characteristics of which are clarity of purpose, holistic people experience, thriving ecosystem [the inter-connected arrangements, facilities and practices present in an organization to promote learning], agile digitally enabled infrastructure, intelligent decision making and continued engagement. All these are important but they are characteristics of any effective approach to L&D and are only broadly related to the original notion of the learning organization.

Comparison of the organizational learning and learning organization concepts

The notion of the learning organization is often associated with the concept of organizational learning. But they not the same. Lau *et al* (2017: 163) offered the following explanation of the differences between the concepts of organizational learning and the learning organization:

> Organizational learning, learning organization and learning culture conceptually overlap, but they are distinct. While organizational learning is defined as the process whereby learning occurs in organizations through creating, sharing, disseminating, storing, and retrieving information to increase organizational competencies; learning organization is defined as a growing entity that evolves in form through organizational learning processes to achieve organizational outcomes These terms are often used interchangeably and simultaneously but inappropriately. The former refers to the processes or activities of learning, while the latter emphasizes the outcomes of learning processes A learning culture is required to facilitate organizational learning processes.

Easterby-Smith and Araujo (1999: 8) explained that the literature on organizational learning concentrates on the observation and analysis of the processes of individual and collective learning in organizations, whereas the learning organization literature is concerned with using specific diagnostic and evaluative tools that can help to identify, promote and evaluate the quality of the learning processes inside organizations. They pointed out that the idea of the learning organization involves the creation of normative models and methodologies for improving learning processes (a normative model is a theory that prescribes a norm or standard pattern as best practice). In contrast, organizational learning is about understanding the nature and processes of learning within organizations. In other words, organizational learning is about how people learn in organizations, while the learning organization notion explains what organizations should do to facilitate learning. The learning organization is an aspiration; organizational learning is a fact. The former concept is prescriptive – it tells you to 'get out and do things'. The latter is descriptive – 'this is what happens; mark, learn and inwardly digest; make use of it'.

Learning organization advocates tend to be management consultants or academics acting as consultants, while organizational learning theorists tend to be academic researchers. Learning organization theory provides a dubious base for action. The idea of a learning culture supported by the understanding of how organizations learn, as provided by the concepts of organizational learning and knowledge management, has more to offer.

KEY LEARNING POINTS

Organizational learning defined

Organizational learning is defined as the development and acquisition in organizations of knowledge, understanding, insights, techniques and practices in order to improve organizational effectiveness.

The purpose of organizational learning

'Organizational learning can be conceived of as a principal means of achieving the strategic renewal of an enterprise.' Crossan *et al* (1999: 522)

'Learning usually, but not always increases an organization's capacity to perform better. Tsang (1997: 79)

The process of organizational learning

Organizational learning can be characterized as an intricate three-stage process consisting of knowledge acquisition, dissemination and shared implementation. As such it is closely related to knowledge management. There have been many descriptions of what this involves. Four of the most convincing ones are:

1   The 4I theory: Crossan *et al* (1999). Organizational learning is a multi-level process: individual, group and organization. These three levels are linked by four social and psychological processes: intuiting, interpreting, integrating and institutionalizing (the 4Is).

2   Organizational learning as a social process. Organizational learning is socially constructed. It occurs when individual knowledge is shared among individuals.

3   Organizational learning as a cyclical process. The cyclical model of organizational learning (Easterby-Smith and Araujo, 1999) describes organizational learning as a continuous process which is helped by working through a series of stages comprising the generation of information, the interpretation of information and the development of action on the basis of these interpretations.

4 Single and double loop learning (Argyris, 1992) Organizational learning occurs under two conditions: first, when an organization achieves what is intended and, second, when a mismatch between intentions and outcomes is identified and corrected. These are described as single-loop and double-loop learning.

Practical implications

Organizational learning theory draws attention to the importance of developing a learning culture and the need to take active steps to improve knowledge management processes.

The concept of the learning organization

A learning organization was described by Senge (1990: 3) as one 'where people continually expand their capacity to create the results they truly desire, where new and expansive patterns of thinking are nurtured, where collective aspiration is set free, and where people are continually learning how to learn together.' Pedler *et al* (1997: 3), who referred to it as an organization that 'facilitates the learning of all its members and continually transforms itself.

The idea of a learning organization incorporates miscellaneous ideas about human resource development, systematic training, action learning, organizational development and knowledge management, with an infusion of the precepts of total quality management. But they do not add up to a convincing whole.

The concept of the learning organization provides a dubious base for action. The idea of a learning culture supported by the understanding of how organizations learn, as provided by organizational learning theory and knowledge management initiatives, has more to offer.

References

Argyris, C (1992) *On Organizational Learning*, Blackwell, Cambridge, MA

Argyris, C and Schon, D A (1978) *Organizational Learning: A theory of action perspective*, Addison Wesley, Reading, MA

Brown, J S and Duguid, P (1991) Organizational learning and communities-of-practice: Toward a unified view of working, learning and innovating, *Organization Science*, **2** (1), pp 40–57

Burgoyne, J (1999) Design of the times, *People Management*, 3 June, pp 39–44

Chartered Institute of Personnel and Development (2020) *Creating Learning Cultures*, CIPD, London

Crossan, M M, Lane, H W and White, R E (1999) An organizational learning framework: From intuition to institution, *Academy of Management Review*, **24** (3), pp 523–37

Cyert, R M and March, J G (1963) *A Behavioural Theory of the Firm,* Prentice-Hall, Englewood Cliffs, New Jersey

Deming, W E (1986) *Out of the Crisis*, Massachusetts Institute of Technology Centre for Advanced Engineering Studies, Cambridge, Massachusetts

Easterby-Smith, M (1997) Disciplines of organizational learning: Contributions and critiques, *Human Relations*, **50** (9), pp 1085–13

Easterby-Smith, M and Araujo, J (1999) Organizational learning: Current debates and opportunities, in (eds) M Easterby-Smith, J Burgoyne and L Araujo, *Organizational Learning and the Learning Organization*, Sage, London

Fiol, C M and Lyles, M A (1985) Organizational learning, *Academy of Management Review,* **10** (4), pp 803–813

Garvin, D A (1993) Building a learning organization, *Harvard Business Review*, July–August, pp 78–91

Huber, G (1991) Organizational learning: The contributing processes and the literature, *Organization Science,* **2** (1), pp 88–115

Huysman, M (1999) Balancing biases: A critical review of the literature on organizational learning, in *Organizational Learning and the Learning Organization,* eds M Easterby-Smith, J Burgoyne and L Araujo, pp 59–74, Sage, London

Kim, D M (1993) The link between individual and organizational learning, *Sloan Management Review,* Fall, pp 37–50

Lancaster, A (2020) *Driving Performance Though Learning,* London, Kogan Page, London

Lau, P Y, McLean, G N, Hsu, Y-C, Lien, B (2017) Learning organization, organizational culture, and affective commitment in Malaysia: A person–organization fit theory, *Human Resource Development International*, **20** (2), pp 159–79

Marsick, V (1994) Trends in managerial reinvention: Creating a learning map, *Management Learning,* **25** (1) pp 11–33

Pedler, M and Hsiu, S-W (2019) Regenerating the learning organization: Towards an alternative paradigm, *The Learning Organization*, **26** (1) pp 97–112

Pedler, M, Burgoyne, J and Boydell, T (1997) *The Learning Company: A strategy for sustainable development*, 2nd edn, McGraw-Hill, Maidenhead

Scarborough, H, Swan, J and Preston, J (1999) *Knowledge Management: A Literature Review*, Institute of Personnel and Development, London

Senge, P (1990) *The Fifth Discipline: The art and practice of the learning organization*, Doubleday, London

Tsang, E W (1997) Organizational learning and the learning organization: A dichotomy between descriptive and prescriptive research, *Human Relations*, **50** (1), pp 73–89

Wick, C W and Leon, L S (1995) Creating a learning organization: From ideas to action, *Human Resource Management*, **34** (2), pp 299–311

05

Individual learning

Introduction

Individual learning is about developing capabilities (knowledge, skills and behaviours) that people do for themselves in the normal course of their work and through their own efforts, supported as necessary by the provision of learning opportunities by the organization.

This chapter covers the characteristics of individual learning and the various learning processes that they undertake or are provided for them to promote that learning, namely: self-directed learning, personal development planning, learning how to learn, lifelong learning and continual professional development. How people learn is covered more thoroughly in Chapter 11 of this handbook.

The characteristics of individual learning

The theory of adult learning developed by Knowles (1984) describes the characteristics of individual learning. He calls adult learning 'andragogy' as contrasted with 'pedagogy' which is about how children learn. His six principles of adult learning – which are just as valid today – are:

1 Adults can make their own decisions about learning,

2 Adults use prior learning and experience to bear on new learning.

3 Adults learn best at work when what is being learnt is relevant to their working life.

4 Adults prefer learning which helps them to carry out tasks.

5 Intrinsic motivation – the self-generated factors affecting people's behaviour which may arise from the work itself – is more effective as a motivator than extrinsic motivation which occurs when things are done to or for people to motivate them.

6 Adults need to know and understand why they should learn something.

Later, Hase and Kenyon (2013) suggested that what they called 'self-determined learning' happens when adults are motivated to learn and decide for themselves what learning they want to undertake irrespective of what is provided by the organization. The associated concept of self-directed learning has become a major feature of the learner-centric approach.

The practice of individual learning is concerned with developing capability. This is the prime aim of all L&D activities which is achieved though self-directed learning and workplace learning as well as the learning programmes provided and encouraged by the organization.

Self-directed learning

Self-directed learning is learning carried out at the discretion of the learner (discretionary learning). It happens when individuals take the initiative to learn something, set their own learning goals and plan for themselves how they are to be attained. As observed by the CIPD (2019:1) 'It is about user choice and co-creation, not just prescription learning.' Self-directed learning is associated with the concept of agency – the ability of people to make independent choices and to learn and retain more if they find things out for themselves (discovery learning). It involves recording achievements and action planning, which means that individuals review and reflect on what they have learnt, what their goals are, how they are going to achieve those goals and what new learning they need to acquire. They can in effect design the content of their own learning programmes which may be 'self-paced' in the sense that learners decide for themselves the rate at which they learn and are encouraged to measure their own progress and adjust the programme accordingly. It also involves:

· finding ways to learn in such ways as making use of curated learning material, completing learning programmes on a digital learning platform (a piece of software designed to assist learning), or taking an online course such as a MOOC;

· trying new ways of doing things and exploring alternative methods;

- asking for help when something is not understood;
- observing more experienced employees at work;
- practising what has been learned already;
- interactive learning on an e-learning programme (see chapter 16); and
- setting up and implementing personal development plans (see later in this chapter).

A survey by LinkedIn (2018) found that 58 per cent of employees wanted to learn at their own pace and 49 per cent at the point of need. A CIPD 2018 survey established that 68 per cent of respondents wanted to be able to access learning 'on the go', ie via their smartphones.

Learners need to learn how to learn. They should be encouraged to define, with whatever help they need, the knowledge and skills required to do their work. They need information on where they can get the material – online and elsewhere (curation) – and guidance that will help them to learn and make good use of their learning. They may need assistance in completing personal development plans as described later in this chapter. They also need support from their manager and the organization with the provision of coaching, mentoring and learning facilities, including digital learning. The use of social media as described in Chapter 16 helps.

The term 'self-managed' learning is often used as an alternative to 'self-directed learning'. But it could be argued that the latter term is more comprehensive because it suggests that learners decide what they want to learn and then learn it, while 'self-managed learning' suggests that individuals are given a lead on what they should learn and only then manage the learning themselves.

Another term often used by academics is self-regulated learning. This happens when individuals take the initiative to learn something, set their own learning goals and plan for themselves how they are to be attained. As Nückles et al (2009: 259) stated, self-regulated learning involves 'the ability to control and influence one's learning processes positively'.

The terms self-managed or self-regulated learning and self-directed learning are often used interchangeably. However, Lourenco and Ferreira (2019) argued that, although these constructs show many similarities, especially with regard to the processes associated with active engagement, goal-directed behaviour, cognitive skills and intrinsic motivation, they are not the same. While self-regulated learning is usually considered to be a learner characteristic, self-directed learning is both a learner characteristic and a design feature of the learning environment: Lourenco and Ferreira (page 119) noted that: 'By defini-tion, self-directed learning means that trainees take the initiative to diagnose their learning needs, formulate their own learning goals, identify the needed resources for learning, find the appropriate learning strategies and finally evaluate their learning [while] self-regulated learning has been viewed as playing a mediating role between performance and contextual variables.'

Lourenco and Ferreira (2019: 118) also commented that:

> There is a body of research showing that training designs that encourage and support more active, self-regulated learning can facilitate the development of complex skills and adaptive performance (Bell *et al*, 2017). Self-regulation also plays an important role in life-long learning in the context of continuing professional development and has been found to predict goal attainment in new training formats, such as massive open online courses (MOOCs).

Their research reinforced the proposition that self-regulation supported learning outcomes such as increase in motivation.

A major contribution to thinking about self-regulated learning was made by Zimmerman (1990: 4) who wrote:

> At one time or another, we have all observed self-regulated learners. They approach educational tasks with confidence, diligence, and resourcefulness. Perhaps most importantly, self-regulated learners are aware when they know a fact or possess a skill and when they do not. Unlike their passive classmates, self-regulated students proactively seek out information when needed and take the necessary steps to master it. When they encounter obstacles such as poor study conditions, confusing teachers, or abstruse text books, they find a way to succeed. Self-regulated learners view acquisition as a systematic and controllable process, and they accept greater responsibility for their achievement outcomes.

CASE STUDY
Self-directed learning in Vestas Blades UK Ltd

Vestas Blades UK Ltd is a wind turbine blade research, development and manufacturer based in the Isle of Wight and Southampton. The L&D policy adopted by Vestas was to give ownership of learning to individuals. Learning needed to be continuous, timely and relevant for people whose roles would present new challenges as the business grew. It wanted employees to have a choice about what they learnt, when and how. A menu of training courses not only seemed unattractive but was also seen to have limited effectiveness in terms of the transfer of learning to the workplace. A requirement of any new approach was that it should motivate employees by serving their own individual learning needs while at the same time meeting those of the business.

The self-directed learning programme began by introducing the concept of personal awareness (via the Myers-Briggs Type Indicator) and its relevance to learning. An inquiry tool was developed to help participants identify their own learning needs, known as the Needs Analysis Process (NAP). Individuals decided the learning goals that would have the greatest benefit to them and their part of the business. The NAP focused attention on the impact that the business's strategic and operational objectives had on each participant's current and future level of performance.

Once participants were made aware of the wealth of learning resources available through books or e-learning, they chose the learning group they wanted to join. Each group consisted of four people from across the organization who would meet regularly every six weeks in confidence – serving as a support structure for its members. Such support was critical. The opportunity to talk about how to apply learning in the workplace not only helped group members make sense of the effect that their learning had but also supported fellow learners in the group working on the same or similar topics. During the first year each group had its own facilitator. The facilitator's role was to accelerate the group's capability to learn.

Self-directed learning and the L&D function

The L&D function can do much to support self-directed learning. This can be at different levels and a model of the stages that might take place produced by Grow (1991: 121) is shown in Table 5.1.

TABLE 5.1   The staged self-directed learning model

Stage	Learner	Trainer	Examples
1	Dependent	Authority Coach	Coaching with immediate feedback Lecture Overcoming deficiencies and resistance
2	Interested	Motivator Guide	Guided discussion Goal setting Developing learning strategies
3	Involved	Facilitator	Discussion facilitated by trainer who participates as equal Seminar Group projects
4	Self-directed	Consultant Delegator	Internship Dissertation Individual work Self-directed study group

SOURCE adapted from Grow (1991: 121)

The L&D function can foster self-directed learning by providing training and guidance on learning how to learn (see later in this chapter), by curating learning material and by making the advice available to interested individuals or generally through smartphones, a learning management system or an enterprise social network as described in Chapter 16. E-learning material can be produced in easily assimilated bites. L&D can let employees have information on the learning opportunities that are available to them and how they can be used. Line managers can be encouraged to get employees to produce self-development plans as part of the performance management process and to follow up on progress in achieving them. L&D specialists can act as facilitators to create 'learning sets' – groups of people involved in collective self-directed learning, or arrange coaching for individuals.

Personal development planning

Personal development planning is a method of formalizing self-directed learning. It is carried out by individuals with guidance, encouragement and help from their managers, usually on the basis of performance and development reviews. A personal development plan sets out the actions people propose to take to learn and to develop themselves. Personal development planning is a method of formalizing self-directed learning. It is carried out by individuals with guidance, encouragement and help from their managers, usually on the basis of performance and development reviews. The purpose is to provide what Tamkin *et al* (1995) called a 'self-organized learning framework.' The stages of personal development planning are:

1 *Analyse current situation and development needs.* This can be done as part of a performance management process.

2 *Set goals.* These could include improving performance in the current job, improving or acquiring skills, extending relevant knowledge, developing specified areas of competence, moving across or upwards in the organization, preparing for changes in the current role.

3 *Prepare action plan.* The action plan sets out what needs to be done and how it will be done under headings such as outcomes expected (learning objectives), the development activities, the responsibility for development (what individuals are expected to do and the support they will get from

their manager, the L&D or HR department or other people), and timing. A variety of activities tuned to individual needs should be included in the plan, for example observing what others do, project work, planned use of e-learning programmes and internal learning resource centres, working with a mentor, coaching by the line manager or team leader, experience in new tasks, guided reading, special assignments and action learning.

4 Formal training to develop knowledge and skills may be part of the plan but it is not the most important part.

5 *Implement.* Take action as planned.

The plan can be expressed in the form of a learning contract, which is a formal agreement between the manager and the individual on what learning should take place, the objectives of such learning and what part the individual, the manager, the L&D function or a mentor will play in ensuring that learning happens. The partners to the contract agree on how the objectives will be achieved and their respective roles. It will spell out learning programmes and indicate what coaching, mentoring and formal training activities should be carried out. It is, in effect, a blueprint for learning.

Learning to learn

People learn all the time and through doing so acquire knowledge, skills and insight. But they will be better at learning if they 'learn how to learn'. As defined by Honey (1998) learning to learn means the acquisition of knowledge and skills about the learning process itself. The aims are to provide a basis for organizing and planning learning (self-directed learning), pinpoint exactly what has been learnt and what to do better or differently as a consequence, share what has been learnt with other people so that they benefit and transfer what has been learnt and apply it in different circumstances to improve the learning process itself.

Learners can be helped to think for themselves about what they need to learn and how they should do it by answering questions like these:

· What knowledge and skills do I need to do my job properly?

· To what extent are there any gaps between the knowledge and skills I need and the knowledge and skills I possess?

· What learning methods are available to fill these gaps?

- How do I set about selecting the most appropriate methods and putting them to use?

- How should I track my progress and evaluate the results?

Learners should be encouraged to work through these questions and take action themselves. But they will benefit from advice on the learning methods available, help in learning from others in learning communities or learning sets (social learning, see Chapter 15) and guidance on where learning material can be obtained (curation), some of which might be provided on a learning experience platform (see Chapter 16).

Lifelong learning

Lifelong learning is a continuing form of self-initiated education that is focused on personal development. Some years ago, government educational policies were geared to promoting it. These have now faded away but the basic notion remains: education should not stop after leaving school, college or university. This applies to everyone, but policies for continuing development should play a part in L&D strategy.

Continuing professional development

Continuing professional development (CPD) is about tracking and documenting the skills, knowledge and experience that people gain both formally and informally as they work, beyond any initial education or training. It includes both the development and the application of that learning. The idea is that everyone, especially professionals, should keep up to date with any new ideas or practices that affect their work and their ability to continue functioning effectively. It makes use of reflective practice as described in Chapter 12.

In a statement in 2020 on its CPD policy the Chartered Institute of Personnel and Development defined it as 'a combination of approaches, ideas and techniques that will help you manage your own learning and growth. The focus of CPD is firmly on results – the benefits that professional development can bring you in the real world. Perhaps the most important message is that one size doesn't fit all. Wherever you are in your career now and whatever you want to achieve, your CPD should be exactly that: yours.'

The CIPD also noted that: 'We operate an outputs-based CPD policy, which means that we're not concerned with how much time you spend on training courses or how many boxes you tick on a form. Instead, our approach is focused on outcomes and results. CPD is about capturing useful experiences and assessing the practical benefits of what you have learned. As a CIPD member, you are required to demonstrate your commitment to CPD and can be asked to submit evidence of CPD at any time.'

KEY LEARNING POINTS

Introduction

Individual learning is the process of acquiring and enhancing knowledge, skills and abilities that people do for themselves in the normal course of their work and through their own efforts supported as necessary by the provision of learning opportunities by the organization.

Adult learning

Adult learning theory describes how adults learn.

Lifelong learning

Lifelong learning is a continuing form of self-initiated education that is focused on personal development

Self-directed learning

Self-directed learning happens when individuals take initiative to learn something, set their own learning goals and plan for themselves how they are to be attained.

Personal development planning

Personal development planning is a method of formalizing self-directed learning. It is carried out by individuals with guidance, encouragement and help from their managers, usually on the basis of performance and development reviews.

Learning to learn

People learn all the time and through doing so acquire knowledge, skills and insight. But they will be better at learning if they 'learn how to learn.'

Continuing professional development (CPD) is about tracking and documenting the skills, knowledge and experience that people gain both formally and informally as they work, beyond any initial education or training.

References

Bell, B S *et al* (2017) 100 years of training and development research: what we know and where we should go, *Journal of Applied Psychology*, **102** (3), pp 305–23

Chartered Institute of Personnel and Development (CIPD) (2019) *Learning and Development Evolving Practice,* CIPD, London,

CIPD (2018) *Driving Performance and Productivity*, CIPD, London

CIPD (2020) *About CPD*, CIPD, London

Grow, G O (1991) Teaching learners to be self-directed, *Adult Education Quarterly,* **41** (3), pp 124–49

Hase, S and Kenyon, C (2013) *Self-determined Learning: Heutagogy in Action,* London,

Honey, P (1998) The debate starts here, *People Management,* 1 October, pp 28–29

Knowles, M (1984) *Andragogy in Action: Applying modern principles of adult learning,* Jossey Bass, San Francisco

LinkedIn (2018) *Workplace Learning Report,* LinkedIn, London

Lourenco, D and Ferreira, A I (2019) Self-regulated learning and training effectiveness, *International Journal of Training and Development,* **23** (2), pp 117–134

Nückles, M, Hübner, S and Enkl, A (2009) Enhancing self-regulated learning by writing learning protocols, *Learning and Instruction*, **19** (3), pp 259–71

Tamkin, P, Barber, L and Hirsh, W (1995) *Personal Development Plans: Case studies of practice*, Institute for Employment Studies, Brighton

Zimmerman, B J (1990) Self-Regulated learning and academic achievement: An overview, *Educational Psychologist,* **25** (1), pp 3–17

06

Learning and development strategy

Introduction

Learning and development strategy sets out what an organization intends to do about developing the capabilities of employees through its learning policies and practices. The creation and implementation of a strategy takes place within the framework provided by strategic L&D as described in the first section of this chapter. The chapter continues with sections dealing with the nature, formulation and implementation of L&D strategy.

Strategic learning and development

Strategic learning and development (strategic L&D) means taking a wide and far-reaching view of what needs to be done about learning and development and ensuring that L&D strategies and activities are aligned with corporate or business priorities (vertical integration or fit) and linked to each other (horizontal integration or fit). It is an overarching concept that links the development of the people in an organization to the business as a whole and its environment and therefore illuminates the process of developing L&D strategies. It is a mindset rather than a collection of techniques.

To paraphrase Dyer and Holder (1988: 13), the purpose of strategic L&D is to provide 'unifying frameworks which are at once broad, contingency based and integrative'. It aims to enhance resource capability in accordance with the belief that the people employed in an organization are a key factor in ensuring its success and, in a business, are a major source of competitive advantage. This aim is achieved by creating a learning culture and by encouraging organizational and individual learning. It is conditioned by the pursuit of strategic fit – the defining feature of strategic learning and development.

Strategic fit is about strategic alignment and strategic integration. Strategic alignment, also known as vertical integration, is the process of developing and positioning learning and development strategy so that it takes into account the implications of the business or corporate strategy on skill requirements, now and in the future, and thus supports the achievement of that strategy.

Strategic integration, also known as horizontal integration, takes place when the various L&D and HR strategies are 'bundled' together, cohere and are mutually supporting. For example, an L&D strategy might be linked to the resourcing and talent management strategies.

Learning and development strategy

Learning and development strategy defines the priorities that should be attached to different aspects of learning and development and, in accordance with the fundamental feature of strategic L&D, how they should be aligned with the corporate or business strategy and integrated – 'bundled' – with each other.

The CIPD (2020a) stated that 'a learning and development (L&D) strategy sets out the workforce capabilities, skills and competencies the organisation needs, and how they can be developed to ensure a sustainable, successful organisation.' It was emphasized that 'L&D strategy has to reflect the overall business strategy and drive progress directly towards that. It must also align with the broad people strategy and with other strategies (for example, recruitment).'

L&D strategy and policy

L&D strategy should be distinguished from L&D policy. L&D strategy is purposeful and dynamic. It provides a sense of direction and constantly adjusts to meet changed circumstances. Learning and development policy guides decisions and actions by defining how it is expected that L&D activities will be planned and carried out. It is more about the here and now. It defines 'the way things are done around here'. L&D policies can cover such matters as access to learning opportunities, equality of opportunity for learning and development, the management of diversity and inclusion and the importance attached to workplace learning and self-development.

The nature of L&D strategy

L&D strategy should be based on the values that govern an organization's approach to people management and learning and development. It defines intentions but these are not simply long-term plans. They should be immediately relevant. It is necessary to bear in mind the dictum of Fombrun *et al* (1984) that business and managers must perform well in the present to succeed in the future. In the words of Boxall (1996: 61) a strategy provides 'a framework of critical ends and means.' It should be treated as a perspective on how things should progress rather than a rigorous procedure for mapping the future. Purcell (2001: 72) observed that: 'Strategy in HR, like in other areas, is about continuity and change, about appropriateness in the circumstances, but anticipating when the circumstances change. It is about taking strategic decisions.'

L&D strategy is driven by the capability needs of the organization – what it requires in terms of people with the necessary knowledge, skills and behaviours to ensure that the organization will be able to respond adequately to any demands made upon it and achieve its strategic goals.

L&D strategy may cover specific areas such as the development of workplace learning, the use of digital learning facilities or the extension of self-directed learning. But it may advantageously consist of a general statement of intent, which provides the framework for more specific strategic plans in individual areas. Mintzberg (1987) referred to this approach as 'umbrella strategy' in which senior management sets out broad guidelines, leaving the specifics to people lower down in the organization. Four key areas for such statements are described below.

Strategy for creating a learning culture

A fundamental objective of L&D strategy is to create a learning culture. This is one in which learning is recognized by top management, line managers and employees generally as an essential organizational process to which they are committed and in which they engage continuously (see also Chapter 3). The strategy should demonstrate how learning benefits individuals and the organization. It should spell out the roles in organizational and individual learning of all the stakeholders. This means encouragement and support from senior management, the active involvement of line managers, the participation of individual employees in self-directed learning and the contributions of members of the learning and development function. It should indicate what approaches will be adopted to facilitate learning in the flow of work, to make use of digital learning and to provide face-to-face training.

Organizational learning strategy

Organizational learning strategies aim to improve organizational effectiveness through the acquisition and development of knowledge, understanding, insights, techniques and practices. This is in accordance with one of the basic principles of L&D which is to recognize the importance of developing capability in order to increase the organization's stock of knowledge and skills and ensure that it has the human capital it requires. As stated by Ehrenberg and Smith (1994: 279–80), human capital theory states that: 'The knowledge and skills a worker has – which comes from education and training, including the training that experience brings – generate productive capital.'

Individual learning strategy

The individual learning strategy of an organization is driven by its skill requirements, and these change. As the CIPD (2020c: 34) noted: 'The shelf life of skills is said to be getting ever more short-term – it is believed that skills now last for two to three years before workers need up-skilling. Sloman (2003: 29) emphasized that learners 'will need to be encouraged to take more responsibility for his or her learning. Efforts will be made to develop a climate which supports effective and appropriate learning.'

An individual learning strategy should take account of these points. It will be based on:

- a systematic programme for identifying learning needs;

- an understanding of how people learn – people learn for themselves but they also learn from other people and they tend to learn better from experience than from what they have been told;

- a belief that most learning happens in the workplace and priority needs to be given to encouraging this;

- the use of training in its complementary role of accelerating learning;
- blended learning – the combination of different approaches to learning (for example, face-to-face training supplemented by digital learning) so that they complement and support one another.

Strategy for high performance working

Organizations achieve sustained high performance through the systems of work they adopt, but these systems are managed and operated by people. Ultimately, therefore, high-performance working is about improving performance through people. This can be done by formulating a strategy for creating a high-performance culture, one in which the achievement of high levels of performance is a way of life and which has the following features:

- Management defines what it requires in the shape of performance improvements, sets goals for success and monitors performance to ensure that the goals are achieved.
- Alternative work practices are adopted such as agile working (responding quickly to new demands), lean manufacturing (reducing waste and speeding up production flows), flexible working, job redesign, autonomous work teams, improvement groups and team briefing;
- People know what is expected of them – they understand their goals and accountabilities.
- People feel that their job is worth doing and there is a strong fit between the job and their capabilities.
- There is a focus on promoting positive attitudes that result in an engaged, committed and motivated workforce.

High performance working can be facilitated by a high-performance work system (HPWS), a bundle of HR and L&D practices that facilitate skill enhancement, motivation and employee involvement. Investments in increasing employee skills, knowledge and ability are an important part of an HPWS.

CASE STUDY
People development strategy statement: Astra Zeneca

A key strategic business objective of Astra Zeneca is: To ensure a well-motivated organization in which people are respected, enjoy their jobs and obtain fulfilment.

1   Our people development strategy applies to all employees, not just to managers or people of high potential. It relates to the continuing development of ability and contribution in each person's current job and, if considered to have the potential to advance further, towards subsequent jobs.

2   People development strategies are vital to the business but it is important that they support the key business strategies. The appropriate resources must be available to meet the key priorities for people development. Expenditure on education, training and development is regarded as a necessary and calculated investment yielding considerable pay-off in terms of enhanced business performance.

3   Managers have a clear responsibility to develop their subordinates. Performance management, which is the key management process that brings together the setting of personal work targets and development plans, is the preferred integrated approach by which employees' learning and development are managed continually in relation to all work activities.

4   All employees must have a personal development plan jointly agreed with their manager and this plan must be progressed and regularly reviewed and updated. It should be derived from the accountabilities of the jobholder and the personal targets for the coming period, plus any anticipated future needs. The plan should cover coaching and on-the-job and off-the job training.

5   All employees are to be encouraged continually to develop their skills and experience both for their own benefit and that of the business through the improved contribution that will result, thus maintaining and extending the business's competitive advantage.

6   Career planning will be a joint activity between the individual and the manager, with employees having a major responsibility for their own career management, including personal development.

7   The development of individuals must take into account that Astra Zeneca is a complex, globally managed business. Particular emphasis should be placed on the need for good business understanding and team work across the business worldwide. The nature of the business requires special attention in the areas of organization development activities, team building, project management and cross-cultural management skills.

8   People development activities will be regularly audited to ensure that appropriate, cost-effective investment is made in all parts of the organization to support current business activities.

Formulating L&D strategy

When formulating L&D strategies the aim is to develop an understanding shared by all stakeholders of the direction it is believed learning and development should go. Proposals should be relevant, realistic and actionable. They should respond to but also anticipate the critical needs of the organization and the people in it. They should be evidence-based – founded on detailed analysis and study, not just wishful thinking, and should incorporate the experienced and collective judgement of top management about organizational requirements while also taking into account the views of line managers and employees generally. L&D strategies should be tailored to reflect the needs of the future rather than mirroring current conditions or past practices. They may fundamentally be business-led but it can be a reciprocal process – an analysis of the needs of the business for skills or a review of the issues facing the business in obtaining those skills can lead to the identification of problems in implementing the business strategy that need to be addressed.

The process of formulating L&D strategy

The process of formulating L&D strategy involves generating strategic options and then making appropriate strategic choices. These will be contingent on the business or corporate strategy of the organization and internal and external contextual factors. Internally, these comprise the characteristics of the organization in the shape of its sector, size, complexity, technology, culture, financial circumstances and, importantly, the type of people it employs. External factors include the state of the financial and labour markets, economic and societal trends, developments in new technology and government legislation and regulations. Conditions of volatility, uncertainty, complexity and ambiguity (YUCA) may have to be taken into account as will major influences such as COVID-19 and, in the UK, Brexit.

An emerging strategy should anticipate the problems of implementation which may arise if line managers are not committed to the strategy and/or lack the skills or time to play their part. Strategy should always be formulated with implementation in mind.

The creation of L&D strategy is not such a straightforward procedure as some people believe. Mintzberg (1987: 66) referred to strategy formulation as an 'emergent process' and stressed that: 'formulation and implementation merge into a fluid process of learning through which creative strategies evolve.' The limitations of excessively rationalistic models of strategic planning were noted by Hendry and Pettigrew (1990). Following Mintzberg, they observed that strategies could emerge from the actions and reactions of managers and others.

This may be so and these factors need to be taken into account when creating L&D strategy but they do not preclude a formal approach to this process. Perkins and Shortland (2006) have highlighted the merits of what they call 'informed premeditation'. And there is everything to be said for thinking ahead about what needs to be done and for planning the changes required. The sequence of activities for formulating L&D strategy as described below is:

1   Conduct a diagnostic review using an evidence-based approach.

2   Consider how strategic fit should be achieved.

3   Set out the L&D strategy.

Conducting a diagnostic review

The purpose of a diagnostic review is to establish the learning and development needs of the organization – its capability or skills requirements – within the context in which it is operating, identify any issues that are inhibiting the satisfaction of those needs and assess strategic priorities. It is these needs that drive the learning strategy. As Birdi *et al* (2007: 267) emphasized:

> Strategic needs analysis processes [are required] to identify the key performance priorities for the organization, the tasks employees need to do differently to meet those priorities, and the underlying knowledge and skills required to undertake those tasks. The information derived from strategic needs analysis can therefore help identify the most appropriate learning practices for changing employee knowledge, skills and behaviour to benefit organizational performance.

An evidence-based approach should be adopted. Evidence-based L&D analyses and evaluates the information available from the data about people and L&D practices in the organization obtained by means of learning analytics (see Chapter 8). It also assesses the messages delivered by benchmarking and research. The purpose is to inform decisions on L&D innovations and improvements to L&D practice and to ensure that such decisions are made by reference to the best available evidence. As observed by Reay *et al* (2009:13), the watchwords are 'evidence before action'. Evidence-based L&D becomes a way of thinking that those responsible for formulating the strategy can use to ask themselves:

- What's important to this organization?
- What are we trying to do here?

- What are the drivers of success?

- How are current L&D practices helping or hindering what we are trying to do and what evidence do we have of this?

- What changes are required to improve the delivery of learning and development?

- How can we best implement improvements and how can we show that they are working?

ACHIEVING STRATEGIC FIT

Strategic fit is the outcome of strategic alignment and horizontal integration. The balanced scorecard can be used to establish priorities.

STRATEGIC ALIGNMENT

It is necessary to ensure that L&D strategy supports the achievement of the organization's goals by being aligned with the organization's business or corporate strategy. As the CIPD (2020b: 43) pointed out: 'Alignment is a critical issue when developing a learning and development strategy. If learning is to positively impact business performance, it has to get much closer to the business and there needs to be greater clarity in the learning team about business drivers.'

It was suggested by Schuler and Jackson (1987) that to achieve the maximum effect it is necessary to match the role characteristics of people in an organization with the preferred strategy. A business may adopt any of the three strategies aimed at achieving competitive advantage identified by Michael Porter (1985):

1 *Innovation* – being the unique producer.

2 *Quality* – delivering high quality goods and services to customers.

3 *Cost leadership* – the planned result of policies aimed at 'managing away expense'.

Other important strategies, curiously omitted by Porter, could be to improve performance and productivity. A not-for-profit organization may also have strategies for innovation, quality, cost reduction, performance and productivity.

Account should be taken of the fact that strategies for change have also to be integrated with changes in the external and internal environments. Fit may exist at a point in time but circumstances will change and fit no longer exists. An excessive pursuit of 'fit' with the status quo will inhibit flexibility, which is essential in turbulent conditions. This is the 'temporal' factor in achieving fit identified by Gratton *et al* (1999). An additional factor that will make the achievement of good strategic fit difficult is that the corporate strategy may not be clearly defined – it could be in an emergent or evolutionary state.

Strategic alignment, as shown in Figure 6.1, starts with the identification of the strategic goals and priorities of the organization and the implications of these on the activities carried out and the knowledge, skills and behaviours required. This will involve the analysis of business or corporate plans to identify areas where proposed innovations or changes in the products, services or operations may require new knowledge or skills or the development of existing ones. It is also necessary to identify any organizational performance problems that could be attributed to skills shortages or deficiencies.

Having established skill requirements, the next stages are to find out what skills are currently available and determine the extent to which they need to be developed and how this should be done. This leads to the formulation of a learning and development strategy which will set out intentions on how learning and development will take place by such means as targeted learning programmes, including both face-to-face and online learning. It is possible that skill requirements can only be satisfied in full by external recruitment and consideration will need to be given to the implications of this in terms of onboarding and follow-up training. This is an example of where it will be necessary to achieve the horizontal integration of L&D and resourcing strategies.

For example, in a government department – the Ministry of Housing, Communities and Local Government – the policy was to give more priority to housing which meant that new skills were required in such areas as scientific expertise, risk management and commercial capability. While people

FIGURE 6.1   Aligning business and L&D strategy

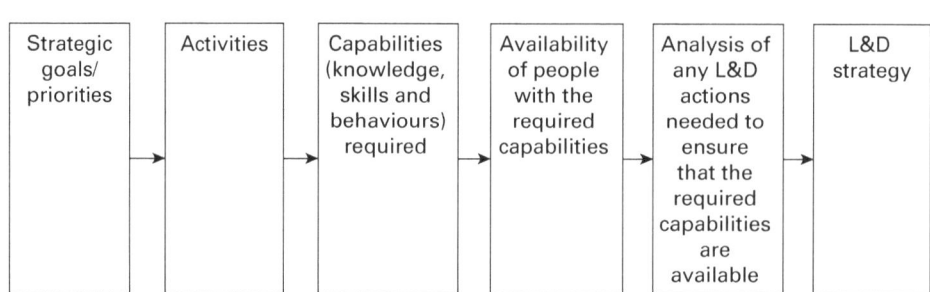

with these skills could be recruited, priority was given to the creation of a strategy for developing them in existing members of staff.

HORIZONTAL INTEGRATION

Horizontal integration or fit means that in order to maximize impact, L&D strategy is linked with associated HR strategies – resourcing, talent management, performance management and organization development and design as modelled in Figure 6.2. Thus they mutually reinforce one another. A joined-up strategy can be developed which arranges for L&D, resourcing and talent management activities to work together. This is sometimes called bundling. High performance work systems as described earlier are in effect bundles of L&D and HR practices.

FIGURE 6.2   Horizontal integration of L&D and HR strategies

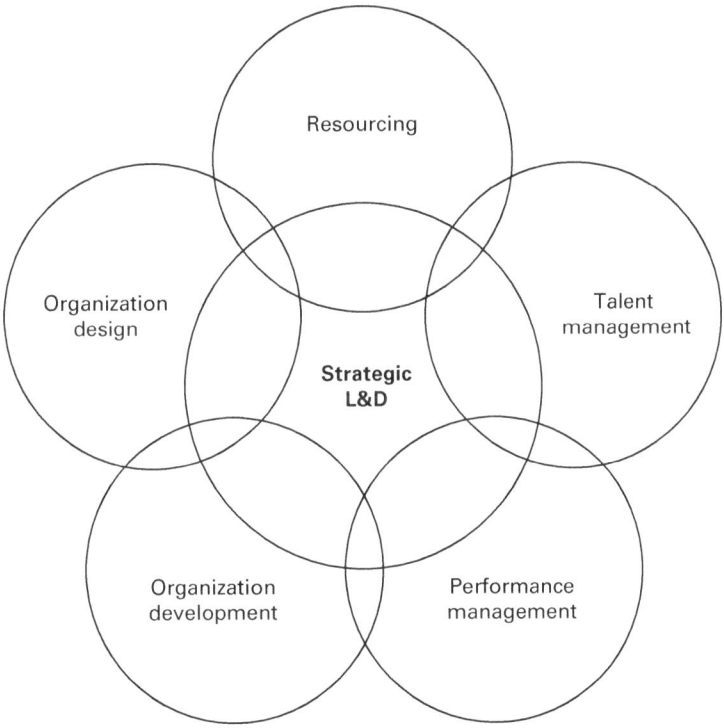

USE OF THE BALANCED SCORE CARD

Strategic priorities can be determined through the balanced score card model which means answering questions about the business from four related perspectives: customer (how do customers see us?), innovation and learning (how can we improve and add value?), internal (what must we excel at?) and financial (how do we appear to our shareholders?). As the originators of the idea, Kaplan and Norton (1992: 79), noted: 'The score-card puts strategy and vision, not control, at the centre. It establishes goals but assumes that people will adopt whatever behaviours and take whatever actions are necessary to arrive at those goals.' They observed later (1996: 83) that the balanced score card enabled businesses to 'identify and align strategic initiatives.'

Shields (2007: 138) commented that the model can be used to define strategic indicators and goals for 'each of the four areas of value creation that cascade down the organization'. He wrote that it 'offers a means of thoroughgoing strategic alignment'. Use of the model enables organizations to identify performance problems and establish how they can be dealt with through L&D initiatives.

Setting out the L&D strategy

The way in which the strategy is set out clearly depends on its content and circumstances of the organization. But the following are the typical areas that might be covered in a formal strategy.

- A definition of guiding principles – the values that have been adopted in formulating the strategy.

- A declaration of intent – the L&D initiatives that it is proposed should be taken.

- A rationale – the reasons why the proposals are being made. It should indicate how they will meet the needs of both the organization and the people it employs. The costs and the benefits should be spelt out.

- An implementation plan – how, when and by whom the L&D strategy initiatives will be implemented. The plan should indicate what steps will be necessary and should take account of resource constraints and the need for communications, involvement and training. The priorities attached to each element of the strategy should be indicated and a timetable for implementation should be drawn up. The plan should state who will be responsible for the development and implementation of the strategy.

Developing a learning strategy for Remploy

Remploy provides employment and development opportunities for disabled people. It operates 83 factories. The company's strategy for learning is explicit and well understood in the organization, and was developed from the bottom-up rather than top-down. Its starting point was recognition that a number of local initiatives in the factories were proving successful and could be developed on a national basis.

The trade unions advocated enhanced opportunities for skill development in basic areas. As a result a national strategy was developed with learning centres as a major element in all 83 sites. Although the use of each learning centre is locally determined, they all have the following in common: a physical location (with at least some PCs); a relationship with a local college whose tutors will visit the site to advise and facilitate; and access to a suite of e-learning programmes, made available from the LearnDirect library (the national e-learning initiative).

Implementing L&D strategy

The ultimate challenge of L&D strategy is putting it to work. As Gratton (2000: 30) remarked: 'There is no great strategy, only great execution.' Strategies cannot be left as generalized aspirations or abstractions. But getting strategies into action is not easy: intent does not always lead to action. Too often, strategists act like the Charles Dickens's character Mr Pecksmith, from *Martin Chuzzlewit*, who Dickens compared (2004: 23) to 'a direction-post which is always telling the way to a place and never goes there.' It is necessary to avoid saying, in effect: 'We need to get from here to there but we don't know or care how.'

Implementation problems

Senior managers in organizations sometimes say they are going to do something and then don't. This is the 'rhetoric-reality' or 'say-do' gap that can easily occur with L&D strategy. Fombrun *et al* (1984: 26) commented that new strategy initiatives often yield only modest results and lack staying power because in many companies 'much time and thought had gone into analysing and planning strategy yet very little time into its implementation.'

Gratton *et al* (1999: 202) commented on 'the disjunction between rhetoric and reality in the area of human resource management, between HRM theory and HRM practice, between what the HR function says it is doing and how that practice is perceived by employees, and between what senior management believes to be the role of the HR function, and the role it actually plays.' These remarks apply equally well to L&D strategy. The factors identified by Gratton *et al* which contribute to creating this gap were:

- complex or ambiguous initiatives that may not be understood by employees or will be perceived differently by them, especially in large, diverse organizations;
- it is more difficult to gain acceptance of non-routine initiatives;
- the initiative is seen as a threat;
- inconsistencies between corporate strategies and values;
- the extent to which senior management is trusted;
- the perceived fairness of the initiative.

To which could be added failure to take account of the strategic needs of the organization (which may be difficult because they are changing too rapidly or no one really understands them), inadequate assessment of the environmental and cultural factors, including internal politics, that affect the content of the strategies, the development of ill-conceived, unmanageable and irrelevant initiatives, possibly because they are current fads or because there has been an poorly digested analysis of 'best practice' which does not fit the organization's requirements, and, importantly, failure to involve stakeholders in the shape of managers and employees in the formulation of strategy. These problems are compounded when insufficient attention is paid to practical implementation problems, particularly where line managers are concerned and there is a need for supporting systems. The role of line managers is vital.

The approach to implementation

Implementation is more likely to be effective if the following approaches are adopted:

1 FORMULATE PRACTICAL STRATEGIES

A practical strategy is one that can be put into effect without too much difficulty and then works. L&D strategy should take into account all the barriers which create the say-do gap. Particularly careful thought has to be given to the practical issues involved in implementing the strategy. It is necessary to consider the role of line managers in delivering people strategy as well as that of L&D specialists. The aims should be to: (1) keep it simple; (2) spell out how the strategy is to be implemented as well as what is to be implemented and (3) ensure that support is given to line managers in the shape of advice, guidance and training.

2 INVOLVE

Involve as many line managers and other employees as possible in formulating the strategy – people support what they help to create. This can be done through formal consultation processes or through workshops and focus groups whose members are representative of the different constituencies in the organization (stakeholders) and who can be encouraged to pass on what they have been doing to their colleagues. It is also possible to involve everyone by conducting an employee survey. The survey should be followed up by discussions with employee groups on its implications for HR strategy and practice.

3 COMMUNICATE

It is essential to communicate details of the strategy to line managers and employees. The communication should explain what is proposed, why it has been proposed (indicating the benefits both to the organization and employees) how it will work, who will be affected and the timetable for introduction. As far as possible it should be by word of mouth to individuals or through team briefing or briefing group arrangements involving everyone in an organization in face-to-face meetings, level by level, to present, receive and discuss information.

4 BUILD SKILLS

New strategies may require the use of new skills or the development of existing ones. This applies to line managers, who should be trained in what they have to do to implement the strategy, and employees generally. Skills can be built through formal off-the-job training courses but there is much to be said for coaching and mentoring.

5 MONITOR AND EVALUATE

The introduction of L&D strategy should be monitored in order to evaluate its effectiveness. Corrective action in the shape of modifications to the strategy or training can then be taken.

6 MANAGE CHANGE

The implementation of L&D strategy involves change, which can be hard to introduce and may be resisted. The problems of implementing strategic change were summed up by Lawler and Mohrman (2003: 24) as follows:

> Most strategies, like most mergers, fail not because of poor thinking, but because of poor implementation. Implementation failures usually involve the failure to acknowledge and build the needed skills and organizational capabilities, to gain support of the workforce, and to support the organizational changes and learning required to behave in new ways. In short, execution failures are often the result of poor human capital management. This opens the door for HR to add important value if it can deliver change strategies, plans and thinking that aid in the development and execution of business strategy.

KEY LEARNING POINTS

Introduction

Learning and development strategy defines where an organization proposes to take L&D. It is formulated and delivered within the framework provided by strategic L&D

Strategic L&D defined

Strategic learning and development (strategic L&D) is concerned with the creation and implementation of integrated learning and development strategies which ensure that the people employed in an organization have the knowledge, skills and abilities required to make a full contribution to the achievement of the organization's strategic goals.

Strategic L&D is a concept that aims to explain what is involved in ensuring that key issues of learning and development are dealt with strategically. It is a process rather than a plan. It explains what is involved in ensuring that key issues of learning and development are dealt with strategically. Acting strategically means taking a broad and longer-term view of what needs to be done and ensuring that strategic fit is achieved, ie that L&D strategies are integrated with business strategies and each other.

L&D strategy

Learning and development strategy describes what the organization intends to do about L&D. This means defining the priorities that should be attached to different aspects of learning and development and how they should be aligned with the corporate or business strategy and integrated with each other.

L&D strategy may cover specific areas such as the development of workplace learning or the use of digital learning facilities. But it may advantageously consist of a broad statement of intent, which provides the framework for more specific strategic plans in individual areas.

Formulating L&D strategy

The formulation of L&D strategy involves the following steps:

1 Conduct a diagnostic review using an evidence-based approach.

2 Consider how strategic fit should be achieved.

3 Set out the L&D strategy.

The approach to implementation

Implementation is more likely to be effective if the following approaches are adopted:

1 formulate practical strategies;

2 involve;

3 communicate;

4 build skills;

5 monitor and evaluate;

6 manage change.

Bibliography

Birdi, K S, Patterson, M G and Wood, S J (2007) Learning to perform? A comparison of learning practices in profit- and non-profit-making sectors in the UK, *International Journal of Training and Development*, **11** (4), pp 265–81

Boxall, P F (1996) The strategic HRM debate and the resource-based view of the firm, *Human Resource Management Journal*, **6** (3), pp 59–75

Chartered Institute of Personnel and Development (CIPD) (2020a) *Learning and Development Strategy and Policy*, CIPD, London

CIPD (2020b) *Learning and Skills at Work 2020*, CIPD, London

CIPD (2020c) *People Profession 2030: A collective view of future trends*, CIPD, London

Dickens, C (1843) *Martin Chuzzlewit*, Chapman & Hall, London

Dyer, L and Holder, G W (1988) Strategic human resource management and planning, in *Human Resource Management: Evolving roles and responsibilities*, ed L Dyer, Washington DC Bureau of National Affairs, pp 1–46

Dyer, L and Reeves, T (1995) Human resource strategies and firm performance: what do we know and where do we need to go? *The International Journal of Human Resource Management*, **6** (3), pp 656–70

Ehrenberg, R G and Smith, R S (1994) *Modern Labor Economics*, Harper Collins, New York

Fombrun, C J, Tichy, N M, and Devanna, M A (1984) *Strategic Human Resource Management*, New York, Wiley

Gratton, L A (1999) People processes as a source of competitive advantage in *Strategic Human Resource Management*, eds L A Gratton *et al* Oxford University Press, Oxford

Gratton, L A (2000) Real step change, *People Management*, 16 March, pp 27–30

Gratton, L A *et al* (1999) *Strategic Human Resource Management*, Oxford University Press, Oxford

Hendry, C and Pettigrew, A (1990) Human resource management: An agenda for the 1990s, *International Journal of Human Resource Management*, **1** (1), pp 17–44

Kaplan, R S and Norton, D P (1992) The balanced scorecard – measures that drive performance, *Harvard Business Review*, January–February, pp 71–79

Kaplan, R S and Norton, D P (1996) Using the balanced scorecard as a strategic management system, *Harvard Business Review*, January–February, pp 75–85

Lawler E E and Mohrman S A (2003) What does it take to make it happen? *Human Resource Planning*, **26** (3), pp 15–29

Mintzberg, H (1987) Crafting strategy, *Harvard Business Review*, July–August, pp 66–74

Perkins, S J and Shortland, S M (2006) *Strategic International Human Resource Management*, Kogan Page, London

Porter, M E (1985) *Competitive Advantage: Creating and sustaining superior performance*, The Free Press, New York

Purcell, J (2001) The meaning of strategy in human resource management, in *Human Resource Management: A critical text*, 2nd edn, ed J Storey, pp 59–77, Thompson Learning, London

Reay, T, Berta, W and Kohn, M K (2009) What's the evidence on evidence-based management? *Academy of Management Perspectives*, November, pp 5–18

Schuler, R and Jackson, S (1987) Linking competitive strategies with human resource management practices, *Academy of Management Executive*, **9** (3), pp 207–19

Shields, J (2007) *Managing Employee Performance and Reward*, Cambridge University Press, Port Melbourne

Sloman, M (1999) Seize the day, *People Management*, 20 May, p 31

Sloman, M (2003) *Training in the Age of the Learner*, CIPD, London

07

The contribution of learning and development to organizational performance

Introduction

Learning and development is fundamentally concerned with performance and it has to justify its existence by its contribution to organizational success. But it has to adopt a multi-stakeholder approach. It must take account of the interests of employees and their managers as well as those of the organization.

The internal factors that shape short and long-term corporate or business performance are the quality of the people working for the organization at every level, the capacity of the organization to innovate and, in a business, compete and the efficiency with which it plans and conducts operations, which includes productivity and cost effectiveness. The external factors are competition in the UK and globally, economic trends, government financial and business policies and legislation, international influences and the pressures exerted by events such as the 2008 financial crisis, Brexit and COVID-19.

But to do well, organizations depend largely on the quality, expertise and skill, dedication and enthusiasm of the people working in them. The message of the resource-based view is that HRM and L&D deliver added value and help to gain 'sustainable competitive advantage' through the strategic development of the organization's rare, hard-to-imitate and hard-to-substitute human resources. As Guest (1997: 269) argued: 'The distinctive feature of HRM is its assumption that improved performance is achieved through the people in the organization.' If, therefore, appropriate L&D policies and practices are introduced, it may be assumed that L&D will impact on firm performance. The problem, however, is that it is difficult to prove a causal connection. Ulrich (1997: 304) contended that:

> HR practices seem to matter; logic says it is so; survey findings confirm it. Direct relationships between performance and attention to HR practices are often fuzzy, however, and vary according to the population sampled and the measures used.

The first section of this chapter provides a backdrop to the remaining parts by examining the 'learning impact' – the factors that link L&D to organizational performance. The next two sections cover respectively, the evidence provided by research on the link and a summary of the impact that L&D can have. Finally, consideration is given to how the contribution of L&D can be measured.

The learning impact

The learning impact is the effect that L&D activities have on the performance of individuals and, ultimately, the organization. The following are the ways in which L&D actions can make an impact:

- Develop a better qualified workforce and extend the skills base of the organization.
- Achieve competitive advantage by having more skilled and engaged employees than competitors.
- Attract high-quality employees by offering them learning and development opportunities, increasing their levels of competency and enhancing their skills, thus enabling them to obtain more job satisfaction, to gain higher rewards, to progress within the organization and increase their employability.
- Improve operational flexibility by extending the range of skills possessed by employees (multi-skilling).
- Facilitate new ways of working.
- Provide those involved in launching new products or developing new markets with the additional knowledge and skills required.

- Increase the engagement of employees by encouraging them to identify with the mission and objectives of the organization.
- Help to manage change by increasing understanding of the reasons for it and helping people to acquire the knowledge and skills they need to adjust to new situations.
- Provide line managers with the skills required to lead, manage and develop their people.
- Help to develop a positive culture in the organization, one that is oriented towards performance improvement.
- Provide higher levels of service to customers.

The CIPD (2018: 34) suggested that:

> A clear characteristic of high performing organisations is that they are effective at translating their business strategy into a compelling people strategy. In such organisations, L&D practitioners are confident and able to understand business priorities and create learning solutions to address those needs.

In his learning-impact model Bontis (2009) claimed that the success of training is not just a function of the course ware and trainer delivery. It is very much the result of the perceived value of the training by the trainee.

How L&D impacts on performance

Views on how L&D impacts on organizational performance are likely to be based on three propositions: (1) that L&D practices can make a direct impact on employee characteristics such as skill, engagement and motivation – employees who know what they are doing, know how to do it and want to do it; (2) if employees have these characteristics it is probable that organizational performance in terms of added value, innovation, efficiency, effectiveness, productivity, quality and the delivery of high levels of customer service will improve; and (3) if such aspects of organizational performance improve, the financial results achieved by commercial organizations will improve (or the overall performance of non-commercial organizations). This can be described as the L&D value chain and is illustrated in Figure 7.1.

FIGURE 7.1   Impact of L&D on organizational performance

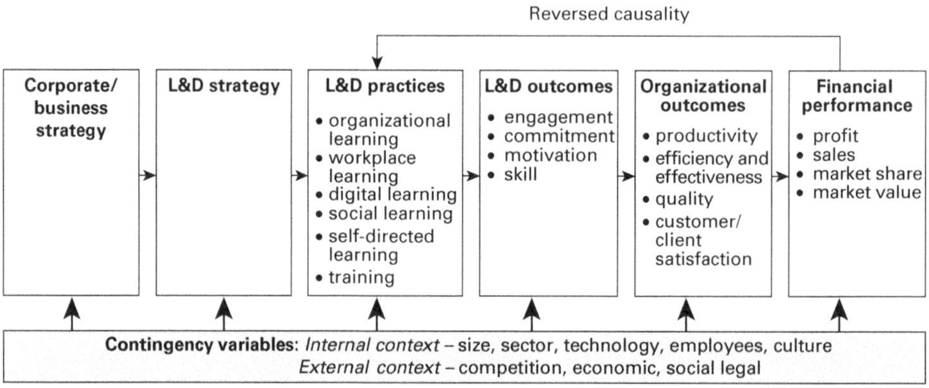

Adapted from Paauwe (2004)

Performance improvement as a result of L&D activities obviously depends on the inherent quality of those activities. But that is not enough. Saks and Burke-Smalley (2014: 105) commented as follows on the significance of transferring learning as a factor in performance improvement:

> There is a paradox about organizational expectations that training interventions will improve firm performance. This is because transfer of training is considered to be the primary leverage point by which training can influence organizational-level outcomes. In other words, without transfer, training efforts cannot contribute to organizational effectiveness. Thus, if training is to have a positive effect on a firm's performance, then employees must first apply learned knowledge and skills on their jobs. However, if the rate of transfer of training in organizations is in fact low, then there exists a training-firm performance paradox because a low rate of transfer of training means that training programs and investments will not lead to an improvement in an organization's performance.

As Choi and Yoon (2015: 2646) emphasized: 'A simple monetary investment in employee training does not automatically improve organizational outcomes; the key factor is whether the investment accompanies a strategically oriented HR [L&D] function in the organization.' And Nishii, *et al* (2008) pointed out that employees who attribute extensive training investment to management's intent for employees' wellbeing will have positive reactions; and those who attribute the same investment to management's motives for exploiting employees will respond with negative attitudes and behaviours.

Evidence from research on the link

An early research project by Russell *et al* (1985) found that the proportion of trained employees favourably affects performance. Research by Bartel (1994) established that financial investment in training can result in productivity growth.

Research by Benabou (1996) examined the impact of various training programs on the business and financial results at 50 Canadian organizations. The conclusion reached was that in most cases a well-designed training programme can be linked to improvements in business results and that return-on-investment in training programmes is very high. A study by Krueger and Rouse (1998) also provided evidence that training is positively related with performance. But Cunha *et al* (2003), using the 1995 CRANET data from several northern European countries, did not find a relationship between training and organizational performance.

On the basis of their research, Mabey and Ramirez (2005: 1068), predicted that 'if an organization carefully cultivates the development of its managerial cadre, this will, in time, lead to improvements in morale, motivation and corporate capability, which will, in turn, and other things being equal, lead to a more productive organization.' They commented that: 'Common-sense logic tells us that the careful development of managers will have a positive influence upon organizational outcomes. The strong probability that employee development will be a driver of growth and add value to the organization in various ways, attitudinal, reputational and financial, has been well articulated (Mayo, 2000).'

In their longitudinal study of 308 companies Birdi *et al* (2008: 107)) found that extensive training produced a gain of nearly 6 per cent in value added per employee. They noted that: 'There is strong support for a positive relationship between the provision of training and firm performance. In fact, one study found that extensive training was more strongly related to organization productivity than operational management practices such as advanced manufacturing technology.'

The research conducted by Aguinis and Kraiger (2009) led them to conclude that training has benefits for individuals, teams and organizations, but that to maximize these benefits firms should pay attention to needs assessment and pre-training stages of trainees, training design and delivery, training evaluation and transfer of training. These actions probably imply the need to invest more resources in training.

Research by Aragon and Valle (2013) into the impact of training on the performance of managers established that firms that train their managers obtain better results than those that do not and that the intensive training contributes to improved performance. As they observed (page 1680):

Training plays a key role in improving the abilities, involvement and innovativeness of one of the most valuable human resources within the company, its managers. Thus, it is worthwhile for the company to train them. In addition, our findings show that what really matters for enhancing those competences is not the proportion of managers who are trained but how much time they are trained and, especially, the amount of resources the firm invests in training. Furthermore, the resources invested in training are the only measure of training that we found to be positively related to a firm's return on assets.

They commented (page 1672) that:

The resource-based view of the firm also provides support for the idea that training has a positive effect on firm performance. According to this perspective, the main sources of competitive advantage for the firm are its intangible resources (Barney, 1991). Among these, human resources, in particular human knowledge, skills and attitudes, are highlighted (Wright *et al*, 1994;) Although all practices of personnel management are involved in the development of these resources, training is considered the main activity in getting qualified, flexible and well-prepared employees (Bartel 1994; Raghuram 1994; MacDuffie and Kochan 1995; Bae and Lawler 2000).

Research in the Spanish hotel industry by Úbeda-Garcia *et al* (2013: 2866) led to the conclusion that 'training policy positively correlates with organisational performance, both using objective result measures (productivity and financial performance) and in... intermediate result measures (human resource outcomes and customer satisfaction).'

The results of the research carried out by Akrofi (2016: 188) on the link between executive development programmes and organizational performance were summarized by him as follows:

This research provide support for the notion that offering executives the opportunity to engage in multi-dimensional L&D events (Activity) will enhance their human capital and dynamic capabilities, resulting in an improvement in the quality of leader-member-exchange, social exchange and in the job demand responses. The corresponding improvement in executive capabilities will culminate in a positive reaction from the employee (Motivation) in terms of better commitment and improvements in levels of productivity, which will eventually translate into positive organisational outcomes (Outcome).

A survey by Esteban-Lloret *et al* (2018: 1222) of Spanish training managers indicated that 'the percentage of trained employees has a positive and significant influence on organizational performance'.

The CIPD (2020:7) claimed that: 'Recent research identifies that organisations in which learning has a deep impact on key behaviours and is supported by learning interventions and programmes experience better growth, transformation, productivity and profitability.'

Measuring the L&D contribution

To ensure that learning and development is making an effective contribution to the achievement of the organization's strategic goals, an attempt should be made to measure the value of that contribution, assess the effectiveness of L&D activities and determine the extent to which L&D processes are aligned with the organization's strategic priorities. As Anderson (2007: 3) commented:

> Traditional approaches to evaluation set out to prove the merit of specific learning interventions and to demonstrate their cost-effective delivery… Whereas a traditional approach to evaluation focuses on the reactions and consequences for learners and trainers resulting from discrete and individual training interventions, a strategic approach requires a focus on the aggregate value contribution made by a more dispersed range of learning processes.

Measuring the overall contribution of L&D in financial terms is not easy. Return-on-investment as described below is one approach which attempts to do this. But there are other ways of assessing at least the effectiveness of L&D, also described below, even if the financial impact cannot be calculated. These comprise return-on-expectations, internal surveys and external benchmarking.

Return-on-investment

Return-on-investment (ROI) measures the value of an investment – the allocation of money in the expectation of some benefit or return in the future. It is expressed as the income derived from an investment expressed as a percentage of the financial value of that investment. Expenditure on learning and development can be regarded as an investment and advocates of this method of measurement such as Kearns and Miller (1997) and Phillips (2011) emphasize the importance of assessing the value of L&D outcomes in financial terms. They argue that such measurements resonate with senior management who rely upon ROI as a means of evaluating their business investments. The ROI for L&D is calculated as:

$$\frac{Benefits\ from\ L\&D\ (\pounds) - costs\ of\ L\&D\ (\pounds)}{Costs\ of\ L\&D\ (\pounds)} \times 100$$

The problem with using ROI for learning evaluation is that while it is easy to record the costs it is much harder to produce convincing financial assessments of the benefits. A return-on-investment model produced by Phillips (2011) aims to overcome this problem. It is mainly concerned with the evaluation of individual learning events and programmes although level five is concerned with the overall evaluation of impact on performance.

The first three levels in this model correspond with those in the Kirkpatrick model of learning evaluation (see Chapter 22). The fourth level, which is concerned with measuring business improvement, is where the Phillips approach differs. He suggests that there are four areas in which performance can be improved and should be measured: (1) routine performance such as meeting production or sales targets; (2) problem solving; (3) innovative applications and (4) personal development. In each case objectives should be set and the means of measuring performance determined. He notes that there are usually other factors besides training that could have contributed to improvements in performance. It is therefore necessary to isolate the impact of training. He lists various means of doing this, the most accurate one being the use of control groups – comparing the results achieved by an experimental group that has undergone training with one that has not. But Phillips acknowledges that the latter method may be difficult to use. He therefore suggests the alternative of obtaining estimates of the contribution of training from participants and their managers. This could be done through questionnaires or interviews and views on the overall contribution would be recorded as a percentage, for example, the contribution of training was 30 per cent of the total performance improvement. He recognizes that this can only be an estimate and some people will be better at doing it than others. But he claims that it is a simple approach that has been adopted in a number of training impact studies.

The next step in the Phillips model is to convert the performance data to monetary data. Where 'hard data' is available in the shape of such traditional measures of performance as units produced, unit costs, productivity, scrap/rejects, items sold, response times and customer satisfaction, conversion is quite straightforward. It is more difficult in the case of 'soft data' such as levels of engagement, grievances, cases of unacceptable behaviour (harassment, bullying, displaying prejudice etc), and 'soft skills' like conducting performance reviews, giving feedback, coaching, dealing with problem employees and handling challenging conversations. The following quantifiable four step method of dealing with soft data issues was proposed by Phillips (2011: 151):

1 Focus on a unit of improvement, eg a programme on handling grievances.

2 Determine a value for each unit, eg an estimate from HR that the cost of handling an average grievance was $6,500.

3 Obtain change in performance data, eg decline in the number of grievances over a period.

4 Calculate annual value of improvement, eg the number established in step three multiplied by the value for each unit (say 8 × $6,500 = $52,000).

If this method is not feasible, Phillips recommends the subjective approach of obtaining estimates of annual value from experts, managers or participants. But he also suggests that it is important to identify intangible measures covering such areas as levels of engagement, customer satisfaction and quality of leadership. The data on these sort of measures can be collected by such means as engagement and customer surveys or, in the case of leadership, 360 degree feedback (the assessment of performance by individuals' subordinates as well as their manager). The levels of improvement expected can be defined when planning the event and these expectations will be the basis for evaluation. The final step (level 5) in calculating ROI proposed by Phillips is to obtain cost data and relate that to the monetary value of the improvement. It is then necessary to reach conclusions about the implications of the analysis and communicate them to stakeholders.

But there are problems with the ROI method. The calculation is complex and usually depends on subjective assumptions about the value of the investment although this is often the case with ROI calculations in other business areas. Fitz-Enz (2010: 14) proposed a way of increasing objectivity by calculating the business value of training. He explained that:

> One way to express training's business value is to survey the trainees, asking them to score their perceived value on a scale of 1 to 100 per cent; the course ware from 1 to 5 points; and the delivery 1 to 5 points. Then you put these factors into an equation such as the one below:

Perceived value	Course ware	Delivery Cumulative score
.80 × 4	× 5	= 16

As any of the ratings change, the cumulative score changes too.

Another problem is that the arithmetic of ROI means that investments in L&D, which are typically much smaller than investments in technology or research, can look superficially impressive. As Phillips noted, it is not unusual for L&D programmes to generate ROIs in the 100–700 per cent range while the target for ROI on other business investments is generally set in the range of 15–20 per cent. Huge L&D returns are likely to be suspect and lead management to question the basis on which they were calculated. And ROI calculations may be possible for individual learning events and projects but are less suitable for overall evaluations of the impact of L&D. These problems explain why only 17 per cent of the respondents to the 2020 CIPD survey used this method.

Return-on-expectations

Return-on-expectations assesses the extent to which people believe that L&D has achieved what it was expected to achieve. It is probably the most practical way of assessing the overall effectiveness of L&D. Objectives such as one or more of these could be considered:

- reflect the strategic goals of the business and support their achievement;
- enable the organization to develop the capable people it needs;
- foster the development of a learning culture;
- enhance learner engagement;
- help to embed organizational learning;
- promote the use of blended learning;
- integrate learning into the flow of work;
- support social learning;
- provide for the extended use of digital (online) learning;
- encourage and support self-directed learning;
- support a curator approach to L&D;
- make use of learning analytics and learning evaluations to guide strategy and practice.

Return-on-expectations is covered in more detail in Chapter 22.

Internal surveys

In the learning-impact model produced by Bontis (2009) the success of training is not treated simply as a function of the course ware and trainer delivery. It is also concerned with the perceived value of the training by the trainee. Internal surveys aim to do this and can also obtain the views of line managers on the effectiveness of the learning and development activities. An example of a survey is given in Figure 7.2.

External benchmarking

An overall assessment of the effectiveness of learning and development processes can be achieved by comparing what is happening within the organization with what can be regarded as 'good practice' in other businesses. This is 'benchmarking' which is defined as a systematic process of making these comparisons and evaluating the results to identify areas for improvement and stimulate change. Benchmarking will cover aspects of learning and development such as these

FIGURE 7.2   Learning and development survey

Rate the extent to which you agree or disagree with the following statements about how learning and development (L&D) operates in this organization on a scale of 1–5 where: 1 = fully agree, 2 = agree, 3 = not sure, 4 = disagree, 5 = strongly disagree					
1 L&D is treated by senior management as one of the key processes for managing the business	1	2	3	4	5
2 Line managers are committed to supporting learning in their departments	1	2	3	4	5
3 Line managers have the skills to facilitate learning	1	2	3	4	5
4 Members of the L&D function help me to learn and provide good support	1	2	3	4	5
5 I am encouraged to manage my own learning and receive good help in doing so	1	2	3	4	5
6 I learn a lot of useful things from the on-line facilities provided by the organization	1	2	3	4	5
7 The training courses I have attended have been well run	1	2	3	4	5
8 I have been able to apply the learning I obtained from courses usefully in my workplace	1	2	3	4	5
9 I was provided with useful guidance and training when I started in my current job	1	2	3	4	5
10 I feel that the L&D provisions in this organization are helping me to develop my career	1	2	3	4	5

listed above and contained in the surveys of L&D by Emerald Works (Daly and Ahmetaj, 2020) and the CIPD (2020).

CASE STUDY

Measuring the contribution of learning to business performance at Lyreco Ltd (UK)

Lyreco UK is part of a large family-owned office supplies group operating extensively in Europe, Canada and Asia. Metrics are a central part of all management processes at Lyreco and these inform the learning investment and planning processes. In field sales, measures include sales turnover, margin and new business, whilst in customer service the performance and productivity metrics include costs per line, abandoned call rate, average call time and average wait time. Monthly performance results in all areas are scrutinized to identify areas for attention, and the learning and development team run learning sessions and activities aimed at helping people to improve their performance. When sales margin was identified as an area for attention, over 150 people attended focused workshops and subsequent performance results were tracked to measure improvements. Similarly, warehouse supervisors with the highest staff turnover attended learning programmes and, as a consequence, staff turnover was at its lowest ever levels.

KEY LEARNING POINTS

How L&D impacts on performance

Views on how L&D impacts on organizational performance are likely to be based on three propositions: 1) that L&D practices can make a direct impact on employee characteristics such as skill, engagement and motivation; 2) if employees have these characteristics it is probable that organizational performance will improve; and 3) if such aspects of organizational performance improve, financial results will improve.

Research

A number of research projects have indicated that there is a link between L&D and organizational performance.

The ways L&D makes an impact

L&D can help the organization to attract high-quality employees by offering them learning and development opportunities, increasing their levels of competency and enhancing their skills, thus enabling them to obtain more job satisfaction, to gain higher rewards and to progress within the organization.

The overall evaluation of the L&D contribution

An attempt should be made to measure the value of the L&D contribution, assess the effectiveness of L&D activities and determine the extent to which L&D processes are aligned with the organization's strategic priorities. Evaluation can be conducted by:

- return on capital employed;
- return on expectations;
- internal surveys;
- external benchmarking.

Bibliography

Aguinis, H and Kraiger, K (2009) Benefits of training and development for individuals and teams, organizations and society, *Annual Review of Psychology*, **60**, pp 451–74

Akrofi, S (2016) Evaluating the effects of executive learning and development on organisational performance: implications for developing senior manager and executive capabilities, *International Journal of Training and Development*, **20** (3), pp 177–199

Anderson, V (2007) *The Value of Learning: A new model of value and evaluation*, London, CIPD

Aragon, I B and Valle, R S (2013) Does training managers pay off?, *The International Journal of Human Resource Management*, **24** (8), pp 1671–1684

Bae, J and Lawler, J J (2000) Organizational and HRM Strategies in Korea: Impact on firm performance in an emerging economy', *Academy of Management Journal*, 4i, pp 502–19

Barney, J B (1991) Firm resources and sustained competitive advantage, *Journal of Management* **17** (1), pp 99–120

Bartel, A P (1994) Productivity gains from the implementation of employee training programs, *Industrial Relations*, **33**, pp 411–25

Benabou, C (1996) Assessing the impact of training programs on the bottom line, *National Productivity Review*, **15** (3), pp 91–99

Birdi, K, *et al* (2008) The impact of human resource and operational management practices on company productivity: a longitudinal study, *Personnel Psychology*, **61** (3), pp 467–501

Bontis, N (2009) *The Predictive Learning Impact Model*, Knowledge Advisors, Chicago

Chartered Institute of Personnel and Development (CIPD) (2018) *Driving Performance and Productivity*, CIPD, London

CIPD (2020) *Learning and Skills at Work 2020*, CIPD, London

Choi, M and Yoon, H (2015) Training investment and organizational outcomes: a moderated mediation model of employee outcomes and strategic orientation of the HR function, *International Journal of Human Resource Management*, **26** (20), pp 2632–51

Cunha, R, *et al* (2003) Market forces, strategic management, HRM practices and organizational performance: A model based in a European sample,' *Management Research*, **1** (1), pp 79–91

Daly, J and Ahmetaj, G (2020) *Back to the Future: Why tomorrow's workforce needs a learning culture*, Emerald Work, London

Esteban-Lloret, N N, Aragón-Sánchez, A and Carrasco-Hernández, A (2018) Determinants of employee training: impact on organizational legitimacy and organizational performance, *The International Journal of Human Resource Management*, **29** (6), p 1208–29

Fitz-Enz, J (2010) *The New HR Analytics*, American Management Association, New York

Guest, D E (1997) Human resource management and performance; a review of the research agenda, *The International Journal of Human Resource Management*, **8** (3), 263–76

Kearns, P and Miller, T (1997) Measuring the impact of training and development on the bottom line, *FT Management Briefings*, Pitman, London

Krueger, A and Rouse, C (1998) The impact of workplace education on earnings, turnover, and job performance, *Journal of Labor Economics*, **16**, pp 61–94

Lancaster, A (2019) *Driving Performance Through Learning*, London, Kogan Page

Mabey, C and Ramirez, M (2005), Does management development improve organisational productivity? A six-country analysis of European firms, *International Journal of Human Resource Management*, **16** (7), 1067–82

MacDuffie, J P and Kochan, T A (1995), Do US firms invest less in human resources? Training in the world auto industry, *Industrial Relations*, **34**, pp 147–68.

Mayo, A (2000) The role of employee development in the growth of intellectual capita, *Personnel Review*, **29** (4), pp 521–33

Nishii, L, Lepak, D P and Schneider, B (2008) Employee attributions of the why of HR practices: Their effects on employee attitudes and behaviors, and customer satisfaction, *Personnel Psychology*, **61**, pp 503–545

Paauwe, J (2004) *HRM and Performance: Achieving long-term viability,* Oxford University Press, Oxford

Phillips, J J (2011) *Return-on-investment on Training and Performance Improvement Programs*, 2nd edn, Routledge, Abingdon

Raghuram, S (1994) Linking staffing and training practices with business strategy: A theoretical perspective, *Human Resource Development Quarterly*, **5**, pp 237–51

Russell, J S, Terborg, J R and Powers, M L (1985) Organizational performance and organizational level training and support, *Personnel Psychology*, **38**, pp 849–63

Saks, A M and Burke-Smalley, L A (2014) Is transfer of training related to firm performance? *International Journal of Training & Development*, **18** (2), pp 104–15

Úbeda-Garcia, M, *et al* (2013) Training policy and organisational performance in the Spanish hotel industry, *International Journal of Human Resource Management*, **24** (15) pp 2851–75

Ulrich, D (1997) Measuring human resources: An overview of practice and a prescription for results, *Human Resource Management*, **36** (3), pp 303–20

Wright, P M, McMahan, G C and McWilliams, A (1994), Human resources and sustained competitive advantage: A resource-based perspective, *The International Journal of Human Resource Management*, **5**, pp 301–26

08

Learning analytics

Introduction

Learning and development strategy and policy should be evidence-based. This means that decision-making is founded on reliable information about what is happening and what is likely to happen to people and L&D in the organization. Providing this data and using it to guide decisions is the function of learning analytics. As the CIPD (2017: 32) commented: 'People professionals will need to have the competency and desire to explore different sources of information to inform their decisions, and to help evidence decisions for key stakeholders.'

The role and purpose of learning analytics is described in the first section of this chapter. In the next section, the way in which learning analytics works is considered in terms of gathering data and using measures. This is followed by an examination of the three levels of analytics and the use of benchmarking. The chapter is completed with a discussion of the scope of learning analytics.

The role and purpose of learning analytics

The role of learning analytics is first to provide guidance on the direction in which L&D strategy should go and assemble and second, to analyse data on learning and development activities and programmes to establish their effectiveness and identify the need for changes or new initiatives. Learning analytics gathers evidence and understanding that can be put to good use. Mattox and Van Buren (2016: 13) defined learning analytics as follows:

> Learning analytics is the science and art of gathering, processing and reporting data related to the efficiency, effectiveness and business impact of development programmes designed to improve individual and organizational performance and inform stakeholders.

They suggested that the purpose of learning analytics was to determine whether a learning experience was effective or not and thus decide what needs to change. In other words, to find out what works and what doesn't work. This implies that learning analytics is mainly about the evaluation of learning events. But it should be more than that. By far the greater amount of learning takes place through experience and in the 'flow-of-work' rather than on formal training courses. Learning analytics needs to be concerned with all forms of learning, not just face-to-face events. It has to cover digital learning and try to assess how effective workplace learning is, although measuring the latter is difficult. It has to attempt to measure the overall impact of L&D in order to support the business case for expenditure on learning including the cost of the L&D function. It has to provide the information necessary to adopt an evidence-based approach to the development of L&D strategy.

The use of learning analytics is an important development in L&D. It enables informed decisions to be made on the type of investments in learning the organization should make. As Mattox and Van Buren (2016: 14) observed, 'learning analytics provides the basis for continuous improvement.'

How learning analytics works

Learning analytics involves the analysis and application of data and measures in order to provide information and enhance knowledge as defined below:

- *Data* consist of the basic facts – which, as interpreted through measures, contribute to information and knowledge;
- *Measures or metrics* (these terms are generally used interchangeably although strictly speaking, metrics are decimalized measures) are means of recording, analysing and interpreting data;
- *Information* is data which have been processed in a meaningful way; as Drucker (1988) wrote, 'information is data endowed with meaning and purpose';

- *Knowledge* is information put to productive use; it is often intangible and it can be elusive – the task of tying it down, encoding and distributing it through knowledge management activities can be tricky.

Data are raw material. Measures or metrics record that raw material so that conclusions can be reached on its value and significance. This may include the analysis of 'big data', defined as data which are too complex to be dealt with by normal statistical techniques. It means translating multiple sources of data into insights about the effectiveness and impact of learning and development inter-ventions. Data come first but establishing the need for a certain measure may indicate what data are required to enable the measurement to take place. The gathering and analysis of data is facilitated by the use of digital learning processes, including learning platforms and artificial intelligence (see Chapter 16).

The steps for the generation of good quality data are:

1 Start with basic data and analysis concentrating on the identification of trends and patterns and their meaning.

2 Demonstrate its integrity by ensuring it is accurate, reliable and of value.

3 Progress to higher levels of data collection and demonstrate the values of particular processes to see how they can impact on performance.

Levels of learning analytics

There are three levels of learning analytics:

1 **Descriptive analytics**: The use of data to record a particular aspect of learning and provide information on what has been happening, for example, the number of people who have undergone training.

2 **Multi-dimensional analytics**: The combination of different sets of data to establish any relationships (correlations) between them and, hopefully, indicate causation (eg that a particular L&D initiative has caused an improvement in performance).

3 **Predictive analytics**: The analysis and use of historical data to predict trends and therefore provide guidance on L&D strategy.

TABLE 8.1   A summary of L&D data and their possible uses

Data	Possible use: analysis leading to action
1 Skills analysis/assessment – graduates, professionally/technically qualified, skilled workers	Assess skill levels against requirements Indicate where steps have to be taken to deal with shortfalls
2 Personal development plans completed as a percentage of employees	Indicate level of learning and development activity
3 Training hours per employee	Indicate actual amount of training activity (note that this does not reveal the quality of training achieved or its impact)
4 Percentage of managers taking part in formal management development programmes	Indicate level of learning and development activity
5 Percentage of employees taking part in formal performance reviews	Indicate level of performance management activity
6 Evaluations of learning events and programmes, ideally covering at least the first three levels of the Kirkpatrick (1994) evaluation system: 1) reaction to the training event; 2) the amount of learning that takes place 3) the extent to which that learning affects behaviour on return to work.	Assess effectiveness of learning events and programmes
7 Return-on-investment (RoI) on L&D activities, overall or individually	Assess effectiveness of learning events and programmes and of L&G activities and the L&G function in general

Descriptive analytics

Descriptive analytics cover data such as those shown in Table 8.1:

Multi-dimensional analytics

Multi-dimensional analytics is a form of descriptive analytics in which different sets of data or 'variables' are compared to show the extent to which there is any relationship between them. A 'dependent variable' is one that may be affected by changes in an 'independent variable'. In effect, when planning the analysis, a hypothesis is made that one or more of the independent variables will impact in some way on the dependent variable. For example, a dependent variable might be the customer satisfaction score achieved by sales assistants and the independent variable might be the hypothesis that this is improved by attending a customer service training course. Regression analysis is used to examine the relationship between the variables and indicate how changes in the level of the independent variable relate to changes in the level of the dependent variable. The analysis may show that the independent variable has a positive effect on the dependent variable. In the example given above, this would mean that following attendance at a training course customer satisfaction levels go up. But this does not mean that the conclusion can be reached that course attendance *causes* higher levels of customer satisfaction. There may be other factors such as price reductions or improved merchandising. Correlations indicate a relationship but do not in themselves establish causation.

However, even if causation cannot be determined with confidence, the existence of correlation can be revealing. At least it can indicate that a positive relationship exists between an L&D initiative and desirable outcomes. This can be used to justify the investment and point the way to further developments.

Stewart and Rogers (2017) gave the following two examples of multidimensional analysis: 1) The cost of each type of learning activity can be divided by the number of employees engaged with each activity to produce the cost per employee of each type; 2) Surveys can produce ratings by employees and their managers of the effectiveness of different types of learning activities that can be compared with the cost of the activity to produce a cost/benefit analysis thus guiding future choice.

A third example is the evaluation of a learning programme for managers on how to conduct performance management sessions with their staff. Prior to the programme a survey of the reactions of employees to their performance management interview would be held (how well it was conducted, how helpful it was etc). Following the programme, when the next performance reviews have been completed, the same questions would be put to employees and any improvements (hopefully) recorded. These could be compared with the cost of the programme to produce a cost/benefit analysis.

Predictive L&D analytics

Predictive L&D analytics involves the analysis and use of historical L&D data to analyse patterns and predict future trends. This enables evidence-based decisions to be made on L&D strategy. It can be used to obtain information on the benefits of innovations that can be included in a business case for them.

Models for learning and development can be produced by predictive analytics. Algorithms determine what courses are needed to fill gaps and advance careers. Learners can enter a learning management system (LMS) and see a customized development plan. They can then take up whatever learning opportunities are on offer.

Benchmarking

Benchmarking is the process of comparing L&D practices with what is happening in similar organizations to establish the extent to which good practices have been adopted and to indicate areas for improvement. Benchmarking information can be obtained from surveys conducted by the Chartered Institute for Personnel and Development, Emerald Works and the Training Journal. For example, the Emerald Works survey, *Back to the Future,* (Daly and Ahmetaj, 2020) found that in the UK the average spend on L&D was £494 per employee and on digital learning £98. The median number of people in the L&D department was 11.

The scope of learning analytics

The scope of learning analytics is sometimes limited to basic data (the first five categories in Table 8.1). It should and often does include category six, the evaluation of learning events. In fact, commentators such as Mattox and Van Buren (2016) have focused much of their work on this aspect of analysis. But a warning on the limitations of this approach has been given by Anderson (2007: 1) as quoted in Chapter 7.

The aim should be to apply more comprehensive analytics to reveal overall trends and requirements and to provide a justification for total spending on L&D as well as expenditure on particular aspects of it. Approaches to measuring and evaluating the overall impact of L&D were discussed in Chapter 7. Let's return to the case study from Chapter 7, which also has relevance here.

CASE STUDY

Measuring the contribution of learning to business performance at Lyreco Ltd (UK)

Lyreco is a large office supplies company with branches in Europe, Canada and Asia. Metrics are a central part of all management processes and these inform learning investment and planning. In field sales, measures include sales turnover, margin and new business, whilst in customer service the performance and productivity metrics include costs per line, abandoned call rate, average call time, and average wait time. Monthly performance results in all areas are scrutinized to identify areas for attention, and the learning and development team run learning sessions and activities aimed at helping people to improve their performance. When sales margin was identified as an area for attention, over 150 people attended focused workshops and subsequent performance results were tracked to measure improvements. Similarly, warehouse supervisors with the highest staff turnover attended learning programmes and, as a consequence, staff turnover was at its lowest ever levels.

KEY LEARNING POINTS

Introduction

The effectiveness of evidence-based L&D is largely dependent on information about what is happening and what is likely to happen to people and learning and development in the organization.

Learning analytics defined

The assembly and analysis of data on learning and development programmes and activities to establish their effectiveness and identify the need for changes or new initiatives. Learning analytics gathers evidence and understanding that can be put to good use.

How learning analytics works

Learning analytics applies measures or metrics in order to guide decision-making on present and future L&D activities. It provides the basis for measuring such things as the impact of L&D practices, the effectiveness of learning programmes and levels of learning engagement. It can demonstrate the return-on-investment achieved by L&D activities.

Levels of learning analytics

1 **Descriptive analytics**: The use of data to record a particular aspect of learning and provide information on what has been happening to, for example, the number of people who have undergone training.

2 **Multi-dimensional analytics**: The combination of different sets of data to establish any relationships (correlations) between them and, hopefully, indicate causation (eg that a particular L&D initiative has caused an improvement in performance).

3 **Predictive analytics**: The analysis and use of historical data to predict trends and therefore provide guidance on L&D strategy.

The scope of learning analytics

The scope of learning analytics is sometimes limited to basic data. But it should make use of more comprehensive analytics to reveal overall trends and requirements and to provide a justification for total spending on L&D as well as expenditure on particular aspects of it. This suggests that a return on investment (RoI) approach is required.

References

Anderson, V (2007) *The Value of Learning: From return on investment to return on expectation*, CIPD, London

Chartered Institute of Personnel and Development (2017) *Human capital metrics and analytics: Assessing the evidence of the value and impact of people*, CIPD, London

Daly, J and Ahmetaj, G (2020) *Back to the Future: Why tomorrow's workforce needs a learning culture*, Emerald Works, London

Drucker, P (1988) *The coming of the new organization*, Harvard Business Review, January-February, pp 45–53

Kirkpatrick, D L (1994) *Evaluating Training Programmes*, San Francisco, CA, Berret-Koehler

Mattox, J R and Van Buren, M (2016) *Learning Analytics*, Kogan Page, London

Stewart, J and Rogers, P (2017) *Studying Learning and Development*, CIPD, London

PART TWO

The responsibility for learning and development

09

The role of the learning and development function

Introduction

The learning and development function is a centre of expertise. Its members exercise the insight required to appreciate the learning strategy needed by the organization. They possess the professional skills and business acumen required to formulate the strategy and to implement it by providing the advice and services required. This chapter starts with reviews of the role and organization of the learning and development function and continues with an analysis of the roles of its members and the considerable range of skills they need to carry out their often demanding duties.

The L&D function: activities and purpose

The L&D function provides advice, guidance and services in order to develop the capability of employees and thus improve individual and organizational performance. Rosemary Harrison (2009: 8) observed that its primary purpose is 'to aid collective progress through the collaborative, expert and ethical stimulation and facilitation of learning and knowledge that support business goals, develop individual potential, and respect and build on diversity.'

What might be called a learning and development revolution has taken place over the last few years. Although formal training courses are still provided where appropriate and formal digital learning is becoming important, the focus is now more on workplace, social and self-directed learning. This has also meant changes in the role of the L&D function and its members. As a local government L&D consultant remarked (CIPD, 2016: 32)

We are moving from courses to resources – becoming a curator of content, building management capability in developing self-directing learning, developing organisational agility and developing key skills to work effectively in a global organisation.

Members of the function are concerned on a daily basis with learning design, delivery and impact. But these activities need to take place withing the framework of a well-understood L&D strategy which is aligned to the business or corporate strategy. This L&D strategy should be designed to provide a comprehensive framework for developing people through the establishment of a learning culture and the encouragement of organizational and individual learning, talent management and knowledge management processes. As the CIPD (2010: 5) put it: 'The aim is to help organizations 'to find new ways of meeting current and future challenges.'

Research by Hird and Sparrow (2012: 7) led to the conclusion that: 'Traditionally L&D departments have been transactional support functions that supply a range of courses that satisfy requests for support from the business. However, the business is increasingly looking for learning support that fits the requirements of knowledge workers – embedded in day-to-day activity, supporting development of professional networks and ultimately ensuring that the business has the knowledge and skills to deliver the business plan.' They also noted (page 8) that: 'The influence of L&D in the organization was expanding, their learning offerings would grow, online learning was set to take centre stage, the majority of learning would become collaborative, and would be delivered in short timescales using micro-modules [micro-learning] to provide more focused learning. This would require significant change in course design and presentation, a move beyond current primary offerings of mainly foundational skills, and the need to embrace more blended learning (ie combining different learning methods).'

CASE STUDY

Remit of the Learning and Education (L&E) function in PricewaterhouseCoopers

1 **Transformation**: leadership of the PwC research and development agenda on learning technologies.

2 **Adoption**: Consultancy with territories and groups on learning strategies and development and delivery of global content.

3 **Foundation**: Management of core systems powering learning across the organization.

Organization of the L&D function

The survey conducted by the CIPD (2020) revealed that in larger organizations the learning and development function is usually incorporated within HR. L&D is either a specialist section of the HR department (29 per cent) or part of generalist HR activities (16 per cent). L&D activities are split between HR and another area of the business in 14 per cent of organizations. In the remaining 41 per cent of organizations, learning and development activities are completely separate from the HR function – having either a separate function and different reporting line (11 per cent), sitting within the business function (10 per cent) or with operations and/or line managers (18 per cent). This pattern is much more common in smaller organizations. The CIPD (2020: 15) argued that positioning L&D outside of HR has benefits in diagnosing performance needs, engaging managers in the design and delivery process, and facilitating learning solutions in the flow of work.

The CIPD survey also established that there is considerable variation in L&D budgets. Just over a third of respondents had an annual budget of less than £150 per employee, while 22 per cent had a budget of more than £750 per employee per annum.

The different types of L&D professionals within the L&D function obviously vary according to the size and complexity of the organization. In a large department under the leadership of a head of L&D they could include:

- *strategic business partners* who work with line managers to help them improve the performance of their departments through L&D activities such as onboarding training, facilitating self-directed learning, skills instruction and development, coaching, mentoring and the use of performance management as a development aid;
- *learning specialists (trainers)* who have specialist skills in the design, delivery and evaluation of learning events and programmes;
- *digital learning specialists* who develop or commission digital learning processes (see Chapter 16) and help to implement them; they may work with content designers;
- *content designers and curators* who may be wholly engaged in creating or commissioning content for e-learning or for more traditional learning events, but, increasingly, may be involved in curating learning material for use by learners, especially self-directed learners;
- *administrators* who operate learning platforms, administrate learning events, maintain records and prepare learning analytics.

These roles could be combined in different ways and in smaller organizations L&D professionals may be concerned to a degree with all or most of them. But they will obviously have to prioritize and will often be almost entirely employed in planning and running learning events with perhaps some e-learning thrown in.

The CIPD 2020 survey found that traditional jobs dominate the L&D function. The most commonly reported jobs are administrator (reported by 49 per cent of respondents), head of L&D/L&D manager (48 per cent), and face-to-face trainer/facilitator (46 per cent).

Evaluation of the function

The prime criteria for evaluating the work of the L&D function are its ability to operate strategically and its capacity to deliver the levels of services required. An evaluation should cover not only the work of the function as a whole but also the effectiveness of the main L&D policies and practices with which the function is concerned. The following questions should be answered when carrying out a review:

1 Does L&D policy and practice clearly support the achievement of the organization's goals?

2 To what extent is what is taking place in accordance with the principle of good practice?

3 How effectively is the policy or practice being implemented?

4 What impact is the policy or practice having on performance?

5 What are the reactions of line managers and employees generally to the policy or practice?

A further review of ways in which the overall contribution of L&D can be measured was included in Chapter 7.

The role of the L&D professional

L&D professionals work to provide the advice and services required to ensure that the learning needs of the organization and its members are satisfied, and in doing so, that the organization achieves its strategic goals. They help to create the learning strategy and develop a learning culture. Within that culture they manage the learning environment (the learning 'ecosystem') and provide whatever advice and services are needed to meet the learning and development objectives contained within the organization's L&D strategy.

The CIPD (2020:13) described the nature of the role of L&D professionals as follows:

- Work with leaders to define a vision for learning and transformation, clearly linked to organizational objectives.
- Support leaders to communicate a vision for learning and transformation.
- Evaluate current systems for knowledge management and learning: are they accessible across multiple devices, fit for purpose and set up for social and informal learning?
- Consider whether there are appropriate channels in place to allow individual and team learning and reflection to feed into organizational decision-making. If not, consider how a feedback loop can be implemented.
- Consider whether dialogue, challenge and reflection are embedded into the organization's approach. If not, consider how reflection and feedback can be encouraged as part of day-to-day activities.
- Examine whether individuals have an appropriate degree of voice and autonomy.

Changes in the role

The role of the L&D professional is changing. Old style training managers were almost exclusively engaged in providing formal courses or supervising formal training programmes and many still do; it is still an important activity. But new style learning and development professionals no longer spend most if not all of their time delivering face-to-face training events or supervising training. Instead, they are increasingly involved in providing some form of digitalized learning and, importantly, encouraging workplace learning.

The trend is for their role to become that of an internal consultant rather than an old-fashioned trainer. They advise on performance issues related to people and promote workplace and social learning. They are more concerned with facilitating learning than with delivering learning. Facilitating learning means guiding line managers on how to get learning done in their departments, encouraging and supporting self-directed learning, curating learning content and providing bite-sized training content (small easily assimilated chunks of learning) which can be accessed by employees on their smartphones.

This was confirmed through research conducted by the CIPD (2015: 3) which noted: 'A key shift is a move away from learning delivery to performance consultancy, underpinned by the need for L&D to be aligned to the business and deliver tangible organisational and individual impact. There is also increasingly a need for L&D to support social learning.' The CIPD commented that: 'L&D roles are becoming more diverse in response to a complex external environment. This represents a challenge for how to best focus roles. Do you build 'performance consultants' able to diagnose, develop and curate? Or do you need experts who are focused entirely on data analytics, coaching or online learning?' (page 15). Specific aspects of the role are examined in more detail below.

The role of L&D professionals in delivering learning

Delivering learning events or providing learning material is still an important L&D activity. The CIPD's 2020 survey found that face-to-face training contributed to between 60 and 100 per cent of the learning provided in 44 per cent of the respondents' organizations. L&D professionals carry out analyses of learning needs, create learning content for learning events and digital learning, plan and manage formal learning events and programmes and evaluate the effectiveness of learning.

The role of L&D professionals in workplace learning

Although most learning may occur in the workplace this does not absolve L&D from any responsibility for its effectiveness; quite the opposite. L&D has to be much more closely involved in what is going on than it was when it lived in a remote learning centre delivering formal courses. This is again a facilitation process and by no means as clear cut as planning and delivering learning events. It is probably the most difficult task facing L&D professionals.

What L&D professionals have to do is to encourage line managers to be fully involved in improving the quality of learning in their departments, advise them on how to set about it and provide coaching as required on how to do so. L&D professionals can advise on learning arrangements, for example, the provision of onboarding (induction) training, skills training, mentoring or buddying. They can help to choose people from within departments who can assist in training departmental members and monitor workplace learning arrangements to ensure that advice and help is given where necessary. They can persuade line managers to use performance management as a means of identifying learning needs and provide guidance on how this should be done. They can encourage managers to enter into learning contracts with their staff which provide for the satisfaction of those needs. They can provide online learning material to support learning in the flow of work.

The role of L&D professionals in facilitating self-directed learning

In self-directed learning as described in Chapter 5, individuals take charge of the whole learning process. They identify their learning needs, decide on their learning objectives, locate the resources needed for learning, initiate learning programmes and finally evaluate their learning. By definition, L&D professionals are not directly involved in delivering the learning but they do have a role to play in providing encouragement and advice, helping people 'to learn to learn' and in curation – advising on the learning material available and enabling it to be accessed online.

The role of L&D professionals in social learning

The role of L&D professionals in social learning is to liaise with work teams to build or enhance existing sharing practices as an integral part of their daily work, not as an extra initiative. 'Supporting social learning involves working closely with teams – not by designing a programme of instruction for them, but by encouraging team members to share their knowledge and engage in new collaborative work practices' (Hart, 2014: 42). L&D professionals may be involved in establishing and managing an Enterprise Social Network (ESN) which can service special interest groups and enable online forum discussions to take place. They can set up and facilitate communities of practice, learning communities and learning sets as described in Chapter 15.

The role of L&D professionals in digital learning

L&D professionals establish which forms of digital learning should be adopted, select and operate learning platforms (integrated sets of e online services that provide information, tools and resources to support and enhance learning delivery), create e-learning content, and oversee the application of digital learning as part of a blended learning approach with particular relevance to self-directed learning.

The role of L&D professionals in content creation

Content creation is what L&D professionals do when they produce original material for learning purposes. The created content is used in formal learning events (training courses) or is made available online (e-learning) or through webinars, blogs, podcasts, social media, videos or infographics (visual representations of information or data). Content creation involves knowing about learning needs and creating visual and text-based learning material that will meet them. There is much to be said for creating content in small easily absorbed pieces – micro-learning – especially when it is presented online. It may be appropriate to use content creation mainly to provide learning material which meets specific learning needs in the organization, for example, onboarding and compliance and to use content curation to provide people with a wide range of information which they can access easily.

The role of L&D professionals in content curation

L&D professionals today are concerned with curating content just as much as they are with content creation, if not more so. Content curation is the process of gathering information from internal or external sources that is relevant to a particular topic or learning need, and then sharing it with employees, often on a learning platform or through a learning app. Sources of information can come via benchmarking, journals, blogs, news items, social media posts, Google, Wikipedia, TedTalks and e-books. Platforms like Buzzsumo can also assemble information. A corporate Twitter account can be set up with Twitter Lists to categorize and organize followers with mutual topic interests and engage and interact with them. Content obtained from other sources can be customized. But when making use of content from disparate sources it is necessary to be clear about what is needed and to evaluate its effectiveness.

The role of L&D professionals in performance consulting

Performance consulting consists of identifying or responding to a business or corporate need, especially one that involves performance, analysing the nature and reasons for the need and deciding how a learning and development initiative could satisfy it. This may mean facilitating workplace learning or planning and implementing a formal learning event or programme. The ultimate purpose is to connect behaviour with corporate or business results in order to engage employees and encourage them to develop the capabilities and carry out the activities that will achieve that purpose. To be effective as performance consultants L&D professionals need to possess business acumen and know the key factors that affect organizational performance and how these factors impinge on the performance expected from individual employees and on the skills they need.

There is a range of possible approaches. Formal training – a course designed to fill a defined gap in the knowledge and/or skills required to achieve high performance – is the most obvious although not necessarily the most effective one. Alternatively, and often preferably, it could mean coaching. Or it could involve enabling someone to broaden their experience (workshop learning). This might be the best alternative, although care would be needed to plan the experience and ensure that learning takes place as a result.

Performance consultants can use a diagnostic devised by Weisbord (1976) which he called the Six Boxes Model. Information is collected and analysed under the following six headings to identify and deal with behavioural problems that negatively affect performance:

1 Expectations and feedback.

2 Tools and resources.

3 Consequences.

4 Skills and knowledge.

5 Selection and assignment (capacity).

6 Motives and preferences (attitude).

The demands of the role

The demands on L&D professionals are considerable. The CIPD's 2018 Towards Maturity Health Check reported that 57 per cent of L&D professionals believed that they were overwhelmed and underequipped. The three areas of core knowledge they need to increase learning effectiveness and organizational impact were identified by the CIPD (2019) as business acumen, analytics and learning culture.

Business acumen means that L&D professionals need to understand the critical factors that determine success in a profit-making firm (how it makes money), its business model and its business strategies, especially those leading to expansion and the development of new products, services and markets which require different skills. In a public sector or not-for-profit organization they need to understand its purpose, how that purpose is achieved, any changes planned in its services and activities and, again, the factors that contribute to its success. But as noted by the CIPD (2019: 10) the findings of its survey 'showed that L&D professionals lack the ability to demonstrate and apply business acumen to a level regarded as satisfactory by the wider organisation. This raises doubts about the competence and professionalism of the function.'

In any organization they need to: 1) possess insight into the people issues relating to capability in order to establish learning and development needs; 2) have the ability to facilitate workplace and social learning; 3) possess technological capability, especially related to the use of digital learning; 4) have the skills required to diagnose problems, develop correct solutions and use learning analytics to help plan and evaluate learning. They should also have the ability to understand how learning cultures are formed and developed. And of course, if they are involved in learning events they need the skills required to plan and deliver them. The CIPD (2016: 37) quoted a Senior Manager, Academy Development in the finance sector as follows: 'We need social learning and collaboration tools. Ability to facilitate learning rather than deliver learning. Using analytics to understand performance improvement. Curating content that exists already rather than buying new.'

The specific skills required by L&D professionals were listed by Daly and Ahmetaj (2020) as:

- learning and development strategy;
- identification of learning needs;
- instructional design;
- digital content development;
- classroom/F2F learning/training delivery;
- live online learning delivery;
- facilitating social and collaborative learning;
- implementing blended learning;
- programme evaluation and data analytics;
- performance consulting.

KEY LEARNING POINTS

The role of the L&D function

The role of the L&D function is to provide advice, guidance and services in order to develop the capability of employees and thus improve individual and organizational performance.

The role of the L&D professional

L&D professionals no longer spend most if not all of their time delivering training events or supervising training programmes although they may still be involved in the development of e-learning programmes. Instead their role is much more that of an internal consultant advising on and promoting workplace and social learning who may act as a coach but not an old-fashioned trainer.

As established through research conducted by the CIPD (2015: 3): 'A key shift is a move away from learning delivery to performance consultancy, underpinned by the need for L&D to be aligned to the business and deliver tangible organizational and individual impact.

Research by the CIPD (2015:15) produced the comment that: 'L&D roles are becoming more diverse in response to a complex external environment. This represents a challenge for how to best focus roles. Do you build 'performance consultants' able to diagnose, develop and curate? Or do you need experts who are focused entirely on data analytics, coaching or online learning?'

L&D professionals:

- analyse learning needs and make proposals on how these can best be satisfied;
- advise line managers on the achievement of workplace learning and coach them on the learning and development skills they need;
- promote social learning;
- develop e-learning and the use of social media to aid learning;
- provide individual coaching;
- plan, implement and evaluate training events and programmes, often outsourcing training to external providers.

The role of L&D in workplace learning

L&D has in effect a consultancy and coaching role – much harder and more demanding than laying on a course but more rewarding,

What L&D has to do is to focus on line managers and their team leaders who need to be briefed on their responsibilities for learning and coached in how to fulfill them.

The role of L&D in social learning

The role of L&D in social learning is basically to liaise with work teams to build or enhance existing sharing practices as an integral part of their daily work, not as an extra initiative.

The role of L&D in digital learning

L&D professionals establish the potential for the use of digital learning, identify the most appropriate forms, develop the content of learning programmes and oversee its application as part of a blended learning approach with particular relevance to self-managed learning.

The skills required

L&D professionals need to understand the business, possess insight into the people issues relating to capability and skill in order to establish learning and development needs, have the ability to facilitate workplace and social learning, possess technological capability, especially related to the use of e-learning, and have diagnostic and analytical skills.

References

Chartered Institute of Personnel and Development (CIPD) (2010) *Next Generation HR*, CIPD, London

CIPD (2015) *Learning and Development: Evolving Roles, Enhancing Skills*, CIPD, London

CIPD (2016) *Preparing for the Future of Learning: A Changing Perspective for L&D Leaders*, CIPD, London

CIPD (2018) *Towards Maturity Health Check*, CIPD, London

CIPD (2019) *Professionalising Learning and Development*, CIPD, London

CIPD (2020) *Learning and Skills at Work 2020*, CIPD, London

Daly, J and Ahmetaj, G (2020) *Back to the Future: Why tomorrow's workforce needs a learning culture*, Emerald Works, London

Harrison, R (2009) *Learning and Development*, 5th edn, CIPD, London

Hart, J (2014) *The Social Learning Handbook* [Online] http://www.c4lpt.co.uk/blog/2014/01/27/social-learning-handbook-pdf-now-available/ (archived at https://perma.cc/8N4C-JEP2)

Hird, M and Sparrow, P (2012) *Learning & Development: Seeking a renewed focus?* White Paper 12/01 Centre for Performance-Led HR, Lancaster University, [Online] http://www.lancaster.ac.uk/media/lancaster-university/content-assets/documents/lums/cphr/LDWP.pdf (archived at https://perma.cc/YW8L-4SFH)

Weisbord, M R (1976) Organizational diagnosis: Six places to look for trouble with or without a theory, *Group Organization Management*, 1, pp 430–47

10

The role of the line manager

Introduction

Line managers show people how to do things and structure and provide learning opportunities. In 2005 the CIPD reported that:

> The role of the line manager is critical to training and development in organisations. Line managers initiate a high percentage of the training that takes place. They are also responsible for over half of the discussions with employees on the effectiveness of training that takes place. Ensuring that line managers have the skills for and are committed to support learning and development is essential.

The message is still the same today. The CIPD (2020a) report on learning culture stated that:

> Our review found evidence that suggests managers play a pivotal role and can be more influential for individual learning than overall learning culture. Managers need to deliver on operational objectives – allowing individuals to take time out of their role to attend training or other forms of development is not often top priority. However, managers stand to benefit by prioritising learning.

In this chapter, the first section deals with what managers can actually do about learning in their department; the second section examines the conditions in which they can carry out their development role and the third covers how the L&D function can help.

The vital role of line managers in L&D

Research by Hutchinson and Purcell (2007) led to the conclusion that:

> Line managers are critical conduits of learning from induction, the organising of 'buddies', the design of jobs that stretch, the learning function of teamworking and problem-solving, the provision of coaching (both for poor, or new, performers and for budding stars), to the assessment of development needs both formally in the annual performance management cycle and informally as is necessary or opportune.

More recently, the CIPD (2020b) observed that:

> Line managers are critical in supporting continuous learning at work and need to be supported to enable them to take more responsibility for the growth and development of their people in their daily working lives. They are key to shaping workplace culture and fostering a work environment that is productive and supportive of learning. This means identifying learning needs, encouraging participation in learning, helping to assess learning impact, supporting both formal and informal learning and valuing non-training ways of learning, adopting modern learning practices themselves, and encouraging the sharing of knowledge and experiences in their teams.

An American view (Hamori, 2018) was that: 'Line managers have the domain expertise to guide course selection for the development of job-relevant skills. They are also well positioned to support individuals' self-directed learning within work hours: They can balance workloads so that people will have time to study.'

But managers and their team members may have different views about how learning should take place. Research by Lilovai and Poell (2019) led to the following conclusion:

> The results of the study provide support for the view that employees and managers differ in the HRD activities they prefer for themselves, respectively, for their direct reports. Although the biggest per cent of both groups did not demonstrate a specific preference, the order in which the activities came after that revealed that employees were more likely to choose formal courses and programs over job experiences, whereas managers preferred job experiences over formal courses and programs.

The research by Hutchinson and Purcell (2007) established that the line manager role was seen as fundamental in:

- Induction (onboarding) activities – providing initial explanations of what the role entails with possibly some instruction or coaching in the skills required, arranging for a 'buddy' to guide and advise the new starter and in encouraging shadowing or working alongside a member of staff to cover key aspects of the work.

• Giving access to challenging work or being a member of a project team – being starved of good work in some instances was an outcome of poor performance. Good performers got the cutting-edge work that provided the best route for learning new things by doing.

• Continuing coaching and guidance – where the line manager works with a member of staff in dealing with a difficult business issue, the use of technology or handling a demanding customer. Coaching staff, particularly poor performers, is a key activity for many line managers.

Performance coaching is particularly important. Heslin *et al* (2006) identified three dimensions of this: guidance, facilitation and inspiration. Managers encourage team members to stimulate the learning of their colleagues. Employees often agree that their colleagues help them learn shortcuts and better ways to do their jobs. As explained by Schleicher *et al* (2018) this occurs amidst the other day-to-day manager-employee interactions.

Following their research, Govaerts *et al* (2017) suggested that managers should exercise their responsibility for meeting the learning needs of their team members by discussing learning needs, agreeing with them performance and learning goals, taking an interest in what they learn by observing and checking their progress, offering opportunities for them to practise newly learned skills and providing them with resources and practical support.

Unfortunately, all this may not happen. The CIPD (2018) concluded from its focus group research that: 'Line managers were viewed as a key gate-keeper to progression and development opportunities. Yet, many [focus group members] cited that their manager either did not have the time or experience to fulfil this role effectively. However, though this role was seen as crucial, most line managers themselves, while enjoying this aspect of their work, had received no training on how to carry this function out effectively.'

The Learning and Skills at Work 2020b survey conducted by the CIPD found that just half (50 per cent) of organizations reported that line managers encourage participation in learning and less than a third report that they facilitate continuous learning and support their teams to transfer what they have learned back into the workplace (29 per cent and 28 per cent respectively). Under a third (31 per cent) of organizations report that line managers are involved in assessing L&D impact and just 39 per cent are involved in determining learning needs.

Supporting line managers

The limited involvement of line managers in L&D activities referred to above indicates the need to provide them with more support, encouragement, guidance and training. The steps that can be taken are to:

- encourage line managers' buy-in and commitment to learning and development by communicating the importance and value of development-related activities, by clarifying their responsibilities in role profiles (it should be a key result area) and through performance management in which L&D goals should be set and reviewed;

- ensure that managers have the time as well as the inclination to carry out their learning and development duties;

- provide ongoing guidance and advice to managers supplemented by coaching and training;

- obtain senior management commitment and encourage leaders to act as role models;

- select line managers carefully, paying particular attention to behavioural competencies that facilitate learning and development in themselves and others.

Much of the onus for doing all this rests with the learning and development function. L&D professionals need to give priority to supporting line managers so that learning and development will happen where it should happen, in the workplace, guided by line managers with L&D support.

KEY LEARNING POINTS

The L&D role of line managers

Line managers play a pivotal role in learning and development. They structure and deliver learning opportunities, provide coaching and guidance and lead teams to stimulate the learning of team members

Providing support

There is a need to provide line managers with more support, encouragement, guidance and training. The L&D function should give this priority.

References

Chartered Institute of Personnel and Development (CIPD) (2005) *Who Learns at Work? Employees' Experiences of Training and Development*, CIPD, London

CIPD (2018) *Over-skilled and underused: investigating the untapped potential of UK skills*, CIPD, London

CIPD (2020a) *Creating Learning Cultures* [Online] *https://www.cipd.co.uk/Images/creating-learning-cultures-1_tcm18-75606.pdf* (archived at https://perma.cc/R4YA-BJKN)

CIPD (2020b) *Learning and Skills at Work 2020*, CIPD, London

Govaerts, N, *et al* (2017) A supervisors' perspective on their role in transfer of training, *Human Resource Development Quarterly*, **28** (4), pp 515–52

Hamori, M (2018) *Can MOOCs solve your training problem?* Harvard Business Review, January–February, pp 71–76

Heslin, P A, VandeWalle, D, Latham, G P (2006) Keen to help? Managers' implicit person theories and their subsequent employee coaching, *Personnel Psychology*, **59**, pp 871–902

Hutchinson, S and Purcell, J (2007) Learning and the Line: the Role of Line Managers in Training, *Learning and Development*, CIPD, London

Lilova, I and Poell, R F (2019) Preferred human resource development activities and their functions: differences in perspective between managers and employees, *International Journal of Training & Development*, **23** (3), pp 185–201

Schleicher, D J, *et al* (2018) Putting the System Into Performance Management Systems: A review and agenda for performance management research, *Journal of Management*, **44** (6), pp 2209-45

PART THREE

The process of learning

11

The nature of learning

Introduction

This chapter contains an overall analysis of the nature of learning as an introduction to the more detailed descriptions of learning processes that follow. It starts with a preliminary look at the basis of learning, including the 70:20:10 model, and continues with an examination of what encourages people learn in terms of how they are motivated and engaged. The rest of the chapter is devoted to a summary of the learning theories that explain how people learn and the lessons that can be learnt from neuroscience.

The basis of learning

Learning is the process by which a person acquires and develops new knowledge, skills, capabilities, behaviours and attitudes. It was defined by Harrison (2009: xxvii) as: 'A qualitative change in a person's way of seeing, experiencing, understanding and conceptualizing something in the real world.' In particular, learning in organizations is concerned with gaining declarative knowledge of facts, developing procedural knowledge about how to do things, and acquiring skills. Learning happens primarily in the domain of the workplace but it also occurs in the other domains of social learning, digital learning and formal training.

As described by Collins (2016: 51): 'Learning is a process by which changes in your brain allow you to behave and respond in particular ways'. People learn by doing (experiential learning) and from each other (social or cooperative learning) and to a smaller extent, by instruction (training). As Brown and Duguid (1991: 48) contended: 'The central issue in learning is *becoming* a practitioner not learning *about* practice.' According to the CIPD's survey *Who Learns at Work?* (2005: 4), the best way to learn is 'being shown how to do things and then practising them'.

But self-directed, discretionary, learning is important. It takes place when individuals of their own volition actively seek to acquire the knowledge and skills they need to carry out their work. The organization helps by providing customized learning that allows people to adapt their learning in a way that enables them to achieve their individual goals. The 70:20:10 L&D model is a widely accepted explanation of the relative significance of experiential, social and formal training, and the nature of learning is clarified by an analysis of the different types of learning.

The 70:20:10 model

The significance of learning from experience and from others (social learning) and the relatively small contribution made by formal training is represented by the 70:20:10 model for learning and development based on research conducted by the Centre for Creative Leadership (Lombardo and Eichinger, 1996). This claims that people's development will be about 70 per cent from work experience, about 20 per cent from social learning and 10 per cent from formal training courses. In other words, by far the most learning takes place informally in the workplace, while formal instruction plays a much less important part.

The model has been criticized by Clardy (2018) on the grounds that it has been under-researched and the evidence for it is therefore weak. In reality, he argued, learning doesn't happen in these three neat boxes and thinking of it in this way can do more harm than good. The model should not be taken too literally and should instead be regarded simply as an illustration of the value of experiential and social learning. And it is still necessary to recognize the importance of formal training which can play an important role in helping people to acquire specific knowledge and skills, especially when it is blended with other forms of learning.

Types of learning

There are three types of learning:

1 *Affective learning* – relates to the learner's interests, attitudes and motivations. In the digital age we are living through, affective learning can be enhanced by technology.

2 *Contextual learning* – is based on the constructivist theory of learning (Piaget, 1973). Learning takes place when people are able to construct meaning based on their own experiences.

3 *Situated learning* – **is learning that is** embedded within activity, context and culture. It is often unintentional rather than deliberate. (Lave, 1988). Social interaction and collaboration are essential components of situated learning – workers learn from their immediate colleagues and become involved in 'communities of practice' consisting of people bound together by shared expertise who exchange information on how to get things done. Situated learning is related to the notion of learning through social development (Vygotsky, 1980).

What makes people want to learn?

People want to learn if they are motivated to learn and engaged with the learning process.

The motivation to learn

As Reynolds *et al* (2002: 34) commented: 'The disposition and commitment of the learner – their motivation to learn – is one of the most critical factors affecting training effectiveness. Under the right conditions, a strong disposition to learn, enhanced by solid experience and a positive attitude, can lead to exceptional performance.'

Two motivation theories are particularly relevant to learning. Expectancy theory states that goal-directed behaviour is driven by the expectation of achieving something that the individual regards as desirable. If individuals feel that the outcome of learning is likely to benefit them they will be more inclined to pursue it. When they find that their expectations have been fulfilled, their belief that learning is worthwhile will be reinforced.

Goal theory states that motivation is higher when individuals aim to achieve specific goals, when these goals are accepted and, although difficult, are achievable, and when there is feedback on performance. Learning goals may be set for individuals (but to be effective as motivators they must be agreed) or, better still, individuals may set their own goals (self-directed learning).

Another relevant concept explaining the factors that affect learning is the AMO model developed by Boxall and Purcell (2003). This states that performance depends on the individual's ability, motivation and opportunity. Employees must have the ability to perform well and the motivation to do so, while organizations must ensure that they are given the opportunity to perform. Boxall and Purcell (2016: 155) formulated the AMO framework as $P = f(A,M,O)$. They noted that someone's ability, motivation and opportunity to perform would depend on two groups of factors: 1) the individual's experience, intelligence, health personality etc, and 2) the situational factors of HR and L&D policies and practices orientated to creating 'AMO' and related variables in the production system and the organizational context.

Learner engagement

Learner engagement takes place when learners want to learn, are committed to their learning activities and go on to make good use of the outcome of those activities. It is about the individual's involvement and satisfaction with as well as enthusiasm for learning. Noe *et al* (2010: 281) referred to the increased recognition that the learner is at least as important as the instructor (the learner-centric perspective) and suggested that this emphasized the importance of learner engagement. They also commented (page 284) that:

> First, engagement may lead to greater knowledge and skill acquisition. That is, when learners are engaged, they may benefit more from learning interventions. Second, engagement may lead to more favourable learner reactions (ie engaged individuals may enjoy the process of learning more). Third, the design and delivery of learning activities may not necessarily promote learner engagement. Due to a variety of constraints, learning activities may not always be designed to immerse individuals in the learning process but rather to maximize efficiency and reduce the cost of instruction.

Shuck *et al* (2014) argued that it is an important psychological experience that connects L&D practices with employee outcomes.

The following types of learner engagement were classified by education psychologist Jenifer Fredericks (quoted by Beevers *et al*, 2020: 262):

- *Behavioural engagement* describing how people actually behave in a learning situation. Do they demonstrate good conduct? If so, how deep does it go?

- *Emotional engagement* referring to the extent to which people enjoy their learning experience. Do they feel happy, comfortable and included?

- *Cognitive engagement* referring to how much people actually apply themselves to the learning and exert the mental effort required to learn.

This classification provides a basis for assessing learner engagement as do the following comments made by Steve George of the CIPD (quoted by Beevers *et al*, 2020: 266): 'Learner engagement is arguably the foundation for all good outcomes that result from the content you create. Engagement is the psychological investment made by a learner; aspects such as the level of curiosity they show, their attention and reflection on the learning, the extent to which they are an active participant in the learning experience and not just a passive observer.'

Learning strategy can include proposals for enhancing learner engagement such as:

- Create a positive learning culture.
- Ensure senior management demonstrates their support for learning.
- Ensure that line managers support and encourage learning.
- Adopt learner-centric policies.
- Encourage and support self-directed learning.
- Provide digital learning support.
- Reward people who are successful learners.
- Ensure that employees know the learning opportunities available to them.
- Respond quickly to requests for help with learning.
- Provide learning 'just in time and just for you' targeted to meet individual learning needs.

How people learn

There are a number of different theories of learning as described below that aim to explain how people learn. Each of them provides a different perspective on the process of learning which has been enhanced by the lessons provided by neuroscience.

Behaviourist learning theory

Behaviourist learning theory is concerned with the behaviour of people and how they can learn to change that behaviour or learn new ones. It is based on the idea of 'stimulus-response' – changes in behaviour take place as a result of an individual's response to events or stimuli and the ensuing consequences (rewards or punishments). This is called 'associative learning'. Thorndike (1898) conducted experiments that produced the 'Law of Effect' which states that when behaviour is followed by something pleasant it is likely to be repeated but behaviour followed by something unpleasant will stop. This led to the concept of reinforcement which is the belief that Individuals can be 'conditioned' to repeat behaviour by positive reinforcement in the form of feedback and knowledge of results. This idea was developed by Skinner (1974) as the notion of 'operant conditioning', the process through which the strength of a behaviour is modified by reinforcement or punishment.

Reservations about behaviourist learning theory were expressed by Doloriert *et al* (2014: 13) who wrote that:

> There are widely accepted criticisms of the behavioural approach. By focusing on observable behaviour, especially in animals, the behavioural approach only provides a partial view of learning in humans. It does not explore those areas which are 'particular and special to humans' (Mullins, 1998, p 361) such as personality, desire, free will and incidental/accidental learning.

But behaviourist theory has had and still has considerable influence on L&D practice. As Beevers *et al* (2020: 271) noted:

> The influence of behaviourism on L&D is easy to see. The systematic approaches taken by the behaviourists can still be seen in how we approach L&D in organizations; seeking a clear and systematic understanding of what needs to be achieved (or changed), directing our efforts and resources at bringing about the change, measuring our effectiveness on an ongoing basis, and making adjustments to achieve the desired results.

Cognitivist learning theory

Cognitivist learning explains learning in terms of how the mind works. It refers to the acquisition of knowledge and understanding by absorbing information in the form of principles, concepts and facts and then internalizing it. Learners can be regarded as powerful information-processing machines. The cognitive processes of rehearsal, organization and elaboration are deployed to understand the concepts, link them together and put them to use. Cognitive learning theory originated in the work of Piaget (1973) who focused on how the development of learning took place.

Information processing theory (Sadler-Smith, 2008: 107) which, amongst other things, is concerned with the learning of skills, divides cognition into four stages:

1 Input processing.

2 Short-term storage and active processing.

3 Encoding and embedding in long-term memory.

4 Output.

A development of cognitive learning theory is constructivism which, as noted by Doloriert *et al* (2014: 15), states that: 'Learning is a process for actively constructing knowledge rather than passively absorbing information.'

Experiential learning theory

Experiential learning takes place when people learn from their experience by absorbing and reflecting on it so that it can be understood and applied. Thus people become active agents of their own learning.

As long ago as 1910 John Dewey defined learning as a continuous reorganization and reconstruction of experience (reflective experience). People only learn when they are able to reflect on their actions and recognize as well as reconstruct experience by a continuous process of reflection. This is thinking as a means of action.

A model was created by Kolb *et al* (1974) to describe how experience is translated into concepts that are used to guide the choice of new experiences. As shown in Figure 11.1, this was expressed as a learning cycle consisting of four stages:

1 *Concrete experience* – this can be planned or accidental.

2 *Reflective observation* – this involves actively thinking about the experience and its significance.

3 *Abstract conceptualization (theorizing)* – generalizing from experience to develop various concepts and ideas that can be applied when similar situations are encountered.

4 *Active experimentation* – testing the concepts or ideas in new situations. This gives rise to a new concrete experience and the cycle begins again.

The key to this model is that it is a simple description of how experience is translated into concepts that are then used to guide the choice of new

FIGURE 11.1   The Kolb learning cycle

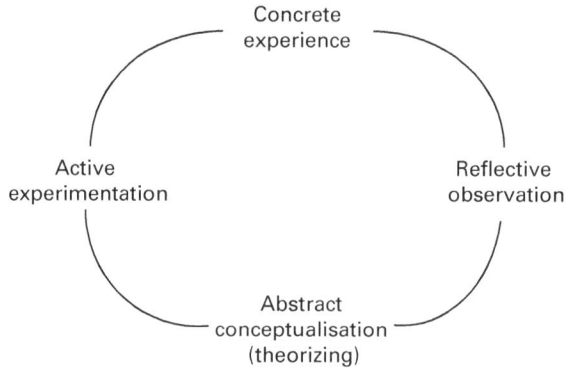

experiences. To learn effectively, individuals must shift from being observ-
ers to participants, from direct involvement to a more objective analytical
detachment.

The concept of 'learning in-the-flow of work' as discussed in Chapter 12 is
associated with experiential learning theory.

Social learning theory

Social learning theory was initiated by Bandura (1977) who viewed learning
as a series of information-processing steps set in train by social interactions.
Behaviours are learnt from experience but also through the example of others
which happens whether or not it is organized. Bandura emphasized the
importance of reflection and self-determination. The six concepts of Bandura's
social learning theory are:

1 *Expectations* – the individual's beliefs about likely results of actions.

2 *Observational learning* – the individual's beliefs based on observing similar
   and visible physical results of desired behaviour.

3 *Behavioural capability* - the knowledge and skills needed to influence
   behaviour.

4 *Self-efficacy* – confidence in ability to take action and persist in action.

5 *Reciprocal determinism* – behaviour changes resulting from interaction
   between a person and the environment; change is bi-directional.

6 *Reinforcement* – Responses to a person's behaviour that increase or
   decrease the chances of recurrence.

Social development learning theory as explained by Vygotsky (1980) states that effective learning requires social interaction, for example, with a more experienced colleague. Wenger (1998) suggested that we all participate in 'communities of practice' (groups of people with shared expertise who work together) and that these are our primary sources of learning.

The Revans contribution

A useful contribution to learning theory was made by Revans (1984) when he defined these assumptions underpinning his concept of action learning for managers (see Chapter 23):

1 Experienced managers are curious to know how other managers work.

2 People learn when they are motivated to learn something worthwhile.

3 Learning about oneself is threatening and is resisted if it tends to change one's self-image. However, it is possible to reduce the external threat to a level which no longer acts as a total barrier to learning about oneself.

4 People only learn when they do something, and they learn more the more responsible they feel the task to be.

5 Learning is deepest when it involves the whole person – mind, values, body, emotions.

6 The learner knows better than anyone else what he or she has learned. Nobody else has much chance of knowing.

The learning curve

The concept of the learning curve refers to the time it takes an inexperienced person to reach the required level of performance in a job or a task, which is sometimes called the experienced worker's standard (EWS). The existence of the learning curve needs to be taken into account when planning and implementing training or instruction programmes. The standard learning curve is illustrated in Figure 11.2.

But rates of learning vary, depending on the effectiveness of the training, the experience and natural aptitude of the learner and the latter's interest in learning. Both the time taken to reach the EWS and the variable speed with which learning takes place at different times affect the shape of the curve, as shown in Figure 11.3.

Learning is often stepped, with one or more plateaus, while further progress is halted. This may be because learners cannot continually increase their skills or speeds of work and need a pause to consolidate what they have already learnt. The existence of steps as illustrated in Figure 11.4 can be used when planning skills training to provide deliberate reinforcement periods when newly acquired skills are practised in order to achieve the expected standards. This is called the 'progressive parts method' of training.

FIGURE 11.2   A standard learning curve

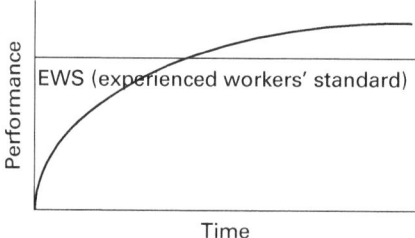

FIGURE 11.3   Different rates of learning

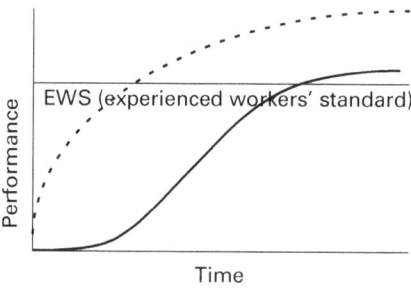

FIGURE 11.4   A stepped learning curve

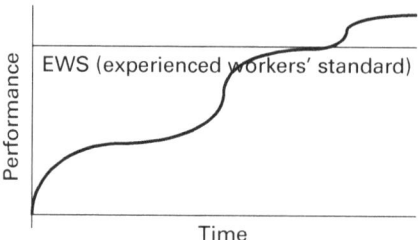

Lessons from neuroscience

Neuroscience is the study of how the brain works. As explained by Collins (2016: 57), it teaches us that learning 'is a physical set of changes in your brain that includes synthesizing new proteins, releasing neurotransmitters and changing your neurons to generate new connections.' The latter process was defined by Hebb (2002) whose 'law' states that 'cells that fire together wire together'. This means that when a new connection has been established it becomes stronger the more frequently it is 'refreshed'. So to learn something difficult you may have to go over it again and again.

Neuroscience also teaches us that our brains work best when they focus on one thing at a time, rather than multitasking. This means that in creating learning content for a learning event or online learning it may be advisable to sequence the learning in stages so that learners are able to grasp one concept before moving on to another. It also supports the idea of micro-learning.

Another key concept of neuroscience is that of neuroplasticity. This suggests that the brain has 'plasticity' in that it is able to keep developing and changing. It challenges the belief that the ability to learn diminishes with age. A frequently quoted study of neuroplasticity involved London taxi drivers, whose intense learning of London routes ('the knowledge') caused measurable development in their brains which changed their brain structure. As Howard-Jones (2014: 6) commented:

> Our brains build our learning, learning builds our brains... Everyone knows we need our brains to learn and sometimes we can even blame any difficulties we face when learning on our brains. However, our brains impose no clearly defined biological limit on our learning potential. Moreover, we can change and develop our brains through learning. Much of the building of our brains comes through the use of skills and experience, which can happen at any age.

The Maritz Institute (Hendel-Giller, 2010: 6) produced the following learning design principles based on research linking the Kolb learning cycle to the structure of the brain:

1 Engage the entire Kolb learning cycle. Make time for reflection, creating and active testing as well as absorbing new information.

2 Make a connection with the learner's prior knowledge and experience.

3 Create opportunities for social engagement and interaction as part of the learning process.

4 Engage both feeling and thinking. Learning needs emotion as well as intellect.

5 Actively attend to attention-gaining, holding and focusing the learner's attention.

6 Engage a maximum number of senses – especially visual – when designing learning.

A report by the Royal Society (2011: v) noted that: 'Biological factors play an important role in accounting for differences in learning ability between individuals.' The Royal Society listed four things that neuroscience has taught about what makes learning effective:

1 Emotional engagement with what is being learnt.

2 Keeping up physical exercise to prepare the brain for learning as well as maintaining learning energy.

3 Stimulating environments, both online and physically.

4 Time to reflect to embed the learning.

The models summarized below describe in different ways the lessons that can be learned from neuroscience on how to create the conditions that lead to effective learning.

RAD

Willis (2007) highlighted the importance of learning being a stress-free and enjoyable experience for effective outcomes. She used the acronym RAD, which relates to specific brain areas and functions, to encourage learning professionals to integrate neuroscience into their practice.

R (Reticular activating system RAS): All information enters the brain through sensory inputs but only a fraction makes it through the unconscious RAS filter. Effective learning content should therefore be non-threatening, novel and engaging.

A (Amgdala): The part of the brain's limbic system which acts as a filter to send information to the reactive or reflective areas of the brain. Learning requires reflection, which is supported by stress-free environments in which positive past experiences and strengths are highlighted. Stressful environments lead to a fight, flight or freeze reaction and should be avoided.

D (Dopamine): This chemical neurotransmitter, linked to our sense of pleasure, is released during pleasurable experiences. Effective learning is supported by creating positive associations with existing knowledge and past success, and through engaging and creative activities.

SCARF

The five factors in the SCARF model produced by Rock (2009) explain how we engage in social, interactive and collaborative settings. The model as set out below proposes that learning increases as threats are minimized and rewards maximized.

1 *S (Status):* Learning that's perceived to enhance status (leading to a promotion, for example), will be motivational.

2 *C (Certainty):* If we lack certainty about a situation our impulse may be to disengage, whereas clear steps and a sense of order can increase learning transfer.

3 *A (Autonomy):* A degree of autonomy in learning is a key factor in reducing stress, as it means we have some influence over what is taking place. There's a contrary impact if we are denied autonomy; effective learning involves some choice and control.

4 *R (Relatedness)*: If we feel trust, empathy and social connection during learning, oxytocin is released in the brain, which increases engagement.

5 *F (Fairness):* A sense of unfairness stirs hostility and threat, but learning which is perceived as fair and justified is motivational.

AGES

The AGES model created by Davachi *et al* (2010) proposes that learning design and delivery is more effective when the following four factors are considered:

A (Attention): We need to ensure minimal distractions and avoid cognitive overload; undivided attention is essential for effective learning. Novelty and varied techniques and approaches enhance attention.

G (Generation): We maximize the likelihood of positive engagement and formation of long-term memories when learning has personal meaning and significance. L&D practitioners should relate learning to existing knowledge and support personal, meaningful associations and applications.

E (Emotion): This is a key factor in fostering attention and enhancing memory function. Generating positive emotional experiences and social activities is key to effective learning transfer. Conversely, if learners have a negative emotion associated with learning, such as a fear of failure, they are less likely to engage.

S (Spacing): It's better to distribute learning in discrete blocks delivered over short time periods than cram lots of content into a prolonged session. 'Chunked' learning results in more effective transfer and aids long-term memory.

Practical implications of learning theory

The practical implications of learning theory are summarized in Table 11.1.

TABLE 11.1   The practical implications of learning theory

Theory	Content	Practical implications
Behaviourist theory	Behaviours can be strengthened by reinforcing them with positive feedback (conditioning).	Reinforcement theory underpins training programmes concerned with developing skills through instruction. In these, the learner is conditioned to make a response and receives immediate feedback and progress is made in incremental steps, each directed to a positive outcome.
Cognitive learning theory	Learners acquire understanding, which they internalize by being exposed to learning materials and by solving problems.	The knowledge and understanding of learners can be enriched and internalized by the use of a variety of learning materials in addition to face-to-face instruction (eg e-learning, case studies, projects and problem-solving activities). Cognitive learning theory also underpins self-directed learning and personal development planning activities.

(continued)

TABLE 11.1 (Continued)

Theory	Content	Practical implications
Experiential learning theory	People learn by constructing meaning and developing their skills through experience.	Learning through experience in the workplace can be enhanced by encouraging learners to reflect on and make better use of what they learn through their own work and from other people. Self-directed learning and personal development planning activities with help from facilitators, coaches or mentors are also underpinned by experiential learning theory, as is action learning.
Social learning theory	Learning is most effective in a social setting. Individual understanding is shaped by active participation in real situations.	Learning can be encouraged in communities of practice and in project teams and networks.
The learning curve	The time required to reach an acceptable standard of skill or competence, varies between people. Learning may proceed in steps with plateaus rather than being a continuous process.	Recognize that progress may vary and may not be continuous. Enable learners to consolidate their learning and introduce reinforcement periods in training programmes to recognize the existence of learning steps and plateaus.
Neuroscience	Understanding the way in which the brain functions provides useful insights into approaches to learning and development	The aids to effective learning include: • Emotional engagement with what is being learnt. • Stimulating environments, both physically and online. • Creating opportunities for social engagement and interaction as part of the learning process. • Time for the brain to reflect to embed the learning

KEY LEARNING POINTS

Learning defined

Learning is the process by which a person acquires and develops new knowledge, skills, capabilities, behaviours and attitudes. It can be described as the modification of behaviour.

The basis of learning

People learn by doing (experiential learning) and from each other (social or cooperative learning) and to a much smaller extent, by instruction (training). Discretionary, self-directed, learning is important.

The 70:20:10 model

The significance of learning from experience and from others (social learning) and the relatively small contribution made by formal training is represented by the 70/20/10 model for learning This claims that people's development will be about 70 per cent from work experience, about 20 per cent from social learning and 10 per cent from formal training courses. But these figures are only guidelines.

Types of learning

There are three types of learning: *affective learning, contextual learning* and *situated learning.*

What makes people want to learn?

People want to learn if they are motivated to learn and engaged with the learning process.

How people learn

How people learn is explained by learning theories (behaviourist, cognitivist, experiential and social learning), the concept of the learning curve and neuroscience.

References

Bandura, A (1977) *Social Learning Theory*, Prentice-Hall, Englewood Cliffs, New Jersey

Beevers, K, Rea, A and Hayden, D (2020) *Learning and Development Practice in the Workplace*, 4th edn, Kogan Page, London

Boxall, P F and Purcell, J (2003) *Strategy and Human Resource Management*, Palgrave Macmillan, Basingstoke

Boxall, P F and Purcell, J (2016) *Strategy and Human Resource Management*, 4th edn, Basingstoke, Palgrave Macmillan

Brown, J S and Duguid, P (1991) Organizational learning and communities-of-practice: toward a unified view of working, learning and innovating, *Organization Science*, **2** (1), pp 40–57

Chartered Institute of Personnel and Development. (2005) *Who Learns at Work? Employees' Experiences of Training and Development*, CIPD, London

Clardy, A (2018) 70-20-10 and the Dominance of informal learning: A fact in search of evidence, *HRD Review*, **17**(2), pp 153–178

Collins, S (2016) *Neuroscience for Learning and Development*, Kogan Page, London

Davachi, L, *et al* (2010) Learning that lasts through AGES, *NeuroLeadership Journal*, **3**, pp 53–63

Dewey, J (1910) *How We Think: A restatement of the Relation of Reflective Thinking to the Education Process,* D C Heath, Boston, Massachusetts

Doloriert, C, Stewart, J and Sambrook, S (2014) Individual and collective learning, in *Designing, Delivering and Evaluating L&D: Essentials for Practice,* eds J Stewart and P Cureton, Kogan Page, London

Harrison, R (2009) *Learning and Development,* 5th edn, CIPD, London

Hebb, D (2002) *The Organization of Behaviour,* NJ, Erlbaum, Mahwah

Hendel-Giller, R (2010) The neuroscience of learning: New paradigms for corporate education [Online] http://www.themaritzinstitute.com/Perspectives/-media/Files/ MaritzInstitute/White-Papers/The-Neuroscience-of-learning-The-Maritz-Institute.pdf (archived at https://perma.cc/P273-3XMX)

Howard-Jones, P (2014) *Neuroscience and Learning,* CIPD, London

Kolb, D A, Rubin, I M and McIntyre, J M (1974) *Organizational Psychology: An experimental approach*, Prentice-Hall, Englewood Cliffs, New Jersey

Lave, J (1988) *Cognition in Practice: Mind, Mathematics, and Culture in Everyday Life,* Cambridge University Press, Cambridge

Lombardo, M M and Eichinger, R W (1996) *The Course Architect Development Planner,* Lominger, Minneapolis,

Mullins, L J (2013) *Management and Organizational Behaviour,* 10th ed, Financial Times/ Prentice-Hall, London

Noe, R A, Tews, M J and Dachner, A M (2010) A new perspective for enhancing our understanding of learner motivation and workplace learning, *The Academy of Management Annals,* **4** (1) pp 279–315

Piaget, J (1973) *Memory and Imagination,* Basic Books, New York

Revans, R W (1989) *Action Learning,* Blond and Briggs, London

Reynolds, J, Caley, L and Mason, R (2002) *How Do People Learn?* CIPD, London

Rock, D (2009) *Your Brain at Work: Strategies for overcoming distraction, regaining focus, and working smarter all day long,* Harper-Collins, New York

Royal Society (2011) *Brain Waves 2: Neuroscience: implications for education and lifelong learning* [Online] https://royalsociety.org/topics-policy/projects/brain-waves/education-lifelong-learning/ (archived at https://perma.cc/P273-3XMX)

Sadler-Smith, E (2006) *Learning and Development for Managers: Perspectives from Research and Practice,* Blackwell, London

Shuck, B D. Twyford, D T, Reio, T G and Shuck, A (2014) Human resource development practices and employee engagement: Examining the connection with employee turnover intentions, *Human Resource Development Quarterly,* **25** (2), pp 239–70

Skinner, B F (1974) *About Behaviourism*, Cape, London

Thorndike, E L (1898) Animal intelligence: An experimental study of the associative processes in animals, *Psychological Monographs: General and Applied*, **2** (4), pp 109

Vygotsky, L S (1980) *Mind in Society: The development of higher psychological processes,* Harvard University Press, Boston

Wenger, E (1998) *Communities of Practice: Learning, meaning and identity*, Cambridge University Press, Cambridge

Willis, J (2007) The neuroscience of joyful education, *Educational Leadership*, **64** (9)

12

Approaches to learning and development

Introduction

Approaches to learning and development are the overall ways in which learning and development takes place, for example through formal or informal learning, rather than specific techniques such as coaching or instruction as dealt with in Chapter 13. The approaches described in this chapter are concerned with:

- recognizing the importance of the distinction between formal and informal learning;
- the concept of learning in-the-flow of work and its significance;
- making the best use of the various methods available in combination – blended learning;
- appreciating that learning is or should be happening all the time, it does not simply consist of one-off training courses – continuous learning;
- ensuring that the learning process takes advantage of the opportunities available in the workplace, including those provided by fellow workers – connected learning;
- recognizing that the capacity to absorb large quantities of information is limited and that it is better to provide it in small chunks – micro-learning;
- fitting learning to the needs of the learner – adaptive learning;
- increasing impact by making use of the procedures adopted in agile project work – agile learning;

- encouraging reflective practice in self-directed learning; and
- making use of performance management.

Formal and informal learning

People learn both formally and informally. Formal learning can occur face-to-face in a lecture room, a training centre or the workplace. It can also happen through various types of remote (digital) learning. Eraut (2000: 114) suggested that the characteristics of formal learning were a prescribed learning framework, an organized learning event or package and the existence of a designated trainer. However, although formal learning is the most popular form of learning provision, research by Josh Bersin (2018) into practices in over 700 organizations found that on average, employees had only 24 minutes a week to do it.

Informal learning occurs mainly in the workplace. Manuti *et al* (2015: 5) noted that

> Informal learning recognizes that the acquisition of knowledge and skills in the work setting does not occur from organized programmes alone. Indeed, learning also occurs during critical moments of need embedded in the context of practice. In contrast to formal learning, informal learning occurs in situations that are not usually intended for learning, most notably in the actual work setting. As a result, informal learning is said to call on and require a blending of individual difference constructs such as intellectual curiosity, self-directedness and self-efficacy.

They also claimed that: 'Informal learning at work is positively correlated with flexibility, employability, adaptability of learning to context, rapid transfer to practice, and resolution of work-related problems through regular review of work practices and performance.'

Sambrook (2005) distinguished between learning *at* work and learning *in* work. Learning at work is associated with planned training and education courses. Learning in work is associated with the more informal processes implied in these activities, such as discussing, observing, asking questions, problem solving.

Hoyle (2015) described formal and informal learning as a continuum (see Figure 12.1). In the south-west quadrant there are traditional courses and programmes. But these sessions only work if a degree of informal learning takes place to effect the change in behaviour that improves performance. In the north-west quadrant there is performance support. This may be provided by the organization in the shape, for example, of e-learning programmes. Support should also be available from line managers and colleagues (social networks). The south-east quadrant covers such activities as coaching and refers to work experiences from which people learn by reflecting, drawing conclusions and planning future actions. This model indicates that there are many varieties of informal learning and that formal training does have a part to play but not in the old way of relying on classroom training and ignoring everything else.

A comparison between formal and informal learning made by Davenport (1999) is shown in Table 12.1

FIGURE 12.1   Formal and informal learning

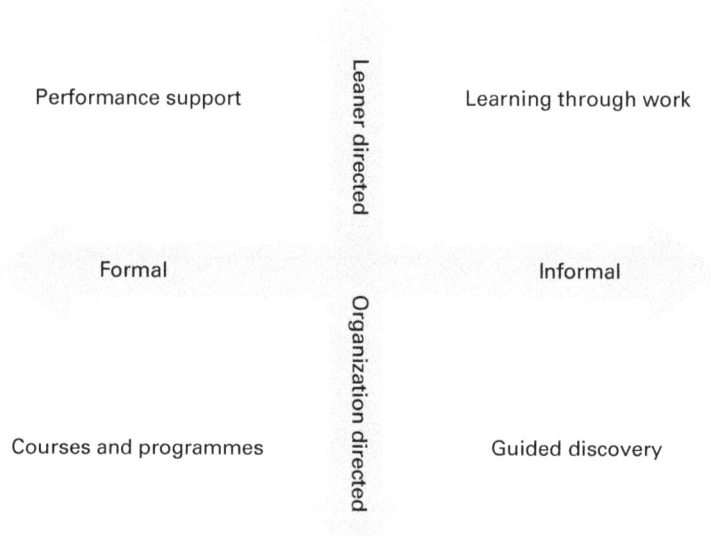

SOURCE Hoyle, R, 2015

TABLE 12.1   Comparison between informal and formal learning

Informal learning	Formal learning
Highly relevant to individual needs	Relevant to some, not so relevant to others
Learners learn according to need	All learners learn the same thing
Learner decides how learning will occur	Trainer decides how learning will occur

(continued)

TABLE 12.1 (Continued)

Informal learning	Formal learning
May be small gap between current and target knowledge	May be variable gaps between current and target knowledge
Immediate applicability ('Just-in-time' learning)	Variable times, often distant
Learning readily transferable	Problems may occur in transferring learning to the workplace
Occurs in work setting	Often occurs in non-work setting

Learning in-the-flow of work

Learning in-the-flow of work, a phrase coined by Bersin (2018), is the learning that takes place when people are doing their job rather than receiving some form of 'off-the-job' training. They are primarily learning from their actions not from what they are told to do. The concept refines that of informal learning by focusing attention on the work itself as a basis for learning. It is about 'learning in the moment'. As Bersin and Zao-Sanders (2019: 3) emphasized:

> Learning in-the-flow of work is a new idea: it recognizes that for learning to really happen, it must fit around and align itself to working days and working lives. Rather than think of corporate learning as a destination, it's now becoming something that comes to us.

The nature of learning in-the-flow of work

People learn by finding out what they have to do and then doing it, particularly when they're faced with unfamiliar situations and challenges. It is a continuous process. People want to work better and look for support in order to perform and move on. They want to get useful information that meets their needs in these situations and provides guidance on what they should do and how they should do it. They appeal to colleagues for advice – tips, recommendations and suggestions. They need quick answers to questions they face right now. They seek information. To get it, they may pursue, often with difficulty, whatever sources in their organization they can identify. Or they may Google – a familiar process to many people but one that may be unfocused. Because they know what they need to know they can in effect take part in the process of designing learning content. Although they are learning for themselves they may still need support. This should be integrated with their work and provided for them where they are.

As noted by Finch (2019: 1) 'traditional classroom-based learning methods take time and effort to organize which means they may take long – perhaps too long – after a need to learn has been identified.' She pointed out that in essence, learning-in-the-flow of work 'takes you away from your regular work as little as possible and might mean not even leaving your desk. It means giving people what they need to be effective in the workplace, but also exactly when they need it, using everything from videos or content on internal social media channels, to connections with colleagues.' It enables people to learn in real time while performing their jobs. As Andy Lancaster, quoted by Finch, remarked, it means that 'we are empowering learners rather than having dependent learners'.

Facilitating learning in-the-flow of work

There are three barriers to the effective facilitation of learning in-the-flow of work: 1) the problem of knowing what is taking place during the process, 2) lack of support from line managers and 3) lack of support from L&D professionals. First, by definition, learning in-the-flow of work happens continuously, informally and without any obvious signs that it is taking place although the results may become apparent if performance improves. This makes it difficult to identify any direct actions that may facilitate it. Secondly, learning may be inhibited if line managers do not provide adequate guidance or support, which they don't always do because they are not aware of the need, don't know how to deal with it even if they are aware that it exists or can't be bothered. Thirdly, L&D professionals may also be unaware of the need and, even if they are aware, don't know how to satisfy it.

To deal with these barriers it is necessary to accept that even if it is difficult to pin down, the process of learning in-the-flow of work exists and is important. It may be difficult to develop specific measures to promote it because of the hidden nature of what is happening. But there are generalized approaches that can help. First, there should be a strong learning culture in the organization, one that is driven by the commitment of management to the encouragement and support of learning. Second, line managers should be made aware of the importance of learning in-the-flow of work and be given guidance and support on how they can promote it by providing a working environment which encourages learning, by coaching, by encouraging self-directed learning and by facilitating social learning. Third, L&D professionals should provide support that can benefit individuals at the point of need as described below.

THE ROLE OF L&D IN SUPPORTING LEARNING IN-THE-FLOW OF WORK

The support provided by should be based on an understanding of what people are trying to do and what they are finding hard to do either at all or well. This understanding can only be obtained if L&D professionals stay close to the business. They have to be out there, talking to line managers and workers; establishing what's going on, what problems individuals have in getting on top of their jobs and what skills are in short supply. Equipped with this knowledge, L&D professionals can initiate actions such as generating small bites of relevant learning content in the form of text or video to be studied on smartphones, pointing the way to information obtainable within the organization and curating information available externally. They can discuss with line managers any individual learning needs they have identified and what can be done about them. They do not simply resort to a formal training programme. But they do provide the guidance and encouragement which will help people to integrate learning with day-to-day work and engage in self-directed learning. They can make sure that corporate knowledge systems are helpful, accurate and easy to use, by, for example, encouraging the digitalization of standard operating procedures. They can distribute learning content by means of internal social media channels, directly to learning apps on smartphones or through emails. They can arrange for learning content to be shared through APIs (application programming interfaces) and even introduce a chatbot. They can arrange for communities of practice or learning sets to be established in a department where there are a number of common learning needs.

Blended learning

Blended learning is the use of a combination of learning methods to increase the overall effectiveness of the learning process. It provides for different parts of the learning mix to complement and support one another and recognizes that the best approach to learning is to accomplish it in a number of different ways, for example, through experience, through other people, face-to face and online.

The most typical method of blended learning is to mix face-to-face training with another delivery method such as online learning. A blended learning programme might be planned for an individual using a mix of any of the self-directed learning activities helped by curation provided by the L&D function.

Generic training for groups of people might include e-learning, planned instruction programmes and selected external courses. Within a learning and development programme a complementary mix of different learning activities might take place, for example a 'soft skills' programme for managers or team leaders might include some instruction on basic principles, but much more time would be spent on simulations, games and other exercises.

Blended learning seems to have a lot to offer but only 34 per cent of the larger employers surveyed by the CIPD (2020) were using it.

Continuous learning

Continuous learning, sometimes referred to as life-long learning, is about the constant expansion of knowledge and skills through self-directed learning and by taking up any learning opportunities offered by the organization. It is what engaged learners do and the role of the L&D function is to encourage and support them. Continuous learning means responding to new developments and demands and absorbing and putting to use new ideas. It is an important aspect of Continuing Professional Development (CPD).

Connected learning

Connected learning involves the creation of knowledge between participants in semi-structured, semi-directed learning activities. It links the individual's need to learn and interest in learning with the opportunities available in the workplace, including those provided by fellow workers (social learning).

Connected learning therefore offers an approach to workplace learning that fits between the directed, structured knowledge transfer (ie training or e-learning) that has been the way that L&D has traditionally operated, and the unstructured, self-directed knowledge sharing that happens in work teams and groups during the flow of work.

Micro-learning

Micro-learning involves small learning units or short-term learning activities. It delivers small bursts of content for learners to study at their convenience. It is also called 'bite-sized learning'. Content can take many forms, from text to full-blown interactive multimedia, but is always short. Micro-learning units usually focus on one learning objective. The characteristics of micro-learning are that:

- the learning takes five minutes or less;
- it is topic or problem based;
- it is provided by text and/or video;
- the learning material is easily sourced;
- searches take place by asking questions;
- it is addressed to individual learners, often for them to pick up on their smartphones.

The advantages of micro-learning are that, compared with the traditional approach to training, it's faster to deliver, less expensive to create, more flexible, more user-friendly and the learning is easier to assimilate and retain. Trainers dealing with complex material can promote transfer by using micro-learning as a follow-up to the original training event. But it is not suitable for complex subjects or in-depth training.

Adaptive learning

Adaptive learning adjusts learning to the needs of individual learners rather than subjecting them to irrelevant training programmes. It can be self-directed, and it may involve the use of computer algorithms or artificial intelligence to make learning content available.

Agile learning

Agile learning is the transfer of agile methods of project work, especially Scrum, to learning processes. Scrum is an agile framework for developing, delivering and sustaining complex products, with an initial emphasis on software development. Agile learning proceeds in incremental steps and through an iterative design which alternates between phases of learning and doing. Agile learners are willing to change by learning from experience and formal training and applying the learning to their work.

Reflective practice

Reflective practice is the ability to reflect on one's actions so as to engage in continuous learning. It was defined by Stewart and Rogers (2017: 94) as 'the process of thinking about an experience, thinking about why it is as it is, then deciding what you have learned from it, and then what to do next time'. They identify three models of reflective practice.

THE GIBBS (1988) MODEL

This model consists of a cycle of five stages as shown in Figure 12.2.

FIGURE 12.2   The Gibbs reflective learning model

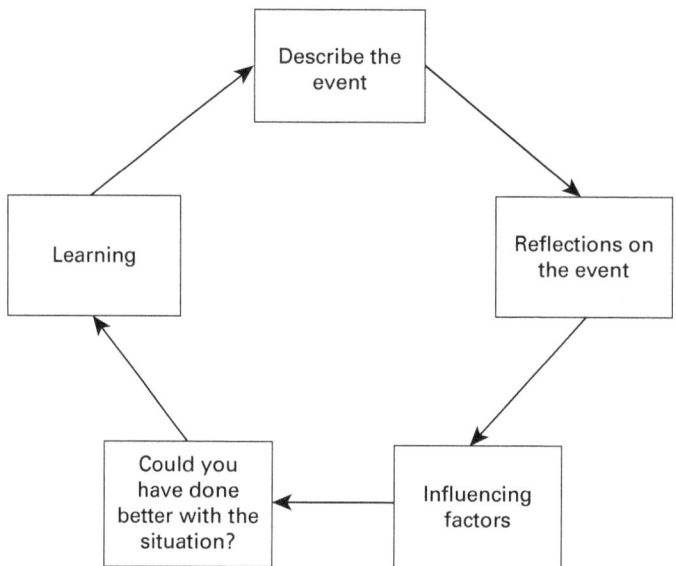

THE DRISCOLL (1994) MODEL

The Driscoll model is limited to just three questions:

1 *What?* Describe the situation in detail.

2 *So what?* Describe the context in which the event occurred.

3 *Now what?* Describe what the outcomes of the situation might be and what is *going to be done about it.*

THE JOHNS (1994) MODEL

The Johns model requires reflective learners to take a real situation and answer as many questions as they can. These questions could include:

- What happened: when, where, who?
- Why did it happen?
- What were you trying to achieve?
- What were the consequences for you of any actions taken?
- What factors influenced decision-making?

Learning and development through performance management

Properly conducted, performance management can be a good way of identifying individual learning needs, agreeing learning goals designed to satisfy the needs and reviewing progress in meeting them. It includes line managers in the whole learning process and provides the incentive for self-directed learning. The approach adopted by the Lloyds Banking Group to development as an important part of their performance management system is set out below.

CASE STUDY

Development though performance management at the Lloyds Banking Group

Purpose

Development plans at the Lloyds Banking Group provide an important way for colleagues to drive personal and business improvement by providing a framework that helps them to build new skills, refine behaviours and acquire different experiences. It is emphasized that line managers have an important role to play in supporting colleagues with their development plans to build on areas of strength, identify skills gaps and support career aspirations.

Process

At the beginning of the year, colleagues agree a development plan with their line manager. The plan is described as 'a living, breathing document that continually evolves. It is reviewed and updated through regular one-to-one conversations

At mid-year and year-end performance rating discussions, the progress of the development plan and the degree of the colleague's development as a result form part of the performance rating decision. Performance rating descriptions explicitly refer to self-development; a key requirement to achieve a good performer rating is to maintain a personal development plan.

The plan

The development plan should contain up to three development areas to focus on to address skills, behaviours or career aspirations. When preparing the plan colleagues are expected to answer the following questions:

- What do you want to achieve this year and longer term?
- What are your greatest strengths and how can you build on them?
- Do you have any development areas that make it difficult to do your job or prevent you from reaching your goals?
- Do you want to learn about a particular department or further develop a skill or area of knowledge?
- What development area will have the greatest impact on your performance?
- What support will you need to undertake development activities?
- In terms of activities, will you be learning on the job or will you need some learning options outside of your role?

Policy and practice implications

This chapter has illustrated the wide number of concepts that have grown up about learning and development policy and practice. The following is an attempt to distil then into a summary of their implications.

Most learning is based on experience and takes place informally during the flow of work – 'learning-in-the-moment'. When putting into practice more formal methods of learning the two basic approaches are face-to-face and online learning. These are best blended together. But learning is not simply an individual matter. People learn by connecting with each other and this has to be catered for. Learning is most readily absorbed if it is available in small chunks rather than extended training programmes. It should adapt to the needs of the learner and be agile, proceeding in incremental steps with alternate learning and doing. When considering learning and development practice, bear in mind that the work context where learning takes place has to be considered when planning learning events.

But it should always be remembered that learning is a continuous process, people should be given the opportunity to go on developing throughout their career. People learn by reflecting on their experience and by modelling their behaviour on others, and they should be encouraged to learn from their mistakes. Performance management practices are an essential aid to the planning and implementation of programmes for individual development.

KEY LEARNING POINTS

Online learning

Online learning takes place over the internet. The learning content is prepared for this purpose and is made available on computers or smartphones.

Formal and informal learning

People learn both formally and informally. Formal learning can occur face-to-face (F2F) in the workplace, lecture rooms or training. It can also take place through various forms of digital learning.

Learning in-the-flow of work

Learning in-the-flow of work is the learning that takes place when people are actually carrying out their work rather than receiving some form of 'off-the-job' training. They are primarily learning from their actions not from what other people tell them to do.

Blended learning

Blended learning is the use of a combination of learning methods to increase the overall effectiveness of the learning process.

Continuous learning

Continuous learning, sometimes referred to as life-long learning, is about the constant expansion of knowledge and skills through self-directed learning and by taking up any learning opportunities offered by the organization.

Connected learning

Connected learning involves the creation of knowledge between participants in semi-structured, semi-directed learning activities.

Micro-learning

Micro-learning involves small learning units or short-term learning activities. It delivers small bursts of content for learners to study at their convenience.

Adaptive learning

Adaptive learning is learning adjusted to the needs of learners.

Agile learning

Agile learning is the transfer of agile methods of project work, especially Scrum, to learning processes.

Reflective practice

Reflective practice is the ability to reflect on one's actions so as to engage in a process of continuous learning.

References

Bersin, J (2018) [Online] https://joshbersin.com/2018/06/a-new-paradigm-for-corporate-training-learning-in-the-flow-of-work/ (archived at https://perma.cc/6M6V-FVRS)

Bersin, J and Zao-Sanders M (2019) *Making learning a part of everyday work the business leadership academy* pp 1–7

Chartered Institute of Personnel and Development (2020) *Learning and Skills at Work 2020*, CIPD, London

Davenport, T O (1999) *Human Capital*, Jossey-Bass, San Francisco

Driscoll, J (1994) Reflective practice for practice, *Senior Nurse*, **14** (1), pp 47–50

Eraut, M (2000) Non-formal learning and tacit knowledge in professional work, *British Journal of Educational Psychology*, 70, pp 113–36

Finch, S (2019) Should your employees be learning as they go? *People Management* [Online] https://www.peoplemanagement.co.uk/long-reads/articles/learn-as-you-go (archived at https://perma.cc/DQT6-QDY8)

Gibbs, G (1988) *Learning by Doing: A guide to teaching and learning methods*, Oxford Further Education Unit, Oxford

Hoyle, R (2015) *Informal Learning in Organizations*, Kogan Page, London

Johns, C (1994) A philosophical basis for nursing practice, in *The Burford NDU Model: Caring in Practice*, ed C Johns, Blackwell, Oxford

Manuti, A, Pastore, S and Scardigno, A F (2015) Formal and informal learning in the workplace: A research review, *International Journal of Training and Development*, **19** (1), pp 1–17

Sambrook, S (2005) Factors influencing the context and process of work-related learning: synthesizing findings from two research projects, *Human Resource Development International*, 8 (1), pp 101–19

Stewart, J and Rogers, P (2017) *Studying Learning and Development*, CIPD, London

13

Learning and development techniques

Introduction

People are helped to learn by the use of learning techniques. While their most prominent users are L&D professionals, skills in job and role analysis, instructing, coaching and mentoring are also needed by line managers. The techniques described in this chapter are:

- the analysis of jobs and roles, competencies and skills;
- directly helping people to acquire knowledge and skills or to make good use of their experience – instructing, behaviour modelling, coaching, mentoring, facilitating and providing feedback;
- conducting learning events;
- content creation for face-to-face learning events and digital learning;
- content curation to support learning, especially self-directed learning

Role analysis

Role analysis finds out what people are expected to achieve when carrying out their work and defines the knowledge, skills and behaviours (capabilities) required to fulfil those expectations. It is an essential technique for identifying learning needs, developing role profiles and learning specifications, creating learning content for learning events or e-learning and planning self-directed learning activities.

When considering role analysis it is first necessary to appreciate the difference between roles and jobs and know what role profiles and learning specifications look like.

Roles and jobs

The terms 'role' and 'job' are often used interchangeably, but they are different. A role is the part people play in their work – the emphasis is on the expected patterns of behaviour to achieve agreed outcomes. A job is an organizational unit consisting of a group of defined tasks or activities to be carried out or duties to be performed. Roles are about people. Jobs are about tasks and duties.

FIGURE 13.1   Example of an individual role profile

Role title: Database Administrator

Department: Information systems

Purpose of role: Responsible for the development and support of databases and their underlying environment.

Key result areas:

- Identify database requirements for all projects that require data management in order to meet the needs of internal customers.
- Develop project plans collaboratively with colleagues to deliver against their database needs.
- Support underlying database infrastructure.
- Liaise with system and software providers to obtain product information and support.
- Manage project resources (people and equipment) within predefined budget and criteria, as agree with line manager and originating department.
- Allocate work to and supervise contractors on day-to-day basis.
- Ensure security of the underlying database infrastructure through adherence to established protocols and to develop additional security protocols where needed.

Need to know:

- The principles of database design and operation.
- The main data manipulation languages.
- The requirements of the Data Protection Act and The General Data Protection Regulation (GDPR).

Able to:

- Analyse and choose between options where the solution is not always obvious.
- Develop project plans and organize own workload on a timescale of 1–2 months.
- Adapt to rapidly changing needs and priorities without losing sight of overall plans and priorities.
- Interpret budgets in order to manage resources effectively within them.
- Negotiate with suppliers.
- Keep abreast of technical developments and trends, bring these into day-to-day work when feasible and build them into new project developments.

Behaviours:

- Aim to get things done well and set and meet challenging goals, create own measures of excellence and constantly seek ways of improving performance.
- Analyse information from a range of sources and develop effective solutions/recommendations.
- Communicate clearly and persuasively, orally or in writing, dealing with technical issues in a non-technical manner.
- Work participatively on projects with technical and non-technical colleagues.
- Develop positive relationships with colleagues as the supplier of an internal service.

FIGURE 13.2 Example of a generic role profile

Generic role title: Team leader

Overall purpose of role: To lead teams in order to attain team goals and further the achievement of the organisation's objectives.

Key result areas:

1. Agree targets and standards with team members which support the attainment of the organization's objectives.
2. Plan with team members work schedules and resource requirements which will ensure that team targets will be reached, or indeed exceeded.
3. Agree performance measures and quality assurance processes with team members which will clarify output and quality expectations.
4. Agree with team members the allocation of tasks, rotating responsibilities as appropriate to achieve flexibility and the best use of the skills and capabilities of team members.
5. Co-ordinate the work of the team to ensure that team goals are achieved.
6. Ensure that the team members collectively monitor the team's performance in terms of achieving output, speed of response and quality targets and standards, and agree with team members any corrective action required to ensure that team goals are achieved.
7. Conduct team reviews of performance to agree areas for improvement and actions required.
8. Promote the learning and development of team members by providing onboarding training, instructing as necessary in specific skills, guidance and coaching.

Behaviours:

- *Achievement/results orientation.* The desire to do things well.
- *Communication.* The ability to communicate clearly and persuasively, orally or in writing.
- *Developing others.* The desire and capacity to fosters the development of members
- *Flexibility.* The ability to adapt to and work effectively in different situations and to carry out a variety of tasks.
- *Leadership.* The capacity to inspire individuals to give of their best.

Role profiles

Role profiles define the key result areas of a role (the outcomes expected) and the knowledge, skills and behaviours required to carry it out effectively. A role profile can be specific, related to an individual role, or generic, covering an occupation rather than one role. Examples of these are given in Figures 13.1 and 13.2.

Learning specifications

Learning specifications, as in the example in Figure 13.3, are based on role analysis and define what someone should learn to achieve proficiency in a role and how that learning should take place. They provide a guide for self-directed learning, a basis for workplace learning in the shape of planned experience and instruction and an indication of what arrangements should

FIGURE 13.3 Example of a learning specification

LEARNING SPECIFICATION	
Role: Product Manager	**Department**: Marketing
What the role holder must understand:	
Learning outcomes	Learning methods
• The product market • The product specification • Market research availability • Interpretation of marketing data • Customer service requirements • Techniques of product management	• Coaching: Marketing Manager and Advertising Manager • Coaching: Operations Manager • Coaching: Market Research Manager • Coaching: Market Research Manager • Coaching: Customer Service Manager • Institute of Marketing courses
What the role holder must be able to do:	
Learning outcomes	Learning methods
• Prepare product budget • Prepare marketing plans • Conduct market reviews • Prepare marketing campaigns • Specify requirements for advertisements and promotional material • Liaise with advertising agents and creative suppliers • Analyse results of advertising campaigns • Prepare marketing reports	• Coaching: Budget Accountant • Coaching: Mentor • Coaching: Market Research Department • Read: Product Manager's Manual • Read: Product Manager's Manual • Attachment to agency • Coaching: Mentor, read analyses • Read: Previousreports; • Observe: Marketing review meetings

be made for coaching, mentoring and formal training. This method of assessing individual learning needs can generate information on common learning needs. The information can be related to the organization's competency framework and used to inform the design of competency-based learning events.

Conducting a role analysis

Role analysis is typically conducted by interviewing role holders and then checking findings with their line managers. The interview should obtain details of the outcomes of the role, which may be expressed as key result areas. It should also find out what knowledge, skills and competencies are needed. The latter may be defined in a competency framework produced for the organization by competency analysis or modelling, as described below.

Interviews provide an opportunity to get at least some preliminary guidance on how the learning needs of the role could be satisfied. Interviews should be planned and systematic with the help of checklists on what to look for. The basic questions to be answered on the content and knowledge and skills requirements of the role are:

- What is the overall purpose of your role?
- What are the key result areas of the role?
- What are you expected to know to be able to carry out your role?
- What skills do you need to carry out your role?
- What do you think are the best ways to acquire and develop the knowledge and skills needed?

Competency analysis

Behavioural competencies (the personal characteristics of individuals that they bring to their roles) can be analysed or modelled based on 'expert' opinion (a L&D specialist or a knowledgeable line manager), structured interviews with role holders, or a workshop consisting of role holders and one or more 'expert'. The aim is to obtain information on the positive or negative indicators of behaviour that result in or prevent high levels of performance. These may be analysed under headings such as those set out below. Instances would be sought for each heading that illustrate effective or less effective behaviour.

- Personal drive (achievement motivation).
- Impact on results.
- Analytical power.
- Strategic thinking.
- Creative thinking (ability to innovate).
- Decisiveness.
- Commercial judgement.
- Team management and leadership.
- Interpersonal relationships.
- Ability to communicate.
- Ability to adapt and cope with change and pressure.
- Ability to plan and control projects.

Skills analysis

Skills analysis determines the skills required to achieve an acceptable standard of performance. It is mainly used for technical, craft, manual and office jobs to provide the basis for devising learning and development programmes. Techniques of skills analysis are described below.

Job breakdown

The job breakdown technique analyses a role into separate operations, processes, or tasks that can be used as the elements of an instruction sequence. A breakdown analysis is recorded in a standard format of three columns:

1 *The stage column* – in which the different steps in conducting the work are described.

2 *The instruction column* – in which a note is made against each step of how the task should be done. This, in effect, describes what has to be learnt by the trainee.

3 *The key points column* – in which any special points, such as quality standards or safety instructions, are noted against each step so that they can be emphasized to a trainee learning the job.

Manual skills analysis

Manual skills analysis is a technique developed from work study. It isolates for instructional purposes the skills and knowledge employed by experienced workers in performing tasks that require manual dexterity. It is used to analyse short-cycle, repetitive but often detailed operations such as assembly and wiring tasks.

The hand, finger and other body movements of experienced operatives are observed and recorded in detail as they carry out their work. The analysis concentrates on the tricky parts of the job which, while presenting no difficulty to the experienced operative, have to be analysed in depth before they can be taught to trainees. Not only are the hand movements recorded, but particulars are also noted of the cues (visual and other senses) that the operative absorbs when performing the tasks. Explanatory comments are added when necessary.

Task analysis

Task analysis is a systematic analysis of the behaviour required to carry out a task with a view to identifying areas of difficulty and the appropriate training techniques and learning aids necessary for successful instruction. It can be used for all types of jobs.

The analytical approach used in task analysis is similar to those adopted in the job breakdown and manual skills analysis techniques. The results of the analysis are usually recorded in a standard format of four columns, as follows:

1 *Task* – a brief description of each element.

2 *Level of importance* – the relative significance of each task to the successful performance of the role.

3 *Degree of difficulty* – the level of skill or knowledge required to perform each task.

4 *Training method* – the instructional techniques, practice and experience required.

Job learning analysis

Job learning analysis, as described by Pearn and Kandola (1993), concentrates on the inputs and process rather than the content of the job. It analyses nine learning skills that contribute to satisfactory performance. A learning skill is one used to increase other skills or knowledge and represents broad categories of job behaviour that need to be learnt. The learning skills are:

- physical skills requiring practice and repetition to get right;
- complex procedures or sequences of activity that are memorized or followed with the aid of written material such as manuals;
- non-verbal information such as sight, sound, smell, taste and touch, used to check, assess or discriminate and which usually takes practice to get right;
- memorizing facts or information;
- ordering, prioritizing and planning, which refer to the degree to which a role holder has any responsibility for and flexibility in, determining the way a particular activity is performed;
- looking ahead and anticipating;

- diagnosing, analysing and problem solving, with or without help;
- interpreting or using written manuals and other sources of information such as diagrams or charts;
- adapting to new ideas and systems.

In conducting a job learning analysis interview, the interviewer obtains information on the main aims and principal activities of the job and then, using question cards for each of the nine learning skills, analyses each activity in more depth, recording responses and obtaining as many examples as possible under each heading.

Faults analysis

Faults analysis is the process of analysing the typical faults that occur when performing a task, especially the more costly ones. It is carried out when the incidence of faults is potentially high. The most commonly occurring faults are identified by a study of the job and questioning workers and team leaders. A faults specification is then produced that provides trainees with information on what faults can occur, how they can be recognized, what causes them, what effect they have, who is responsible for them, what action the trainees should take when a particular fault occurs and how a fault can be prevented from recurring.

Error management training

Error management training uses behavioural modelling techniques as described below to help learners to understand how they should correct mistakes. The aim is to get trainees to solve their own mistakes instead of being overwhelmed by them. They learn how to anticipate potential issues and acquire the knowledge and skills needed to handle problems.

Job instruction

Job instruction is training people to carry out specific tasks, especially those requiring basic manual or administrative skills. L&D professionals may take part in providing direct instruction in formal training programmes, but they also help line managers and others taking part in workplace learning to develop their job instruction techniques using the sequence described below.

Preparation

Preparation for each instruction period means that the trainer must have a plan for presenting the subject matter and using appropriate teaching methods, visual aids and demonstration aids. It also means preparing trainees for the instruction that is to follow. They should want to learn. They must perceive that the learning will be relevant and useful to them personally. They should be encouraged to take pride in their job and to appreciate the satisfaction that comes from skilled performance.

Presentation

Presentation consists of a combination of telling and showing – explanation and demonstration. Explanation should be as simple and direct as possible. The trainer explains briefly the ground to be covered and what to look for and makes the maximum use of charts, diagrams and other visual aids. The aim should be to teach first things first and then proceed from the known to the unknown, the simple to the complex, the concrete to the abstract, the particular to the general and the whole to the parts and back to the whole again.

Demonstration

Demonstration is an essential stage in instruction, especially when the skill to be learnt is a 'doing' skill. Demonstration takes place in three stages:

1 The complete operation is shown at normal speed to show the trainee how the task should be carried out eventually.

2 The operation is demonstrated slowly and in correct sequence, element by element, to indicate clearly what is done and the order in which each task is carried out.

3 The operation is demonstrated again slowly, at least two or three times, to stress the how, when and why of successive movements.

Practice

The learner then practises by imitating the instructor and constantly repeating the operation under guidance. The aim is to reach the target level of performance for each element of the total task, but the instructor must strive to develop coordinated and integrated performance – that is, the smooth combination of the separate elements of the task into a whole job pattern.

Follow up

Follow up continues during the training period for all the time required by the learner to reach a level of performance equal to that of the normal experienced worker in terms of quality, speed and attention to safety. During the follow-up stage, the learner will continue to need help with particularly difficult tasks or to overcome temporary setbacks that result in a deterioration of performance. The instructor may have to repeat the presentation for the elements and supervise practice more closely until the trainee regains confidence or masters the task.

Behaviour modelling

Behaviour modelling takes place when people observe the behaviour of another person or other people and then imitate and learn from that behaviour. It is what happens as people learn by example from colleagues, individually or collectively (social learning). This is experiential and vicarious learning in which direct instruction need not occur.

Behaviour modelling can be used as an instruction technique – behaviour modelling training (BMT). It involves describing, showing and practising new actions and giving feedback. The four steps are:

1 Trainers describe specific actions.

2 They show trainees how to use them.

3 Trainers make time for practice.

4 They support trainees with feedback and encouragement.

Taylor *et al* (2005) evaluated the effects of behaviour modelling training. BMT effects were largest for learning outcomes, smaller for job behaviour and smaller still for results outcomes. Although BMT effects on knowledge decayed over time, training effects on skills and job behaviour remained stable or even increased. Skill development was greatest when learning points were used and presented as rule codes (phrases about what to do and why) and when training time was longest. Transfer was greatest when mixed (negative and positive) models were presented, when practice included trainee-generated scenarios, when trainees were instructed to set goals, when trainees' superiors were also trained and when rewards and sanctions were instituted in trainees' work environments.

Coaching

Coaching is a personal (usually one-to-one) approach that helps people to learn by providing guidance, structure and effective feedback. Clutterbuck (2004: 23) noted that: 'Coaching is primarily focused on performance within the current job and emphasizes the development of skills.' And Whitmore (2002: 8) suggested that: 'Coaching is unlocking a person's potential to maximize their own performance. It is helping them to learn rather than teaching them.'

Coaching is often provided by specialists from inside or outside the organization who concentrate on specific areas of skills or behaviour, for example, leadership. But it is something that line managers should do and L&D professionals need to provide them with guidance which might include formal training. And, of course, L&D specialists have to be prepared to carry out coaching as part of their normal duties.

The approach to coaching

The role of a coach is to help people to learn and ensure that they are motivated to learn. The people being coached should be aware of the advantages to them as well as the organization of developing their present level of knowledge or skill or modifying their behaviour. Individuals should be given guidance on what they should be learning and feedback on how they are doing and, because learning is an active not a passive process, they should be actively involved with their coach. As far as possible, coaching should take place within the framework of a general plan of the areas and direction in which individuals will benefit from further development. Coaching plans should be incorporated into personal development plans.

Mentoring

Mentors offer guidance, pragmatic advice and continuing support to help those allocated to them to develop. Mentoring is a method of helping people to learn as distinct from coaching, which can be a relatively directive means of increasing people's capabilities. L&D professionals may act as mentors although experienced managers are best if they have the skills and enthusiasm required.

The role of a mentor is to provide people with:

- guidance on how to acquire the necessary knowledge and skills to carry out their role;
- general help with learning programmes;
- coaching in specific skills;
- advice in drawing up self-development programmes or learning contracts;
- advice on dealing with any administrative, technical or people problems individuals meet, especially in the early stages of their careers;
- information on 'the way things are done around here' – the corporate culture in terms of expected behaviour;
- help in tackling projects – not by doing it for them but by pointing them in the right direction, helping people to help themselves;
- a parental figure with whom individuals can discuss their aspirations and concerns and who will lend a sympathetic ear to their problems.

Mentors need to adopt a non-directive but supportive approach to helping the person or persons they are dealing with.

Facilitating

Facilitating is helping people to learn for themselves. It guides thinking rather than simply imparting new knowledge. People will perform better in a learning environment when they are empowered to make their own decisions, respected as individuals and trusted with personal responsibility. The essential role of a learning and development professional is that of a facilitator – helping people to learn and helping to make learning happen in the workplace, 'on the move' and in formal learning events. Facilitators are educators in the full sense of the word – 'education' is derived from the Latin 'educere' meaning to draw out.

The facilitator of a learning group unobtrusively stimulates group members to talk, moves the discussion along (there must be a plan and an ultimate objective) and gives interim and final summaries. Help in reaching conclusions is provided by asking questions that encourage people to think for themselves. These can be challenging and probing questions but the facilitator does not provide the answers – that is the role of the people involved. Neither do facilitators allow their own opinions to intrude – they are there to help people to learn not to enforce their own ideas.

Providing feedback

Feedback is the provision of information to people on how they have performed in terms of results, events, critical incidents and significant behaviours. It is an important part of the learning process. It is carried out during the course of work, in performance and development reviews, after someone has performed a task following instruction, or after an exercise such as a case study or role-play in a learning event. Feedback can be positive when it tells people that they have done well, constructive when it provides advice on how to do better and negative when it tells people that they have done badly. Feedback reinforces effective behaviour and indicates where and how behaviour needs to change.

The following are guidelines on giving feedback:

- *Provide positive and constructive feedback* – People are more likely to work positively at developing their skills or improving their performance if they feel empowered by the process. Provide feedback on the things that the individual did well in addition to areas where things could have been done differently. Focus on what can be done to improve rather than on criticism.

- *Describe, don't judge* – The feedback should be presented as a description of what has happened; it should not be accompanied by a judgement.

- *Provide feedback on actual events* – Feedback should be given on results or observed behaviour. It should be as specific as possible and backed up by evidence. It should not be based on supposition about the reason for the behaviour. When providing comments, define what is believed to be effective behaviour or good work with examples.
- *Emphasize the 'how' not the 'what'* – Focus attention more on how the task was tackled than on the result.
- *Ask questions* – Ask questions rather than make statements – 'Why do you think this happened?'; 'On reflection is there any other way in which you think you could have handled the situation?'; 'How do you think you should tackle this sort of situation in the future?'
- *Select key issues* – There is a limit to how much criticism anyone can take. If you overdo it, the shutters will go up and you will get nowhere. Select key issues and restrict yourself to them.
- *Ensure feedback leads to action* – Feedback should indicate any actions required to develop performance or skills.

Giving feedback is a skill that L&D professionals need to possess and line managers need to learn and practise.

Learning event techniques

The main techniques used in learning events (formal training courses) are presentations, discussions, case studies, role-playing, context-based learning, simulations, group exercises and gamification. The digital techniques of virtual and augmented reality as described in Chapter 16 are also used.

Presentations

A presentation is in effect a lecture, generally with little or no participation except a question-and-answer session at the end. It is used to transfer information to an audience with controlled content and timing. The effectiveness of a presentation depends on the ability of the speaker to put across material with a judicious mix of words and visual aids. But there are limits on the amount an inert audience can absorb. However good the speaker is, it is unlikely that more than 20 per cent of what was said will be remembered at the end of the day and, after a week, all will be forgotten unless the listeners have at least begun put their learning into practice. For maximum effectiveness, the presentation should never be longer than about 30 minutes. Better still, in line with the principle of micro-learning, it should be a 'talk' – a brief, sharp, informal summary of the considerations affecting a single learning point that lasts no more than 10 minutes and can form the basis of a subsequent discussion on the significance and practical implications of the point (not just a question-and-answer session).

When the audience is large there may be no alternative to a 'straight lecture' unless it is possible to break up the audience into small discussion groups. This can be done most easily if the course members are seated at separate tables – no more than about six people on each table. The speaker can then deliver a talk as described above and put forward one or two questions for the people on each table to discuss and then report back their conclusions. A brief general discussion can follow.

Discussions

Discussions give course members the opportunity to:

- explore points in depth to increase understanding;
- participate actively in learning;
- learn from the experience of others;
- appreciate other points of view;
- develop powers of self-expression.

The aim of the trainer is to guide the group's thinking and the discussion may be more about shaping attitudes than imparting new knowledge. The trainer uses facilitation skills to stimulate people to talk, guide the discussion and ensure that the group reaches a conclusion. The following techniques can be used by the trainer to gain active participation:

- ask for contributions by direct questions;
- use open-ended questions that will stimulate thought;
- check understanding; make sure that everyone is following the argument;
- encourage participation by providing support;

- prevent domination by individual members of the group by bringing in other people and asking cross-reference questions;
- avoid dominating the group – the role of the trainer is simply to guide the discussion, summarize from time to time and help the group reach a conclusion, not to do it for them
- maintain control – ensure that the discussion is progressing along the right lines towards a firm conclusion.

Case studies

Case studies for learning purposes are descriptions of an event or sequence of events in a real-life setting. They may be fictional but must be realistic. A case study is analysed by learners in order to learn something by diagnosing the causes of a problem, working out how to solve it and drawing conclusions on the lessons learned. The use of case studies in a learning event is in accordance with the principle of context-based learning which advocates the use of real-life examples during training sessions in order to learn from practice rather than theory.

Case studies should aim to promote enquiry, the exchange of ideas and the analysis of experience so that learners can discover the underlying issues that the case study is designed to illustrate. They are not light relief. Nor are they a means of reducing the load on the trainer. The latter have to work hard to define the key learning points that should emerge from a case (a key learning point is a succinct piece of information conveyed through a learning process that refers to a learning principle or practice which can significantly affect the ability to carry out work effectively and which is therefore important for learners to learn). And they must work even harder to ensure that the points *do* emerge.

The problem with case studies is they can be perceived by learners as irrelevant to their needs, even if based on fact. Consequently, the analysis may be superficial and the conclusions unrealistic. It is the trainer's job to avoid these dangers, first by using realistic cases and, second, by seeing that the participants are not allowed to get away with half-baked comments. Trainers have to challenge assumptions and persuade people to justify their reasoning. Above all, they have to seize every chance to draw out the principles they want to illustrate from the discussion and get the group to see how these are relevant to their own working situation.

Role-play

A role-play is a training technique in which people practise and develop interactive skills and gain insight into how people behave and feel by acting out a situation and assuming the roles of the characters involved. The situation will be one in which there is interaction between two people or within a group such as interviewing, conducting a performance review meeting, handling conflict, discussing a performance problem, dealing with a grievance or holding a challenging conversation. A role-playing exercise will contain briefs for each participant explaining the situation and their role in it.

The technique of 'role reversal' in which a pair playing, say a manager and a team leader, run through the case and then exchange roles and repeat it, gives extra insight into how people behave and feel.

Role-playing enables learners to practise interpersonal skills and get advice and constructive criticism from the trainer and colleagues in a protected learning situation. It can help to increase confidence as well as develop skills in dealing with people. But a problem with role-playing is that the learners may be embarrassed and reluctant to take part. Beevers *et al* (2020: 117) suggest that a more positive response may be obtained if the request is to do 'skills practice' or 'try-outs' rather than a role-play. Another problem is that the participants do not take the exercise seriously and overplay their parts. If that is happening the trainer has to step in to persuade them to change their behaviour.

Context-based learning

Context-based learning is the term for the use of real-life examples during training sessions in order to learn from practice rather than theory. It uses synthetic learning environments (SLEs) which deploy simulations, games and computer-based virtual worlds to place individuals in learning environments that are physically and/or socially similar to those they experience at work. These provide learners with a safe environment to try out new skills and the similarity between the learning environment and the work environment helps to ensure that the learning is transferred.

Simulation

A simulation is a recreation of a situation in a learning environment that is as close as possible to real life. It requires those involved to analyse, problem-solve and make decisions that mimic what they would have to do in their day-to-day jobs. Simulations can be based on games (gamification) or the use of virtual or augmented reality (see Chapter 16). They can also make use of case studies and role-plays but these must be as realistic as possible.

Gamification

Gamification is the use of video game design and operation elements to motivate people to learn through competition, incentives and rewards. The latter may include the use of 'leader boards' (tables listing game leaders), the award of points for achieving higher levels and the provision of 'badges' (digital indications of the level of skills reached).

Seaborn and Fels (2015: 17) defined gamification as: 'The intentional use of game elements for a gameful experience of non-game tasks and contexts.' They went on to observe (pages 27–28) that: 'Gamification has two key ingredients: it is used for non-entertainment purposes and it draws inspiration from games, particularly made-up games, without engendering a fully-fledged game. In this way, gamified systems are game-like, but not a game… Gamified systems may need to be selectively designed given the individual makeup of the end-user population or even be designed flexibly and inclusively, allowing for personalization and customization, to accommodate individual users.' Howard-Jones (2014: 11) claimed that off-the-shelf action video games have shown themselves surprisingly effective at developing a range of cognitive skills.

Gamification may be appropriate where it is believed that the desire for feedback and recognition needs to be recognized as a means of motivating learners and reinforcing learning. It can be used where the learning need is to develop analytical and problem-solving skills or to assist in team-building. As in the case study given later in this chapter, specially constructed games can help to develop understanding of organizational or management requirements or issues.

The steps for introducing gamification are:

1 Define objectives – the sort of behaviours the game is intended to develop.

2 Select or produce a game that will focus on those behaviours and fits the people who are going to play it.

3 Decide on any help that can be provided through e-learning.

4 Define to participants how they should analyse their performance in the game under such headings as problem-solving, teamwork and leadership.

5 Ensure that participants carry out this analysis and draw up a list of lessons learnt.

6 Get participants to define what action they intend to take at work to apply the lessons learnt.

Armstrong and Landers (2018: 163) stated that: 'Gamification does not replace any existing training methods but gamification can frequently be used to improve such methods. With a strong design foundation already in place, gamification can often be used to improve learning outcomes further through a variety of specific redesign choices inspired by video game and psychological research.' They recommended that when considering the use of gamification, training designers must first establish the aim of the training in terms of the knowledge and skills to be acquired or improvements in performance achieved. Once training goals and needs are identified, the means of meeting them can be considered. If at this stage it appears that the addition of game elements would better achieve learning goals than other methods, such elements should now be introduced. For example, if training designers develop excellent content but are confident that trainees will not find it engaging, gamification may be an appropriate alternative. After conducting the first training sessions, data should be collected and analysed to evaluate the effectiveness of the training. If game elements are included in the training, their effectiveness should be evaluated explicitly, in comparison to and in combination with other training features and designs. If the training is found to be ineffective, the instructional system is repeated, iterating on the needs, design and evaluation methods until the desired outcomes are reached.

CASE STUDY

Gamification at KPMG

To build a more comprehensive understanding of what KPMG, the accountancy and consulting firm, offers clients, the organization developed KPMG Globerunner. This gamified, Web-based learning app is used during onboarding and also is available for all employees to play. In the learning experience, single players figuratively travel the world, learning points for correctly answering such questions as, 'A CFO needs help with X. Which offering can help?' As players progress, questions become more difficult, players unlock access to new locations, complete missions, earn achievements and gain ranking on the global leader board. Learners can play singly or as teams for global competition.

CASE STUDY

Gamification at SAP

SAP, the enterprise resource management firm, designed the game *Road Warrior* to keep their sales team up to date. In *Road Warrior* sales professionals are required to make sales, challenge each other and collect points to be the best sales professional. While competing and playing, employees learn about new products and methods to close deals.

Videos

Video clips can be easily created to meet a specific learning need. They can illustrate and enliven a session in a learning event or be uploaded onto smartphones.

Group exercises

In a group exercise teams of learners analyse a problem and devise solutions to it. The problem could be one entirely unrelated to everyday work so that it simply becomes an exercise in developing analytical and group problem solving abilities. Or it could make use of cases studies or simulations. A group exercise provides an opportunity for people to work together and gain understanding of the dynamics involved and how groups can function effectively.

Content creation

Content creation is the process of putting together the information required to meet a learning need and creating visual or text-based material. This will be used in a formal learning event or through digital learning where it can be made available by such means as a learning platform or through blogs, podcasts, social media, videos or infographics (visual representations of information or data). Content curation rather than content creation can be used to provide people with a wide range of information which they can access easily.

The AGES model (Davachi *et al*, 2010) suggests that learning design and delivery is more effective if these factors are considered when creating content:

- *Attention* – ensure minimal distractions and avoid cognitive overload.
- *Generation* – relate learning to existing knowledge and support personal, meaningful associations and applications.
- *Emotion* – generate positive emotional experiences and encourage social activities to achieve learning transfer.
- *Spacing* – distribute learning in discrete blocks delivered over short time periods rather than cram lots of content into a prolonged session.

Method of creating content for e-learning and formal learning events or courses are covered in Chapters 16 and 19 respectively.

Content curation

Content curation is the process of gathering information that is relevant to a particular topic or learning need and that can then be shared with employees. Internal sources of information consist of codified knowledge stored in data-banks, manuals, libraries, presentations, policy documents and statements of prescribed practices. External data incudes magazines and journals, books, especially e-books, blogs, podcasts, reports, social media posts, news items, Google, Wikipedia and benchmarking. Platforms like Buzzsumo can also assemble information. A corporate Twitter account can be set up with Twitter Lists to categorize and organize followers with mutual topic interests and engage and interact with them. Content obtained from other sources can be customized. But when making use of content from disparate sources it is necessary to be clear about what is needed and to evaluate its effectiveness. Content curation is particularly appropriate as a means of supporting self-directed learning but it is also used in workplace and leadership development programmes.

Content curation is carried out by learning and development profession-als. It starts with an analysis of what needs to be learnt which may be expressed in the form of key learning points. The next step is to find out where the information required to achieve the learning can be acquired – within the organization or elsewhere. Arrangements can then be made to communicate the information to individuals – on a learning platform, through an enterprise social network on their smartphones or directly when giving advice on a learning programme where it can be integrated with other learning activities. In each case the information is aligned to the predeter-mined learning points. This is an aspect of self-directed learning where support from L&D professionals is particularly helpful.

KEY LEARNING POINTS

Role profiles

Role profiles define key result areas (the outcomes required) and what role holders should know and be able to do and how they need to behave in order to meet them.

Learning specifications

A learning specification is based on role analysis and defines what someone should learn to achieve proficiency in a role and how that learning should be carried out.

Gamification

Gamification is the use of video game design and operation elements to motivate people to learn.

Role analysis

Role analysis establishes what people are expected to achieve when carrying out their work and the knowledge and skills they need to meet those expectations.

Skills analysis

Skills analysis determines the skills required to achieve an acceptable standard of performance. It is mainly used for technical, craft, manual and office jobs to provide the basis for devising learning and development programmes.

Job instruction

Job instruction involves training people to carry out specific tasks especially those requiring basic manual or administrative skills.

Behaviour modelling

Behaviour modelling can be used as the basis for instruction. It happens when people observe the behaviour of another person or other people and then imitate and learn from that behaviour.

Coaching

Coaching is a personal (usually one-to-one) approach that helps people to learn by providing guidance, structure and effective feedback.

Mentoring

Mentors offer guidance, pragmatic advice and continuing support to help those allocated to them to learn and develop.

Facilitating

Facilitating is helping people to learn for themselves. It guides thinking rather than simply imparting new knowledge.

Providing feedback

Feedback is the provision of information to people on how they have performed in terms of results, events, critical incidents and significant behaviours. Feedback reinforces effective behaviour and indicates where and how behaviour needs to change. It is an important part of the learning process.

Learning event techniques

The main techniques used in learning events (formal training courses) are presentations discussions, case studies, role-playing, context-based learning, simulations, group exercises and gamification.

Content creation

Content creation is the process of putting together the information required to meet a learning need and creating visual or text-based material.

Content curation

Content curation is the process of gathering information that is relevant to a particular topic or learning need and that can then be shared with employees.

References

Armstrong, M B and Landers, R N (2018) Gamification of employee training and development, *International Journal of Training and Development*, **22** (2), pp 162–68

Beevers, K, Rea, A and Hayden, D (2020) *Learning and Development Practice in the Workplace*, 4th edn, Kogan Page, London

Clutterbuck, D (2004) *Everyone Needs a Mentor: Fostering talent in your organization*, 4th edn, CIPD, London

Davachi, L, Kiefer, T, Rock, D and Rock, L (2010) Learning that lasts through AGES, *NeuroLeadership Journal*, **3**, pp 1–11

Howard-Jones, P (2014) *Neuroscience and Learning*, CIPD, London

Pearn, K and Kandola, R (1993) *Job Analysis*, IPM, London

Seaborn, K and Fels, D I (2015) Gamification in theory and action: A survey, *International Journal of Human-Computer Studies*, **74**, pp 14–31

Taylor, P J, Russ-Eft, D F and Chan, D W (2005) A meta-analytic review of behavior modeling training, *Journal of Applied Psychology*, **90** (4), pp 692–709

Whitmore, J (2002) *Coaching for Performance*, 3rd edn, Nicholas Brealey, London

PART FOUR

Areas of learning

14

Workplace learning

Introduction

Workplace learning happens when people learn where they work ('on-the-job') by gaining experience, observation (social learning), formal training (instruction) or coaching. As Charles Jennings of the 70:20:10 Institute cited by Daly and Ahmetaj (2020: 42) commented: 'In an ever-changing world, learning leaders need to focus their efforts where they can have greatest impact. This is not in the classroom or through e-learning modules. It's in the daily flow of work. We learn far more from working than we do in other ways.' A study at the Research Center for Education and the Labor Market quoted by Daly and Ahmetaj (2020) found that 96 per cent of time spent learning occurs in the daily flow of work and only 4 per cent of time occurs away from the flow of work. In the words of Paine (2015: 46): 'Instead of putting learning *into* work (which is what a course essentially is) you extract learning *from* work and ensure it is accessible and shared.' Extracting learning from the flow of work is more critical for organizational performance than adding learning into the flow of work. This chapter covers the nature of workplace learning, how it can be enhanced and how it can be made effective.

The nature of workplace learning

Learning in the workplace is mainly informal although line managers have an important part to play in facilitating it through coaching and by arranging supporting activities, including formal training sessions. Much of it is experiential learning – learning by doing (learning in-the-flow of work as described in Chapter 12), working with colleagues (social learning) and reflecting on experience so that it can be understood and applied. Workplace learning involves self-directed learning and is enhanced by planned experience and e-learning. But some more formal training activities take place there. These include instruction, coaching, mentoring and onboarding (induction) training. The latter aims to provide new starters with the knowledge and skills they require. Additional formal training may be provided later to develop new skills or enhance existing ones.

A study by Eraut *et al* (1998) established that in organizations adopting a learner-centred perspective, formal education and training provided only a small part of what was learnt at work. Most of the learning described to the researchers was non-formal, neither clearly specified nor planned. It arose naturally from the challenges of work. Effective learning was, however, dependent on the employees' confidence, motivation and capability. Some formal training to develop skills (especially induction training) was usually provided, but learning from experience and other people at work predominated.

Reynolds (2004: 3) explained that:

> The simple act of observing more experienced colleagues can accelerate learning; conversing, swapping stories, cooperating on tasks and offering mutual support deepen and solidify the process... This kind of learning – often very informal in nature – is thought to be vastly more effective in building proficiency than more formalized training methods.

The characteristics of workplace learning were explained by Stern and Sommerlad (1999: 2) as:

- *The workplace as a site for learning* – in this case, learning and working are spatially separated with some form of structured learning activity occurring off or near the job. This may be in a 'training island' in the department or on the shop floor where the production process is reproduced for trainees.

- *The workplace as a learning environment* – in this approach, the workplace itself becomes an environment for learning. Various on-the-job activities such as coaching, mentoring, job rotation, job shadowing and cross-functional or cross-site project work can be conducted. These are structured to different degrees. Learning is intentional and planned and the aim is to support, structure and monitor the learning of employees.

- *Learning and working are inextricably mixed* – in this case, learning is informal. It becomes an everyday part of the job and is built into routine tasks. This is learning in-the-flow of work. A long time before Bersin coined this phrase, Zuboff (1988) commented that learning was at the heart of productive activity. Workers develop skills, knowledge and understanding through dealing with the challenges posed by the work which can be described as continuous learning.

But there are disadvantages. Learning on-the-job was once anathematized as 'sitting by Nellie' (this was when Nellie was a fairly common name), meaning that trainees were left to their own devices to pick up bad habits from their neighbours. It can be argued that formal training has its limits but at least it is, or should be, planned and systematic and a better way of learning a skill than simply hoping that it will be acquired by some form of osmosis. The systematic training movement of the 1960s was a reaction against traditional laissez-faire approaches.

A further difficulty is that while much of the learning that occurs in the workplace is self-regulated, learners still benefit, indeed depend to a certain extent, on the support and guidance of their line managers. Some managers will provide this support; many won't. This crucial aspect of learning may therefore be neglected unless the L&D function does something about it. And that isn't easy.

Approaches to workplace learning

Experiential learning in the workplace is important but it should not be left to chance. It needs to use such approaches as induction (onboarding) learning, planned experience, coaching, mentoring, 'buddying', shadowing, performance management, personal development planning, e-learning and the development of connected learning approaches as described below.

Induction (onboarding)

Induction or onboarding training aims to equip new starters as quickly as possible with the knowledge and skills required to carry out their work. Many new starters other than those on formal training schemes will learn on-the-job, although this may be supplemented with special off-the-job courses. On-the-job training can be haphazard, inefficient and wasteful. A planned, systematic approach is desirable. This can include new starters being told what they are expected to do (their roles), an assessment of what they need to learn (a learning specification), instruction in how to carry out the work (the knowledge and skills required), the use of designated and trained colleagues to act as guides and mentors and coaching by team leaders or specially appointed and trained departmental trainers. A planned experience programme as described below may be desirable. These on-the-job activities can be supplemented by self-directed learning arrangements that involve access to the learning materials available on learning platforms.

Formal induction courses can be provided away from work in a training centre. However, the problem with many such courses is that too much content is provided in too short a space of time and then people are left to figure things out for themselves. It is best to intersperse the formal training provided on induction or onboarding courses with on-the-job experience. Following that experience, the employee can return to the classroom for a review of the learning that has been achieved.

Planned experience

Planned experience is the process of deciding on a sequence of experience that will enable people to obtain the knowledge and skills required in their jobs and prepare them to take on increased responsibilities. Planned experience enables experiential learning to take place to meet a learning specification. A programme is drawn up that sets down what people are expected to learn in each department, section or job in which they are given experience. This should spell out what they are expected to discover for themselves. A suitable person (a mentor) should be available in order to see that people in a development programme are given the right experience and opportunity to learn. Arrangements should be made to check progress. A good way of stimulating people to find out for themselves is to provide them with a list of questions to answer, a form of heuristic learning. It is essential, however, to follow up each segment of experience to check what has been learnt and, if necessary, modify the programme.

Planned experience can take place through job rotation – moving people to different jobs where they can develop their capabilities or learn new ones.

Coaching

Coaching is a personal (usually one-to-one) approach to helping people develop their skills and knowledge and improve their performance. It has an important role in workplace learning. The need for coaching may arise from formal or informal performance reviews, but opportunities for coaching will emerge during everyday activities.

Mentoring

Mentoring is the process of using specially selected and trained individuals (mentors) to provide guidance, pragmatic advice and continuing support that will help the person or persons allocated to them to learn and develop while working.

Buddy system

In a 'buddy system' an individual works alongside someone with more experience. The buddy will be charged with providing guidance on how best to get the job done and assisting when necessary.

Shadowing

Shadowing is a type of buddying except that the trainee is simply observing what an experienced colleague does. It will only work if the colleague is briefed on how to ensure that the trainee is really learning what needs to be learnt. To this end, coaching sessions need to be held regularly so that the trainee can reflect on and learn from the experience.

Performance management

Performance management processes enable managers and individual members of their teams to work together to identify L&D needs.

Personal development planning

Personal development planning is carried out by individuals with guidance, encouragement and help from their managers, usually on the basis of performance. A personal development plan sets out the actions people propose to take to learn and to develop themselves.

Digital learning

Digital learning involves the use of computer, networked and web-based technology to provide learning material and guidance to individual employees. It can be delivered to a computer or a smartphone through a learning management system, a firm's enterprise social network (see Chapter 16) or an intranet system.

Connected learning

Connected learning is concerned with the learning needs and interests of individuals and how these can be linked with opportunities for learning in the workplace, including those provided by fellow workers (social learning).

Making workplace learning effective

Workplace learning of a sort will take place even if nothing is done about it. But it may well be haphazard and incomplete. People will pick up bad habits and will be lucky if they acquire the skills to do the work properly. Some or all of the various activities described in this chapter need to take place. And it is mainly line managers and supervisors – the people on the spot – who do this. In large departments, where the requirement for workplace learning is considerable, departmental learning advisers and trainers can be appointed on a full-time or part-time basis. In smaller departments a team leader can be given additional responsibilities and rewarded accordingly for promoting learning by, for example, managing induction training and the buddy system. It should be made clear to departmental managers and their supervisory staff that promoting learning is an important part of their role and that their effectiveness in doing it will be taken into account when assessing their performance.

The L&D function has an important part to play in promoting workplace learning by advising line managers generally on managing the learning environment, by giving line managers specific guidance and help with induction and continuation training, by encouraging managers to coach their staff and make use of performance management to identify learning and development needs and enter into learning contracts with employees to meet those needs and by providing managers with coaching and more formal training on their L&D responsibilities.

The following guidelines were produced by Vaughan (2008) on how to make workplace learning effective:

- it is aligned or reflects the workplace culture;

- the strategic directions of the business and the nature of its challenges and opportunities are reflected in the aims and processes of workplace learning;
- learning is adequately resourced with the right people and the right tools;
- the organization is committed to everyone's learning;
- there is sufficient time for learning to be meaningful;
- innovation and thought risk-taking are encouraged;
- opportunities to learn are part of everyday work (not add-ons);
- formal and informal learning are integrated;
- learning is recognized;
- talent is identified and nurtured.

CASE STUDY

Career coaching at Orange

Within Orange, coaching is used in various ways to support people on-the-job and in leadership and personal development programmes. The career coaching programme uses volunteer line managers who have been trained to provide coaching to staff with whom they have no reporting relationship.

The two objectives for career coaching are: 1) as part of its overall talent management strategy Orange wants to see employees take greater responsibility for their own careers; 2) Orange is in a competitive market as far as skills and resources are concerned and this effort is intended to help with employee retention by engaging employees in conversations about their careers before they look elsewhere. Career coaching is offered to all staff, regardless of grade. The programme consists of three sessions of 90 minutes each, with a line manager coach trained specifically in career coaching.

Employees complete an online application, which must have their line manager's approval, and commit to the time required for the coaching process over an 8–10 week period. Included on this form is the question, 'Why do you want to be coached?' with some examples of the reasons that someone might choose.

The coaching process is tightly structured. The planned outcome is for the employee to develop career goals, which are discussed with the individual's manager at the next performance review. Coaches give employees exercises to work on between the meetings, drawn from a large selection offered by the talent management team.

After the process is completed, individuals are asked to complete an evaluation form describing their experience of the scheme, their coach's style and the outcomes they have achieved.

CASE STUDY

Coaching at Marks & Spencer

Traditionally Marks & Spencer (M&S) trained its customer assistants by taking them off the shop floor for classroom-style training, but the company has introduced a new role, that of coach. When trainees join M&S, their coaches take them through all of the training required for their immediate role, as well as any additional training they may need once qualified. Formal coaching cards are used, which address both service and technical skills and tell the coaches what to assess and what the learning should be. Each trainee is also provided with a booklet summarizing the main learning points.

KEY LEARNING POINTS

The nature of workplace learning

Learning in the workplace is mainly informal although line managers have an important part to play in facilitating it through coaching and by arranging supporting activities, including formal training sessions.

Much of it is experiential learning – learning by doing and by reflecting on experience so that it can be understood and applied.

Workplace learning involves self-directed and self-managed learning and is enhanced by coaching, mentoring, e-learning and planned experience. But some more formal training activities can take place there.

Enhancing workplace learning

Experiential learning in the workplace is important but it should not be left to chance. It needs to be enhanced by such means as induction learning, planned experience, coaching, mentoring, 'buddying', shadowing, performance management, personal development planning and e-learning.

Making workplace learning effective

Workplace learning of a sort will take place even if nothing is done about it. But it will be haphazard and incomplete. People will pick up bad habits and will be lucky if they acquire the skills to do the work properly. Some or even all of the various activities described above have to take place. And it is only line managers and supervisors – the people on the spot – who can do this.

References

Bersin, J (2018) Online] https://joshbersin.com/2018/06/a-new-paradigm-for-corporate-training-learning-in-the-flow-of-work/ (archived at https://perma.cc/P273-3XMX)

Daly, J and Ahmetaj, G (2020) *Back to the Future: Why tomorrow's workforce needs a learning culture*, Emerald Works, London

Eraut, M J, *et al* (1998) *Development of Knowledge and Skills in Employment*, Economic and Social Research Council, London

Paine, M (2015) *The Learning Challenge*, Kogan Page, London

Reynolds, J (2004) *Helping People Learn*, CIPD, London

Stern, E and Sommerlad, E (1999) *Workplace Learning*, Culture and Performance, IPD, London

Vaughan, K (2008) *Workplace Learning: A literature review*, Council for Educational Research, New Zealand

Zuboff, S (1988) *In the Age of the Smart Machine*, New York, Basic Books

15

Social learning

Introduction

Social learning, sometimes called collaborative or connected learning, takes place when people learn by observing and imitating others. Learning 'is not something that people possess in their heads, but rather, something that people do together.' (Gergen, 1991: 270). Some form of social learning happens continually in the workplace as individuals and groups work together. Groups solve problems jointly and learn in doing so. Project teams do the same. Individuals learn by seeing what their colleagues do. Social learning is an important aspect of workplace learning but it also takes place in formal training events.

In this chapter consideration is given to:

- the nature of social learning;
- the background provided by social learning theory;
- the concept of communities of practice;
- how social learning takes place;
- what can be done to encourage social learning.

The nature of social learning

As defined by Hart (2014: 14): 'Social learning is about people connecting, conversing, collaborating and learning from and with, one another on a daily basis at work... It's about helping teams learn as they work, rather than taking them out and forcing them to endure a learning "experience".' She conducted a survey into how people valued ten different forms of learning which established the following order of preference from respondents:

1 Collaborative working within your team

2 Web search for resources

3 General conversations and meetings with people

4 Personal and professional networks and communities

5 External blogs and news feeds

6 Content curated from external sources

7 Self-directed study of external courses

8 Internal job aids

9 Internal documentation

10 Company training and e-learning

This shows that social and collaborative learning activities – and in particular self-organized activities – are the main ways that the survey respondents preferred to learn. Jane Hart noted that, in particular, knowledge workers prefer to learn as an integral part of their daily job and like to learn continuously from the constant flow of information they encounter from other people – which may come from both internal and external channels. Knowledge workers want to be able to find answers to their learning and performance problems as soon as they encounter them. They don't want to have to wait to go on a course or get some other response. If when sitting at their desk or in front of a computer at home they encounter a problem with a task they are working on, they tend either to seek help from their professional network or go straight to Google and search for a solution. She also noted (page 35) that:

> It is in the area of workforce collaboration where there are plenty of new opportunities for L&D to support work teams and groups. Since people learn from one another as a consequence of working together, rather than focusing exclusively on the learning, it is more about helping them work collaboratively and enabling continuous learning to take place as part of that process. It is also important to reiterate that supporting continuous learning in the flow of work is not about providing them with courses as they do their work, helping them to find their own courses, or even helping them to create their own courses... rather it is about helping them share their knowledge, experiences, ideas and resources as part of their daily workflow.

Brown and Duguid (1991) thought that formal instructions about how to do jobs are always inadequate. It is necessary to look at the way new entrants into organizations learn the unwritten information on how to perform effectively. This is achieved through informal exchanges between experienced and less experienced people and through the use of anecdotes and war stories.

Social learning theory and the concept of communities of practice show how social learning works.

Social learning theory

As explained by Bandura (1977) social learning theory regards learning as a series of information-processing steps set in train by social interactions and emphasizes that effective learning requires such interaction. Learning is about imitation which takes place in a social environment. The core beliefs of social learning theory were set out by Jordan *et al* (2008: 79) as follows:

- learning does not occur in isolation; it is socially constructed;
- learning has both sociological and psychological implications;
- society regulates social life through institutions and systems;
- learning is a process of socialization mediated through membership of various groups;
- intra-and inter-group process are important in forming individual identity;
- there is a dynamic relationship between individual self-esteem, the social environment and the learner's action;
- there is a tension between structure (the extent to which societal structures shape individuals) and agency (the extent to which individuals determine their own destiny).

What can be done to encourage social learning

Social learning can be encouraged by teambuilding activities in or out of the workplace, facilitating social networks, online learning and setting up communities of practice, learning communities and learning sets. The effectiveness of formal training courses can also be increased if there is a strong element of social or collaborative learning.

Team building

Team building is an activity which can support collaborative working and its outcome, social learning. It involves developing the effectiveness of teams through training (group dynamics) and indoor or outdoor exercises or games. The processes include clarifying a team's purpose and goals, getting team members to work well together in order to strengthen the team's collective skills, enhancing commitment and confidence and, importantly, creating opportunities for team members to learn from one another. Team building is the immediate responsibility of line managers but L&D can help by providing encouragement, support and training in the necessary 'soft skills'.

Research by Hart et al (2019: 148–149) found that team building may enhance self-efficacy and motivation of learners throughout the training process and offers a realistic training environment in that it models real-world business settings with employees functioning in team or group settings where their actions are dependent on and influenced by others.

Social learning networks

Social learning networks enable people to benefit from the knowhow of others. The learning is not structured but it is real – based on the actual experiences of colleagues – and therefore more effective than a formal presentation by a trainer on a course. Learning is no longer seen as a separate activity from working and it can become a continuous, social experience. The process of sharing knowledge with colleagues as part of the natural process of work is in effect a social learning network although it will not have been established or be known as such. Networks can also be created online.

Online social learning

Online social learning tools enable people to share with others what they know and what they have learnt. The learning can take place in an online discussion forum as described in Chapter 16 or by using an enterprise social network (ESN) such as Yammer. ESN technology is similar to public social networking tools like Facebook in that it supports a constant flow of real-time, threaded conversations through user updates and replies. Within an organization people can share their experiences and thoughts and learn from one another. In using an ESN an individual's personal activity stream will consist of all their activity streams -– from all their learning initiatives as well as from their work teams and communities. Alternatively, a learning experience platform can be used. Products such as Microsoft Teams, Slack, Trello and Google hangouts can facilitate informal group learning.

Communities of practice

Communities of practice are groups of people bound together by shared expertise who meet together to share knowledge. The concept was originated by Wenger (1998) who suggested that they are our primary sources of learning. He defined them as follows (2011: 1):

> Communities of practice are formed by people who engage in a process of collective learning in a shared domain of human endeavour: a tribe learning to survive, a band of artists seeking new forms of expression, a group of engineers working on similar problems, a clique of pupils defining their identity in the school, a network of surgeons exploring novel techniques, a gathering of first-time managers helping each other cope.

He stated (page 31) that communities of practice in organizations operate by:

- enabling practitioners to take collective responsibility for managing the knowledge they need, recognizing that, given the proper structure, they are in the best position to do this;
- creating a direct link between learning and performance, because the same people participate in communities of practice and in teams and business units;
- enabling practitioners to address the tacit and dynamic aspects of knowledge and sharing, as well as the more explicit aspects;
- creating connections among people across organizational and geographic boundaries – they are not limited by formal structures.

Learning communities

Learning communities are groups of people, the members of which get together to learn from one another. They may be self-generated and will work best if the community itself decides on what its members need to learn together and how they will learn it. But L&D professionals can provide them with encouragement and support and may appoint a community facilitator who provides guidance and help but does not dictate what the community members discuss. Learning communities may be linked to a community of practice or may become communities of practice in which further learning possibilities can be explored and agreement reached on how they should be pursued by the community itself or with help from L&D.

Learning communities are sometimes described as self-managed learning sets. These usually consists of between 8 and 12 people from different parts of the organization who meet to learn together. As described by Page-Tickel (2014) the starting point is for individual members to consider what they want to learn and set learning goals. The goals are discussed by the members of the set and each member agrees the initial steps they will take to achieve them. At the next meeting, the members tell each other what they have done since the initial meeting and the set will offer support or challenge individuals who have underachieved. Specialist speakers may be invited to address the set. The set will be facilitated, probably by a L&D specialist, who will monitor progress and provide encouragement and support. The set will finally confirm and celebrate what has been achieved.

Learning communities can be established by L&D before a training course to prepare participants and give them some preliminary material to absorb. After the course community members can get together to discuss what they have learnt and how they are applying it. Problems can be raised and solutions considered. The emphasis is on interaction, sharing and conversations between the participants.

KEY LEARNING POINTS

The nature and significance of social working

As defined by Hart (2014): 'Social learning is about people connecting, conversing, collaborating and learning from and with, one another on a daily basis at work.'

Some form of social learning happens continually in the workplace as individuals and groups work together. Groups solve problems jointly and learn in doing so. Project teams do the same. Individuals observe what their colleagues do and learn from their observations. But it cannot be left to chance.

Learning theory

Social learning theory regards learning as a series of information-processing steps set in train by *social interactions*.

What can be done to encourage social learning

Social learning can be encouraged though teambuilding activities in or out of the workplace, developing social networks, online learning and setting up learning communities. The effectiveness of formal training courses can also be increased if there is a strong element of social or collaborative learning.

References

Bandura, A (1977) *Social Learning Theory*, Prentice-Hall, Englewood Cliffs, New Jersey,

Brown, J S and Duguid, P (1991) Organizational learning and communities-of-practice: Toward a unified view of working, learning, and innovation, *Organization Science*, 2 (1), pp 40–57

Gergen, K J (1991) *The Saturated Self: Dilemmas of identity in contemporary life*, New York, Basic Books

Hart, J (2014) *The Social Learning Handbook* [Online] http://www.c4lpt.co.uk/blog/2014/01/27/social-learning-handbook-pdf-now-available/ (archived at https://perma.cc/RY34-HV3E)

Hart, S L *et al* (2019) Team-based learning and training transfer: A case study of training for the implementation of enterprise resources planning software, *International Journal of Training and Development*, **23** (2), pp 135–52

Jordan, A *et al* (2008) *Approaches to Learning: A guide for teachers*, Open University Press, Maidenhead

Page-Tickel, R (2014) *Learning and Development: A practical introduction*, 2nd edn, Kogan Page, London

Wenger, E (1998) *Communities of Practice: Learning, meaning and identity*, Cambridge University Press, Cambridge

Wenger, E (2011) *Communities of Practice: A brief introduction*, Scholars' Bank, Oregon

16

Digital learning

Introduction

Digital learning is the delivery and administration of learning opportunities and support via computer, networked and web-based technology. As described in this chapter, digital learning covers a wide range of activities and techniques all of which involve some form of online learning. These can broadly be divided into two groups: 1) the provision of overall learning approaches and environments and 2) the application of various learning resources and techniques, either independently or associated with an overall approach.

Overall approaches consist of the use of e-learning and learning platforms and the development of virtual learning environments. Digital resources and techniques comprise the use of smartphones and learning apps, social media, enterprise social networks, web searches for knowledge acquisition, virtual and augmented reality and online courses. The chapter starts with an analysis of the nature of digital learning and continues with a description of the main areas of digital learning as listed above.

The nature of digital learning

Digital learning was defined by the CIPD (2020a) as 'learning that's facilitated, enabled or mediated using electronic technology for the explicit purpose of training, learning or development in organisations.' It has an increasingly important part to play in learning and development. Digital learning technology provides the basis for online learning which is defined as learning that takes place through material made available on a computer, tablet or smartphone. Content is provided to users in accordance with their roles and algorithmic recommendations on the sort of content they consumed before. Virtual learning environments using webinars or virtual classrooms became popular when remote learning was more or less obligatory as a result of COVID-19. The use of cloud technology has enabled organizations to deliver learning according to user needs via the Internet rather than by in-house computing systems.

In operational and safety training there are now adaptive learning solutions (ie fitting the needs of the individual) that deliver small two-to-three minute videos each day when an operator checks into work. The learning is carefully curated, spaced and designed to deliver an outcome – and the employee answers questions (including questions about their confidence in the answers) to give the system enough information to decide what should come next. Digital learning systems cater for people learning their jobs but also cater for those who understand basic requirements but want pinpoint information and quick answers to questions they face right now.

The CIPD (2020b) L&D survey found that online learning was the second most popular delivery method (behind on-the-job learning), with more than half of organizations using it. The proportions of respondents to the survey using different forms of digital learning were:

- webinars, virtual classrooms – 36%
- learning management system – 27%
- online education – 22%
- video – 20%
- mobile – 12%

Three broad categories of digital learning practices have been identified by the CIPD (2020a):

- *Formal digital* – where technology is used to deliver formal course-based content.
- *Informal digital* – where technology provides opportunities to support informal workplace learning, mainly through forums.
- *Blended or supported learning* - where formal and/or informal learning may be combined ('blended') with other types of learning. For example, the majority of learning content might be delivered through face-to-face lectures or coaching and/or through text material, but dialogues with

other learners, collaborative activities and searching for access to supporting material are all conducted online. A popular blend is the 'flipped' classroom model where the knowledge transfer is carried out online separately from the discussion on that learning done face-to-face.

E-learning

E-learning is the delivery and administration of learning material and support in a discrete package via computer, networked and web-based technology. It is usually managed through a learning management system (LMS) as described in the next section of this chapter. The term e-learning originally referred to any form of digital learning but is now generally treated as a sub-set which is often used for such purposes as compliance training in, for example, health and safety, hygiene or data protection, and onboarding (induction) training. But it can deliver any other form of learning. This can be provided in small easily assimilated nuggets lasting up to ten minutes or so (bite-sized training or micro-learning) and may cater for interactive learning. It can be 'blended' with other forms of learning such as face-to-face learning, and it can support informal learning in the workplace and adaptive and self-directed learning. It is accessible anytime from anywhere, especially when using smartphones.

Creating content for e-learning

E-learning content may be created within the organization from existing or new material. Or it can be outsourced – there are many providers – which saves time and trouble but may be expensive. In the latter case care has to be taken to brief the provider on the aims, the subject areas to be covered and in what depth, and the characteristics of the learners who will use the material.

If digital content is being created within the organization, a piece of software called an E-learning Authoring Tool enables trainers to create learning content using text, PowerPoint slides and media. Provision can be made for interactive learning – this takes place when learners are asked to respond to questions or carry out tasks that are presented to them in the e-learning programme.

Course authoring tools come in many shapes and sizes. For example, some learning management systems as described later in this chapter come with built-in authoring tools. These can often only be used to produce fairly basic content although they are a relatively easy and cheap option if no more is required. On the other hand, 'standalone' course authoring software specially developed for the production of digital learning gives instructional designers scope to create high-quality, customized content. This type of software can be desktop-based or cloud-based. Providers of e-learning authoring tools include Elucidate, Evolve and Gome. When choosing a supplier, the main considerations are the speed and ease with which good quality learning content can be produced, the level of customization available and the variety of formats to choose from.

When a course has been developed using an authoring tool, it is exported to a learning platform as a SCORM file (SCORM stands for Shareable Content Object Reference Model), which enables the LMS to read the interactive elements of the course and deliver them to learners.

The principles of creating content for learning events as described in Chapter 19 also apply to the design of e-learning or digital material. These include ensuring that it meets defined learning needs, limiting content to what learners can and will want to absorb and sequencing the learning in steps that the learner can readily assimilate. E-learning works best when it caters for clearly defined areas of knowledge that can be presented in easily digestible bites. This is why it is often used for compliance training and onboarding programmes and for conveying information about new products or services. The content for these should be available within the organization.

Traditionally, e-learning courses were carefully built by instructional designers. The courses had many chapters, were often quite long and were accessed through a learning management system. Progression was linear (it was called 'page turning') and each page had visuals, audio and perhaps a small amount of video. The aim now is to provide content in small digestible chunks and to embed learning into the platform in which people work so that coaching is provided when needed. This is adaptive learning in action.

The content may be presented as a text document and/or in the form of PowerPoint slides. The material can be interactive, for example, by getting learners to answer multi-choice questions. Videos can be used to demonstrate how to carry out a task or deal with a problem, such as a customer complaint. Subject experts can appear on them to make mini-presentations or answer questions. Videos can be developed in-house or by production companies.

Evaluating e-learning

The impact of e-learning should be evaluated. The overall approach may be based on the evaluation of learning methodologies described in Chapter 22. A learning management system can monitor the use of e-learning and obtain reactions from learners not only to the quality of the material but also on how helpful it was at work. Learners and their managers can be interviewed to obtain their views about its usefulness.

Advantages and disadvantages of e-learning

The advantages of e-learning are that it makes learning available both at the point of need (in the workplace) and elsewhere to a dispersed workforce. It can be made readily accessible through the use of apps on smartphones. People can learn at their own pace when and where they want to (learning on the move). They can tailor the learning to their own needs, for example by fast forwarding through content that is already familiar to them or of limited relevance to their roles. It can complement and supplement face-to-face learning and sometimes replace it. The focus of learning can readily be directed to meeting immediate learning needs and people can be encouraged to seek the information they want. The scope for providing the learning in small 'bites' can make it easily digestible.

The disadvantages are the time, effort and money required to develop and update material and the problem of providing adequate support to learners. It may be difficult to ensure that the learning material is being used effectively although learning management systems can monitor its use. E-learning packages tend to be standardized and do not therefore necessarily satisfy the learning needs of different people. For those who like to learn through face-to-face interaction, the learning experience can be inferior. There are limits to how much learning material can be made available. And the technical demands involved in developing and using it may be daunting.

The advantages can outweigh the disadvantages if e-learning is developed and used judiciously. But the drawbacks seem to have put many organizations off. The CIPD (2020b) L&D survey found that while digital learning including e-learning was used by 47 per cent of the respondents it delivered less than 20 per cent of the learning. A fifth of organizations continue to rely on classroom-based training. The CIPD (page 19) commented that: 'With the desire to facilitate accessible, personalized learning in the flow of work and to support remote working, this is a concern, highlighting the pressing need for digital transformation.'

Integrated e-learning at Cable & Wireless

E-learning at Cable & Wireless is based on the establishment and promotion of a single platform for learning. This has been delivered through an outsourcing arrangement with the e-learning company SkillSoft. The core platform is a learning management system that is available to Cable & Wireless colleagues as a portal labelled 'iLEARN'. All training delivery channels are linked to this portal. The library of generic material consists of some 15,000 items plus about 60 modules commissioned by Cable & Wireless. In the first year since the e-learning system was launched, three-quarters of the workforce used it and this penetration figure is rising. Some 20,000 e-learning activities were accessed and 15,000 hours of e-learning undertaken in total.

Learning platforms

A learning platform is an integrated set of interactive digital services that provides L&D professionals, managers and learners with the information, tools and resources they need to support and enhance learning. The original learning platform was the learning management system (LMS) and it is still popular today – 37 per cent of the respondents to the CIPD 2020 L&D survey had one, although Andy Lancaster (2020: 146) thinks they are often outdated. Newer learning platforms use paths or tracks to arrange content by role or competency and can provide machine-driven recommendations. A fairly recent development welcomed by Lancaster is the Learning Experience Platform (LEP). The features of both these platforms and the differences between them are described below.

Learning management systems

Learning management systems (LMSs) are software applications for the administration, documentation, tracking, reporting, automation and delivery of e-learning and other types of L&D programmes. As Page-Tickel (2020: 181) noted: 'They are the shell within which your learning is held and offered to learners'.

Dagger *et al* (2009) grouped LMSs into two main categories:

- Open source (granted under licence) systems include Moodle, Sakai, Atutor and Whiteboard. These may allow users to incorporate extensible frameworks that let them adjust and modify the systems to suit their needs.

- Proprietary systems include Blackboard, Desire2Learn and Learn.com

There are many versions of learning management systems provided by a multitude of suppliers but typical features include:

- all relevant L&D data (numbers attending programmes, individual learning activities, outcomes of learning evaluations and surveys etc) are stored for easy access;
- learner progress, performance and interactions, for example use of e-learning material, are tracked;
- specific e-learning content and programmes (onboarding, compliance, product knowledge etc) are incorporated in one location for unlimited access by employees;
- adaptive learning materials for ongoing skill development can be included.

CASE STUDY

The new LMS at St Leger Homes

At St Leger Homes, which maintains housing stock for Doncaster Council, the priority was to get better information about what was happening to face-to-face learning. But what was also wanted was to give people the opportunity not only to attend essential courses but also to do things that interested and developed them. As Vikki Chamberlain, the people development manager, said: 'We want to get to the point where employees can access learning 'just in time', so if you're looking at a boiler, our specialists can download the latest information about that equipment on their phone. We want to use e-learning to enhance and embed what people did in the classroom – for example, doing some reading beforehand and then following up with further resources.'

SOURCE Faragher (2018)

CASE STUDY

LMS features at Whole Food Market

The LMS at Whole Food Market comes with the standard features of all LMSs: assigning training, hosting e-learning content, tracking completions, reporting on training. In addition, it provides built-in learner experience technology, artificial intelligence driven.

Tips on choosing an LMS

The following tips on choosing a LMS were produced by Weinstein (2020a: 24)

- Select a system that helps track and organize learner assignments, creating simple, automatic formulas for determining which learner gets which assignments to best prepare them for their responsibilities.

- Create a more compelling learner experience that enables the ease of Google searches for needed learning and information.

- Look for an LMS that provides a fluid digital experience in which the technology fits seamlessly into users' workflow.

- Find technology that offers more intra-company and network communication among learners, content sharing, and enhanced ability to create secure course links that can be utilized and sent outside of the LMS to allow promotion to learners, as well as the ability to launch and track course activity.

- See if you can add an LMS to your organization that includes artificial intelligence capabilities that both enhance learners' experience and free administrators from repetitive, tedious tasks.

- Put a priority on finding a system that is intuitive for learners, allowing them to use technology for learning at work that is similar to the technology they use in the rest of their lives.

Learning experience platforms

Learning experience platforms (LEPs) create personalized learning experiences by integrating, consolidating and customizing for employees formal and informal learning initiatives from across the organization. Learners have a single point of access to discover, gain and share knowledge. The L&D function can create, curate and aggregate content on LEPs but there is also scope to include user-generated material – employees can recommend content for sharing with their colleagues. When learners find a helpful resource that answers a commonly asked question, they can submit that resource so it's easily accessible to others. And when learners feel that they are involved in the process, they're more likely to engage with and explore learning opportunities. LinkedIn Learning is a good example of an LEP.

As Bersin (2018) points out, LEPs offer a significant shift from prescriptive learning to subscription learning, from a top-down approach to learning to an essentially learner-driven model. An LEP's content is designed to be experienced just like any digital content found on the Web, and to be as intuitive and easy-to-consume as the apps with which most people are familiar. The LEP is a new way of thinking rather than a new LMS. It means that people are not forced to learn in just one way or have to wait to be assigned content by a manager or L&D specialist.

CASE STUDY

Learning system innovation at Rentokill

Rentokill introduced its revolutionary U+ platform in order to move away from classroom training to a new era of blended learning, allowing employees to develop at their own pace using digital resources. Crucially, these resources needed to cater for colleagues in 64 countries, speaking more than 31 different languages, 34 per cent without an email address or personal technology in a highly decentralised organization.

What's the difference between an LEP and an LMS?

At first glance, an LEP can sound similar to a traditional LMS. Both are used to disseminate learning programmes and both provide options to track progress and certifications and achievements. But there are some important differences, the key one being that an LEP focuses on putting learning experience first, whereas the LMS concentrates more on learning management.

An LMS is a closed system that does not allow users to go beyond a set track or learning pathway. It organizes and delivers formal learning content which has been created using a content management system or authoring tool. It allows organizations to track and evaluate learners' activity and progress, but its closed systems prevent it from being able to encourage and monitor informal learning.

In contrast, LEPs are open systems which operate more flexibly – employees are free to pick and choose their courses, study them at their leisure and complete certifications (or not, if they so choose). LEPs pull learning from a wide array of sources into one central location. This allows organizations to deliver mandatory training – such as compliance or onboarding courses – that they could provide through an LMS. But, in addition, they enable educational content from other sources and third-party providers to be assembled. Furthermore, the flexibility of an open system allows the L&D team to grow and diversify their content library rapidly.

However, the distinction is not always clear, especially when a traditional LMS has been modified to include LEP features.

Virtual learning environment

A virtual learning environment or virtual learning system provides learning online (remote learning) rather than in a training centre or classroom. Dillenbourg *et al* (2002: 4) suggested that a virtual learning environment is a designed information space in which learners are not only active but also actors: 'they co-construct the virtual space' and 'turn spaces into places'. A virtual learning environment can include any of the following features:

- *virtual classrooms* – environments that allow trainers and learners to connect online in order to provide and receive instruction; the environment can be either web-based and accessed through a portal, or software-based and therefore require a downloadable executable file;
- *webinars* (short for web-based seminar) – seminars, workshops or presentations that are transmitted over the Web using video conferencing software and are interactive, enabling trainers and learners to give, receive and discuss information;
- *wikis* – websites which allow modification of their content and structure directly from a web browser;
- *video conferencing* – conferences conducted online using a platform such as Zoom;
- *online discussion forums* – learners are connected to each other so they can share ideas, discuss concepts, work on projects and solve problems; they can use blogs in the shape of observations or experiences posted on a website;
- *threaded discussions* – these link together topics raised by participants in online discussion forums and track them as the discussion progresses;
- *blogs* – websites on which individuals or groups post their observations and experiences;
- *microblogs* – miniature blogs posted on sites such as Twitter; microblogs can be captured and distilled into learning points and harnessed for corporate learning through knowledge-sharing tools like Yammer;

- *podcasts* – digital audio files made available on the internet for downloading to a computer or smartphone;
- *integrated learning* – tools such as Moodle take learners through a whole system of learning experiences and integrate their online interactions;
- *online support* – communications to the learner by such means as e-mails or WhatsApp.

Smartphones and learning apps

Learning material in short 'bites' can be easily distributed on smartphones, usually through a learning app. By 2024 smartphone penetration in the UK is predicted to be 88 per cent. The development of smartphone technology has enabled mobiles to become an important part of the learning environment. This trend has accelerated through the increased use of apps.

Research by Hird and Sparrow (2012) found that in one organization apps were used in three ways:

1 Follow-ups to a learning intervention, broadening access out to different 'layers' of sites that provide basic information and access to broader communities of practice.

2 Awareness-building material, for example, enhancing leadership models with provision of additional guidance, support tools that lay out different options for development, provide feedback and progress checks

3 Process confirmation, where learners can record information, and the L&D function can check for process alignment and behavioural reinforcement.

The following tips on creating and using learning apps were produced by Weinstein (2020b: 23):

- Create or offer an app that gives employees the ability to map out their own development plans. Show them the resources that are available to help them develop their careers.
- Offer videos and podcasts for smartphones and tablets through mobile technology on an app so that employees can use a free moment here and there to catch up on important information.
- Make it easier to complete compliance training. Provide the material in small 'bites' so that employees can absorb it in their spare time.

- Use the app to create greater connectivity with learners about their course work.

- Integrate the app with whatever learning platform is used to ease access to learning material.

CASE STUDY
Learning apps at McDonald's

The app gives restaurant employees a way to see beyond their day-to day responsibilities. It has a range of content promoting career growth and educational opportunities. The app builds on the Archway to Opportunity programme. There is a working style quiz, a list of career pathways, scope to set learning goals and a chatbox for questions about the programme. Opportunities to take up coaching are available.

Social media

Social media such as Facebook, LinkedIn and Twitter are interactive computer-mediated technologies that facilitate the creation or sharing of information. Social media can be used as platforms for learning, acting as conduits for locating expertise and information. They provide a source for learning content which can be generated by users as well as L&D specialists and they help to locate expertise within the organization and to catalogue insight and information for future reference. Employees can gain access to bite-sized learning material so that they can learn in slots of five minutes or so. Forums can be created where employees can discuss training materials with the experts who created them, giving the employees greater clarity on how to use them. These activities can be conducted with the help of an Enterprise Social Network (an internal social network, see below).

As the CIPD (2013: 14) reported: 'The main benefit of social media as a learning tool lies not in hosting formally designed tools and programmes, but supporting informal learning. Through building relationships with new people and joining communities of interest, social media can help us locate the expertise we are looking for or, indeed, lead us to stumble upon.' On the basis of its research, the CIPD (2014: 4) concluded that: 'While there will always be a place for face-to-face learning interventions, social media can transform many aspects of learning and development, being used to curate knowledge, locate experts and facilitate peer-to-peer support, support self-directed learning and help employees prepare for and embed learning from training courses.' The CIPD also commented that: 'Social media blurs the traditional boundaries of learning and development. Sharing information and pointing to resources naturally leads to learner-led development, whereby people find out what they need to know when they need to know it.' (page 19)

Enterprise social networks

Learning, especially learning in-the-flow-of work and social learning, can be encouraged by the use of an enterprise social network (ESN) such as Yammer. ESNs are open communication tools that are in effect internal social media channels. They can combine various functions, including posting announcements, comments, micro-blogs, questions and resources, enabling people to take part in online forum discussions and setting up and servicing online special interest groups. They can engage employees with learning events before and after they take place, thus boosting interest and focusing attention in the first instance and helping to embed learning in day-to-day work afterwards. ESN technology is similar to public social networking tools like Facebook in that it supports a constant flow of real-time, threaded conversations through user updates and replies. Learning is no longer seen as a separate activity from working and it can become a continuous, social experience.

Web searches

Web searches using Google are, of course, a way of life for lots of people seeking information and is the first call for many learners who need to know something about a particular subject. However, there is the problem of sorting the wheat from the chaff. It is possible to be overwhelmed by the sheer quantity of information, a lot of which is provided by vendors promoting their wares rather than offering a dispassionate picture of a subject. L&D can help to overcome this problem by curation – identifying where relevant and reliable information can be obtained.

Virtual and augmented reality

Virtual reality is a computer-generated, fully artificial virtual environment where a learner is fully immersed. Freedom is provided for learners to move within the digital environment which lets them develop and practise skills safely. The digital content is displayed through headsets on a tiny screen in front of users with the real world around them. The headsets may be connected to a computer but there are also standalone VR headsets that work with apps through a smartphone.

Augmented reality is a different technology that operates by overlaying virtual objects onto the real-world environment. For example, it can provide engineering learners with the names of parts in an engine as they scan it with their mobile phones which provides them with more complete information than a line drawing in a manual or on a slide.

Artificial intelligence (AI)

The following ways in which artificial intelligence (AI) can be applied in learning and development have been identified by Eubanks (2019):

- helping with the scheduling, planning and resource allocation involved in delivering learning programmes;
- developing fully automated learning management systems;
- identifying skills gaps and skill development needs;
- analysing the adoption rates of learning programmes to asses impact and indicate where changes may be required.

Another possible application is personalization, which involves tailoring an instructional programme to the needs of learners based on their responses to prior test questions and other known information about the learner. AI could also be deployed for tutoring, which involves a dialogue-like experience in which the computer diagnoses learning challenges and presents support tailored in response to the diagnosis.

Chatbots can be used to simulate a real conversation with a real person through speech or text in which the system rather than a person responds to the prompts. Chatbots rely on a knowledge base filled with responses to anticipated questions and requests.

The problem with AI is the technology itself: AI needs hundreds, if not thousands, of example materials to 'train' the system. But this is costly, and thus favours courses taken by large quantities of learners, which few training programmes have.

Online courses

Online learning for individuals as part of a self-directed learning process can be achieved by online courses. The best known one, MOOC (Massive Open Online Course), offers online courses on topics ranging from machine learning and Java programming to communication and leadership.

Online courses include a combination of videos, activities and online discussions, and most are designed to generate interaction between students. The majority of courses are relatively short – four to six weeks – and are therefore attractive to people who are interested in a specific topic and do not want to commit to a long period of learning. These short courses generally offer certificates and micro-credentials on successful completion. MOOCs provide a personalized learning experience and can readily be incorporated into L&D programmes. Hamori (2018: 72) believes that more use could be made of MOOCs by businesses. She observed that: 'By failing to leverage MOOCs, companies are missing out on an effective way to increase employee commitment, especially for young high potentials.' Other providers include LearnDirect, and useful material is available on Ted Talks.

KEY LEARNING POINTS

Digital learning

Digital learning is a learning technology that involves the use of any sort of learning method that is accessed by means of a computer or electronic device.

E-learning

E-learning technology provides for online learning in the form of training courses or 'bite-sized' learning material accessed through a computer or smartphone.

Virtual learning environment

A virtual learning environment (VLE) is a set of learning tools designed to enhance an individual's learning experience by including computers and the internet in the learning process.

Social media

Social media such as Facebook, LinkedIn and Twitter are interactive computer-mediated technologies that facilitate the creation or sharing of information. They can be used as platforms for learning, acting as conduits for locating expertise and information.

Smartphones and apps

The development of smartphone technology has enabled mobiles incorporating apps to become an important part of the learning environment.

Web searches

Web searches using Google are the first call for many learners who need information about a particular subject.

Artificial intelligence

Artificial intelligence (AI) can be used to personalize learning by tailoring an instructional programme to the needs of learners based on their responses to prior test questions and other known information about the learner. AI can also be used for tutoring, which involves a dialogue-like experience in which the computer diagnoses learning challenges and presents support tailored in response to the diagnosis.

References

Bersin, J (2018) https://joshbersin.com/2018/06/a-new-paradigm-for-corporate-training-learning-in-the-flow-of-work/ (archived at https://perma.cc/6M6V-FVRS)

Chartered Institute of Personnel and Development (CIPD) (2013) *Social Technology – Social Business*, CIPD, London

CIPD (2014) *Putting Social Media to Work: Lessons for employers*, CIPD, London

CIPD (2020a) *Digital Learning*, CIPD, London

CIPD (2020b) *Learning and Skills at Work 2020*, CIPD, London

Dagger, D, *et al* (2009) *Service-Oriented E-Learning Platforms: From monolithic systems to flexible services*, IEEE Computer Society, Washington DC

Dillenbourg, P, Schneider, D and Synteta, P (2002) *Virtual Learning Environments*, 3rd Hellenic Conference Information & Communication Technologies in Education Rhodes, Greece, pp 3–18

Eubanks, B (2019) *Artificial Intelligence for HR*, Kogan Page, London

Faragher, J (2018) Why fresh approaches to L&D are presenting new problems, *People Management Online*, 25th October

Hamori, M (2018) *Are organisations making enough of MOOCS?* Harvard Business Review, January-February 2018, pp 70–76

Hird, M and Sparrow, P (2012) *Learning & Development: Seeking a renewed focus? White Paper 12/01 October 2012 Centre for Performance-Led HR*, Lancaster University, [Online] http://www.lancaster.ac.uk/media/lancaster-university/content-assets/documents/lums/cphr/LDWP.pdf (archived at https://perma.cc/Z49R-HCRU)

Lancaster, A (2020) *Driving Performance Though Learning*, Kogan Page, London

Page-Tickel, R (2014) *Learning and Development: A practical introduction*, 2nd edn, Kogan Page, London

Weinstein, M (2020a) *The future of the LMS*, Training, September/October, pp 22–25

Weinstein, M (2020b) *An APPetite for learning*, Training, May/June, pp 22–23

17

Training

Introduction

Training is the process of ensuring through instruction that people have the knowledge, skills and abilities required to carry out their work effectively. It can take place 'off-the-job' as a formal face-to-face training event or intervention. It can also take place less formally 'on-the-job' whenever someone is given instructions on how to do the work. Increasingly, training is being provided online.

Reynolds *et al* (2002: 9) emphasized that training and learning should be distinguished from one another. 'Learning is the process by which a person constructs new knowledge, skills and capabilities, whereas training is one of several responses an organization can undertake to promote learning.' It can be said that 'Learning is what individuals do; training is what organizations do to individuals'. Brown and Duguid (1991:47) argued that: 'Training is thought of as the transmission of explicit, abstract knowledge from the head of someone who knows to the head of someone who does not in surroundings that specifically exclude the complexities of practice and the communities of practitioners. The setting for learning is simply assumed not to matter.'

As Reynolds (2004: 45) pointed out, training has a complementary role to play in accelerating learning: 'It should be reserved for situations that justify a more directed, expert-led approach rather than viewing it as a comprehensive and all-pervasive people development solution.' He also commented that the conventional training model has a tendency to 'emphasize subject-specific knowledge, rather than trying to build core learning abilities'.

Approaches to training

The most typical form of training is a face-to-face (F2F) training event or intervention. But it can also be provided online. A training programme can consist of a sequence of planned experiences, each of which contribute to achieving the learning required.

A training event or programme can be 'blended' by, for example, mixing both F2F formal courses and online learning in a way which maximizes the range and impact of the learning content as illustrated in the case study at the end of this chapter. It can be 'just-in-time' or 'bite-sized'.

Just-in-time training

Just-in-time training is training that is closely linked to the pressing and relevant learning needs of people by its association with immediate or imminent work activities – 'learning in-the-flow of work'. It provides for 'learning in the moment' by being delivered as close as possible to the time when the activity is taking place. The training will be based on an identification of the latest requirements, priorities and plans of the participants, who will be briefed on the live situations in which their learning has to be applied. The training programme will take account of any transfer issues and aim to ensure that what is taught is seen to be applicable in the current work situation.

Bite-sized training

Bite-sized training involves the provision of opportunities to acquire a specific skill or a particular piece of knowledge in a short training session focused on one activity, such as using a particular piece of software, giving feedback or handling an enquiry about a product or service of the company. It is also called micro-learning which involves small learning units or short-term learning activities. It is often carried out through e-learning.

Bite-sized training can be a useful means of developing a skill or understanding through a concentrated session or learning activity which can then be readily put to use in the workplace. But it can be weak in expanding individuals' intellectual capacity and their understanding of the business – essential qualities to enable employees to respond creatively to the challenges of today's knowledge economy. It can also be facile and too restricted and reliant on the support of line managers, which is not always forthcoming. It is best for training employees in straightforward techniques that they can use immediately in their work.

Learning areas covered by training

Training events or programmes can be concerned with any of the following:

- 'hard' skills – technical, manual, administrative and IT;
- leadership, management and interpersonal skills including 'soft skills' such as motivating, enhancing engagement and team building and the people management skills required for selection interviewing, conducting performance reviews and providing feedback, promoting workplace learning, handling disciplinary issues and conducting difficult conversations with employees;
- personal skills, for example, assertiveness, coaching, communicating, problem-solving, time management;
- compliance training which covers what employees need to know about legal and behavioural requirements such as health and safety, data protection, equal opportunity, managing diversity, inclusion policy and practice, bullying and harassment;
- relevant knowledge about the organization's operations, products and services and the environment in which it functions.

The 2011 Workplace Employment Relations Survey (van Wanrooy *et al*, 2013) found that the proportion of employers conducting different types of training were as follows:

- health and safety – 67%
- operating new equipment – 49%
- communication – 44%
- customer service – 41%
- team working – 39%
- quality control – 31%

The justification for training

Formal training is only one of the ways of ensuring that learning takes place, but it can be justified in the following circumstances:

- The knowledge or skills cannot be acquired satisfactorily by experiential learning in the workplace or by self-directed learning.

- Different skills are required by a number of people, which have to be developed quickly to meet new demands and cannot be gained by relying on experience.

- The tasks to be carried out are so specialized or complex that people are unlikely to master them on their own initiative at a reasonable speed.

- When a learning need common to a number of people has to be met that can readily be dealt with in a training event or programme. For example: onboarding, compliance, IT skills.

Requirements for effective training

Formal training is not the only way or even the best way for people to learn but if it is justified for any of the reasons set out above it should be designed, planned and implemented to meet defined needs. The purpose of the training should be clearly defined in terms of the behaviour required as a result of it (terminal behaviour). Learning will only be effective if learners are fully engaged in the process. This means providing them with the motivation to learn by convincing them of the benefits that will be forthcoming. The focus of the training should be on developing transferable skills which are put to good use in the place of work. The issue of transferring learning to the workplace should be addressed. Outcomes of training should be evaluated on the basis of the extent to which it has achieved its purpose.

The concept of systematic training as developed for the industrial training boards in the 1960s was an attempt to model a successful approach to training. As illustrated in Figure 17.1, it consisted of a four-stage cycle:

1 Identify training needs.

2 Plan the training required to satisfy these needs.

3 Deliver training using experienced and trained trainers to implement training.

4 Evaluate training to ensure that it is effective.

This systematic training model seems to be logical. It looks right to start by understanding what is to be achieved (the need) and proceed through planning and delivery stages to an evaluation of the extent to which the need has been satisfied, leading to a revised plan. But it is simplistic. The stages in the cycle may overlap and contextual issues may affect the way in which the event is

FIGURE 17.1 The systematic training cycle

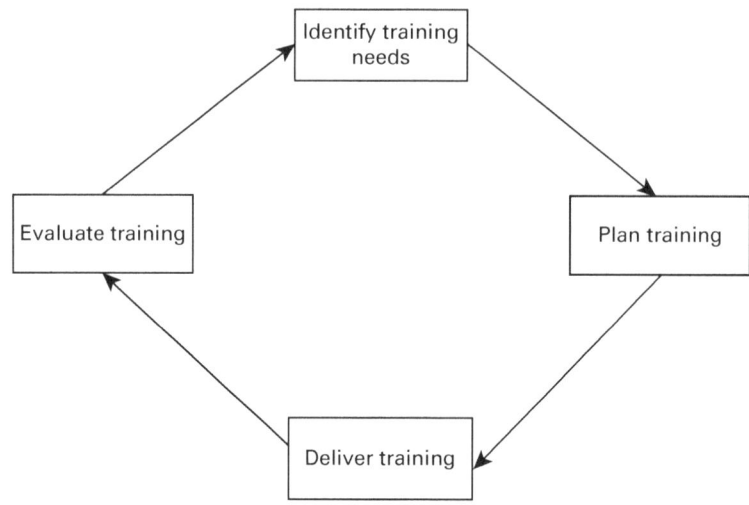

planned and delivered. Doubts about the cycle were expressed by Rosemary Harrison (2009: 17) as follows:

> The major criticism of the cycle is that it presents training as operating in a free-standing closed system dominated by functional tasks. The underlying assumption is that these tasks should and can take place in a predetermined sequence, requiring only the application of specialized expertise to ensure their success. No matter how perfect its design and delivery it can still fail if it does not pay enough attention to that context. When it does fail it is usually because it lacks the support of key stakeholders – especially front-line line managers of learners and the learners themselves – whose buy-in is essential to its success.

Moreover, the systematic training model ignores the problem of getting the learning transferred from the training centre to the workplace.

Transferring learning

The problem of transferring learning following a training course was raised by Reynolds (2004: 47) as follows:

> Some types of intervention disrupt self-directed learning by paying insufficient attention to the needs of the learner in the work context. Methods that rely heavily on the transfer of external expertise or content to employees… carry the

highest risk in this regard, since their design is often removed from the context in which work is created. As a result, it is impossible to meet learning needs adequately.

This is a fundamental problem and applies equally to externally and internally run training courses where what has been taught can be difficult for people to apply in the entirely different circumstances in their workplace. Training can seem to be remote from reality and the skills and knowledge acquired can appear to be irrelevant. Transfer of learning problems often occur after management or supervisory training, but even the manual skills learnt in a training centre can be difficult to transfer. Issues concerning learning transfer are explored in more detail in Chapter 21.

Planning and delivering formal training

A process for planning and delivering training or learning events and programmes is provided by the ADDIE model, which was developed in Florida State University in the 1970s. It has the following five phases:

1 *Analysis* – learning goals are defined as criterion or terminal behaviour (what participants will learn and be able to do as a result of the training) and the learning environment and learners' existing knowledge and skills are identified.

2 *Design* – the subject matter and methods to be used are determined and the programme outline is prepared.

3 *Development* – the detailed programme is constructed as conceived in the design phase.

4 *Implementation* – the programme is implemented as planned.

5 *Evaluation* – each session is evaluated by the programme director and participants. The impact of the programme on performance is measured and the degree to which it met expectations assessed.

Again, this is logical but it suffers from the same flaws as the systematic training model.

An alternative approach is provided by the training sequence, as illustrated in Figure 17.2.

FIGURE 17.2   The training sequence

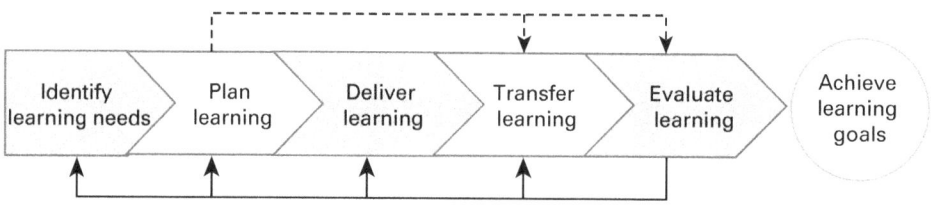

This model adds transfer of learning considerations to the activities included in previous models. But while it represents the process as basically a logical sequence of activities it recognizes that in practice a flexible approach is required. For example, when planning a training course the first consideration will be the contents of that course and the methods to be used. But attention needs also to be given at this stage to what needs to be done to ensure that learning is transferred and the plan should also refer to the basis upon which the learning event will be evaluated.

The stages in this sequence are examined in Part 5 of this book (Chapters 18 to 22). Although they apply to the planning and delivery of formal face-to-face training events they are also relevant when developing and implementing digital learning, especially e-learning.

CASE STUDY
Training overhaul for Scottish police

A radical overhaul of training for the Scottish police has created more opportunities for promotion and culminated in a prestigious National Training Award. The improved training scheme uses facilitated learning delivery, where trainees pre-read all information before attending sessions and then discuss issues and learn from each other. Responsibility for learning is now firmly placed on the shoulders of the individual – you have got to want to be a police officer and you have got to want to learn. After 15 weeks of initial training, a two-week 'reconvention' period helps staff with the areas they particularly need to address. This training is tailored to individual requirements: syndicates of recruits with similar needs are put together to receive it. This 'partnership approach' had helped the participants to focus on communication and problem-solving skills. A Certificate of Higher Education in policing, accredited by the University of Stirling, is awarded on completion of the programme. There are also opportunities to take a diploma in management skills.

CASE STUDY

Training and learning at a customer support centre

This customer support centre employs 300 people. Customer service agents work in a group of five, known as a 'pod.' One of the pod members will be a team coach who provides support and advice to his or her agent colleagues.

A working knowledge of each customer support system is essential to do the job and one of the central tasks of the training department is to bring new entrants up to competence as quickly as possible. The following pattern is adopted. New entrants join in cohorts of 8 to 10 and spend their first week in the training room. As the week progresses they spend periods in a pod sitting next to a 'buddy', listening to calls. At the end of that week they are allocated to a pod team and receive close ongoing support from the pod team coach.

Given the emphasis on learning in the workplace, the role of the team coach is critical and there are a number of steps in place to support and enhance their role. A set of skills and needs have been defined and these are delivered to the 30 centre team coaches in 90 minute modules in the training room.

CASE STUDY

London Underground transformation through blended learning

The London Underground which is managed by Transport for London, employs about 5,000 staff. A number of significant new technologies have been introduced which have meant considerable changes to working arrangements. The business strategy was focused on achieving even better customer relations with the help of these changes. A learning strategy was formulated to support this business strategy. With the help of external providers Kallidus and Interact, a comprehensive learning programme was constructed based on practice-based experiential learning, workshops and e-learning, the latter consisting of a six-week online programme involving 'learning by discovery' (learners finding out for themselves the features of the new technologies and working arrangements and how they would be affected by them). To assist learning, six virtual underground stations were set up and 40 short 'dramas' were created showing what was going to happen and demonstrating the skills required. A dedicated learning platform was introduced and each of the 5,000 employees was issued with an iPad mini to access the e-learning material on a learning app. A special game (gamification) was devised to reinforce understanding of station operations and customer service requirements.

SOURCE *Training Journal*, February 2016

KEY LEARNING POINTS

Training defined

Training is the process of ensuring through instruction that people have the knowledge, skills and abilities required to carry out their work effectively.

Approaches to training

- The most typical form of training is that of a face-to-face (F2F) training event or intervention.

- Just-in-time training is training that is closely linked to the pressing and relevant needs of people by its association with immediate or imminent work activities.

- Bite-sized training involves the provision of opportunities to acquire a specific skill or a particular piece of knowledge in a short training session focused on one activity.

Types of training

Training programmes or events can be concerned with any of the following:

- manual skills, including apprenticeships;

- IT skills;

- team leader or supervisory training;

- leadership and management training;

- interpersonal soft skills, eg leadership, team building, group dynamics, neurolinguistic programming;

- personal, eg assertiveness, coaching, communicating, time management;

- training in organizational procedures or practices, eg induction, health and safety, performance management, equal opportunity or managing diversity policy and practice.

The justification for training

Formal training is only one of the ways of ensuring that learning takes place, but it can be justified in the following circumstances:

- The knowledge or skills cannot be acquired satisfactorily by experiential learning in the workplace or by self-managed learning.

- Different skills are required by a number of people, which have to be developed quickly to meet new demands and cannot be gained by relying on experience.

- The tasks to be carried out are so specialized or complex that people are unlikely to master them on their own initiative at a reasonable speed.

- When a learning need common to a number of people has to be met that can readily be dealt with in a training event or programme.

Effective training practices

The purpose of the training should be clearly defined in terms of the behaviour required as a result of it (terminal behaviour). Learning will only be effective if learners are fully engaged in the process. This means providing them with the motivation to learn by convincing them of the benefits that will be forthcoming. The focus of the training should be on developing transferable skills which are put to good use in the place of work. The issue of transferring learning to the workplace should be addressed. Outcomes of training should be evaluated on the basis of the extent to which it has achieved its purpose.

The sequence of formal training

Training in the shape of formal learning events or interventions is planned and delivered by means of the following sequence of activities:

1 Identify learning needs.

2 Plan learning.

3 Deliver learning.

4 Transfer learning.

5 Evaluate learning.

References

Brown, J S and Duguid, P (1991) Organizational learning and communities-of-practice: toward a unified view of working, learning and innovating, *Organization Science*, 2 (1), pp 40–57

Harrison, R (2009) *Learning and Development*, 5th edn, CIPD, London

Reynolds, J, Caley, L and Mason, R (2002) *How Do People Learn?* CIPD, London

Reynolds, J (2004) *Helping People Learn*, CIPD, London

van Wanrooy, H, Bewley, B H, Bryson, A, Forth, J and Freeth, S (2013) *The 2011 Workplace Employment Relations Survey*: First findings, City University, London

PART FIVE

Planning and delivering learning events

18

Identifying learning needs

Introduction

Learning strategy is driven by the learning needs of the organization – its capability requirements. Learning activities need to be planned and implemented in the light of an understanding of what should be done and why it should be done. That is the purpose of analysing and identifying learning needs at organizational, team and individual levels. This chapter covers the nature and basis of learning needs analysis and the processes of analysis and diagnosis.

Learning needs

Learning needs are related either to maintaining current capability (maintenance needs) or to meeting future needs (developmental needs). A learning need at organizational level exists in three circumstances. First, when it has been established that it is necessary to enhance organizational capability by developing new skills to meet any demands emerging from revised business or corporate goals or developments; second, when there are business, operational, productivity or quality problems affecting overall performance; and third, when there are skill shortages. A learning need at team or group level exists when it is evident that poor teamwork is a problem. At individual level, the need to develop capabilities exists in any of the following circumstances: when starting or moving to a new job; to meet different work demands arising from such factors as new technology, product developments or changes in policies and practice; to satisfy talent management requirements and help people to develop their careers; to overcome deficiencies in performance and to ensure compliance with legislation or company policy.

The CIPD (2020) distinguishes between an ongoing learning needs analysis (LNA) and a training needs analysis (TNA). An LNA is defined as a health check on the skills, talent and capabilities of the organization (or part of the organization) and is carried out with multiple stakeholders. It's based on the systematic gathering of data and insights about employees' capabilities and organizational demands for skills, alongside an analysis of the implications for capability requirements of new and changed roles. A TNA is more of one-off event looking at the needs for a specific learning event.

The process of identifying learning needs

The following model for identifying learning needs was adapted by Harrison and Auluck (2014) from the work of McLelland (1993).

1 Define assessment goals.

2 Determine assessment group.

3 Determine availability of qualified resources to conduct and oversee the project.

4 Gain senior management support and commitment.

5 Review/select assessment methods/instruments.

6 Determine critical time frames.

7 Schedule and implement.

8 Gather information – this stage is a formal or informal process to identify performance issues or areas for development.

9 Analyse information – analyse, interpret and conclude from the data gathered.

10 Draw conclusions.

11 Create a development plan by using the information that has been analysed to resolve the performance issue or development needed.

The key stages in this process are: 1) analysis of learning needs; 2) diagnosis of the factors that govern learning needs as established by the analysis and 3) action planning.

Analysis of learning needs

The RAM approach (CIPD, 2020) can be used when analysing learning needs. This sets out the requirement for:

- *Relevance* – How existing or planned learning provision will meet new opportunities and challenges for the business.

- *Alignment* – If the L&D strategy takes an integrated blended approach, it's critical for L&D practitioners to work with stakeholders about their performance needs and how to achieve them. Aligning with broader organizational strategy gives focus, purpose and relevance to L&D.

- *Measurement* – L&D effectively and consistently measure the impact, engagement and transfer of learning activities as part of the evaluation process.

The three interconnected areas in which analysis takes place are shown in Figure 18.1.

Corporate learning needs relate to what should be done to ensure that the organization thrives and any problems in doing so are overcome. They are established by analysing business or corporate and workforce plans and performance and by surveys.

Collective learning needs are those that are shared by a number of people in the organization in occupational groups. They can be satisfied by learning events addressing these needs that are established through the analysis of corporate or individual learning needs, role or skills analysis or by surveys. As the needs of individual employees are analysed separately, common needs emerge, which can be dealt with on a group basis. For example, at corporate level, the introduction of a new product could indicate that a product knowledge programme is required for sales representatives. The skills needed to use a revised performance management system may have to be learnt in a training course or through coaching. At individual level, performance reviews may show that a number of managers are deficient in leadership skills and that a leadership development programme should be introduced for them.

Individual learning needs relate to the capabilities (knowledge, skills and behaviours) individual employees need to perform their jobs satisfactorily and develop their potential. Gap analysis is used to identify any deficiencies between the capabilities people possess and what they need to have. The needs can be analysed under the headings of:

- *Knowledge* – What people need to know now to carry out their work and also to comply with corporate policies in such areas as diversity and inclusion, health and safety and quality control and government regulations such as those dealing with data protection. Additionally, what people will need to know to deal with future demands arising from organizational initiatives in the shape of new or changing products or services, different markets or customers, or new technologies and from external developments arising from government policies, financial crises and events such as COVID-19 and Brexit.

- *Hard skills* – What people need to be able to do to carry out their work now and in the future in the shape of technical and manual skills (for example, operating new equipment or systems).

- *Soft skills* – The interpersonal skills needed to lead, manage and relate to and work with other people.

- *Behaviours* – How people are expected to behave in their roles: as managers or team members, in relation to others (for example, harassment, bullying, consideration), complying with ethical standards, supporting diversity and inclusion and care for the environment policies and, in general, the exercise of corporate social responsibility

In analysing these areas, especially those concerned with knowledge and skills, the aim should be to relate them to organizational strategies and requirements so that L&D strategies can be aligned with them and therefore support their achievement.

The use of the various analytical methods and of surveys as shown in Figure 18.1 is examined below.

Analysis of business or corporate plans

An analysis of business or corporate plans should reveal any areas where future innovations or changes in the products or services provided by the

FIGURE 18.1 Learning needs analysis – areas and methods

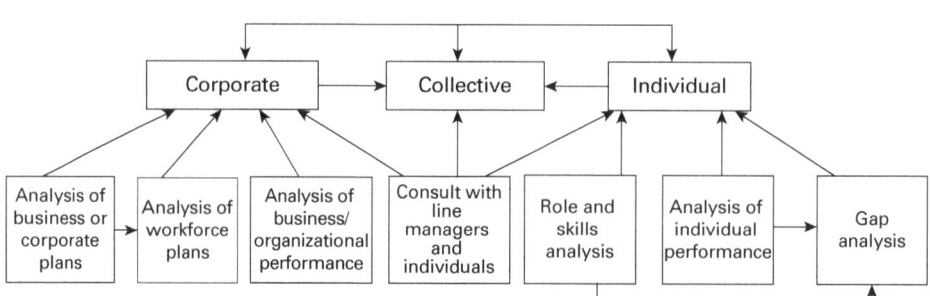

organization, the markets in which it operates or the customers it serves, may require new knowledge or skills or the development of existing ones. Knowledge and skills needs may also be affected by proposed changes in work processes, methods or job responsibilities. These broad indicators have to be translated into more specific plans that cover, for example, the outputs from training programmes of people with particular skills or a combination of skills (multiskilling).

This analysis is an important part of the process of developing learning and development strategy as described in Chapter 6. As was emphasized there, it is necessary to ensure that L&D activities further the objectives of the organization by aligning L&D strategy and business or corporate strategy. The notion of strategic L&D implies that L&D strategy is aligned in linear fashion with and driven by the corporate or business strategy (strategic fit) and translates the learning and development implications of that strategy into a plan for action designed to support the achievement of the organization's strategic goals.

Analysis of workforce plans

Business or corporate plans provide the basis for the development of workforce plans. The latter establish an organization's people requirements in terms of numbers and skills so that steps can be taken to satisfy them. Workforce planning is an integral part of corporate planning. The strategic planning process defines projected changes in the types of activities carried out by the organization and the scale of those activities. It identifies the core capabilities or competences that the organization needs to achieve its goals and therefore its skill requirements. A gap analysis can be conducted to establish the extent that the organization has the level or quantity of skills required and indicate if any remedial learning and development activities are needed. The learning needs analysis should include the key stakeholders – senior management, line managers and employees.

Analysis of organizational performance

The purpose of an analysis of organizational (business) performance is to establish the extent to which outcomes such as the achievement of goals, the creation of shareholder value, productivity, efficiency, quality, innovation, cost control, customer service and the exercise of corporate social responsibility meet or exceed expectations. Below standard results may identify an issue such as lack of required knowledge or skills, poor management and leadership or inappropriate behaviour and these in turn will indicate learning and development needs.

Consulting line managers

Line managers make a significant and indispensable contribution to the satisfaction of learning needs. They are close to the ground. They know what skills they need in their departments and what skills they have. They know about any skills deficiencies that need to be remedied. Their views should be sought systematically. The best way of doing this is to talk to them, individually as far as possible, but if that is difficult, in focus groups. Opinions can be sought by surveys but the personal touch is much better. Increasingly, this is what L&D professionals must do if they are to make an effective contribution to the achievement of L&D goals. It all happens in the workplace and that's where they should spend most of their time.

Consulting employees

In his foreword to the CIPD report on *Driving Performance and Productivity* (2018: 4) Andy Lancaster wrote that: 'Learners, as the most important people in the process, should be intimately involved in learning design. As key stakeholders, their views on what learning is needed, how it's provided and when it's accessible are central to effective development.'

Again, the best way to do this is to talk to them in the workplace. Talk to people who have recently started in their job. Ask them how they were acquiring the knowledge and learning the skills they need. Who told them what they had to do and how to do it? How did they do this? How helpful was it? To what extent do they now feel that they are up to the job? What problems do they have in getting things done? Talk also to more experienced employees and ask them to describe the knowledge and skills they need to their job (required capability) and the knowledge and skills they have (actual capability) in order to reveal any gaps and to discuss what can be done to fill these gaps by them as well as their managers and the organization. This will all take time but it will be time well spent.

Role and skills analysis

Role analysis as described in Chapter 13 is used to prepare role profiles that provide the basis for analysing and identifying learning needs. The profiles set out the key result areas of the role and the knowledge, skills and behaviours or competencies required to carry it out. The output of role analysis could be a learning specification, as illustrated in Figure 13.3 in Chapter 13. Skills analysis techniques as described in Chapter 13 are mainly used for manual jobs

Analysis of individual performance

Performance management is a prime source of information about individual learning and development needs. It is based on an analysis of role requirements as set out in a role profile. Performance reviews, which should be held whenever appropriate rather than simply being an annual event, will include discussions on the extent that the individual would benefit, in career progression as well as performance terms, from some form of learning and development activity. Problems of performance arising from lack of knowledge or skill or inappropriate behaviour can be identified so that remedial action can be taken. A joint assessment can then be made of what sort of development programme is required. This can lead to a personal development plan and a learning contract which include action plans, self-directed learning and an agreement on what support will be provided to the individual by the organization and the manager. An overall analysis of performance and development review reports can reveal any common learning needs that can be satisfied by tailored learning events.

Gap analysis

Gap analysis involves establishing the extent to which there is a difference between what is happening and what should happen, as illustrated in Figure 18.2.

Information on the nature of the gap can be obtained by role and individual performance analysis. When the analysis has been completed the learning needed to fill the gap is specified. But this 'deficiency model' – only putting things right that have gone wrong – is limited. Learning is much more positive than that. It should also be concerned with identifying and satisfying development needs – fitting people to take on extra responsibilities, acquire new skills to deal with changing work demands or develop a range of skills to facilitate multitasking.

FIGURE 18.2   The learning gap

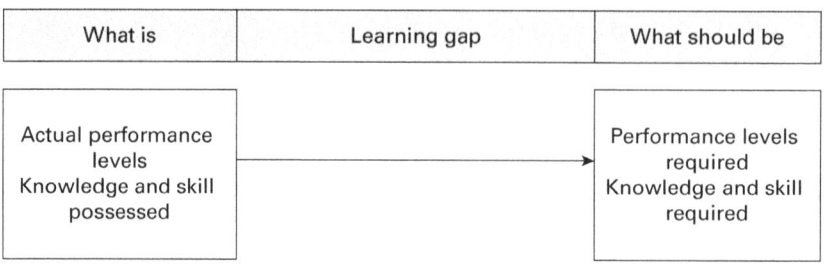

Diagnosis

On completing the analysis, the second stage is a diagnosis of the main factors influencing corporate, communal and individual learning needs. The diagnosis should identify any problems that affect how they can be met and the underlying factors that create those problems. It should indicate the approach that can be adopted to doing so. In effect, the diagnosis is a summary of all the lessons learnt from the analyses under the different headings and it therefore provides the basis for the final stage.

Action planning

Action planning involves drawing conclusions on the implications for learning and development policy and practice of the analyses and diagnosis and preparing a learning and development strategy and implementation for approval by senior management. The following steps are necessary:

1 List the learning activities required as identified from the analyses and diagnosis. These could be formal learning events or 'interventions' on specified subjects for different categories of people, enhancing the quality of 'onboarding' training' and experiential learning in the workplace, making more use of digital learning techniques, satisfying talent management requirements, including the use of extended development programmes, or supporting self-directed learning

2 Assess for each activity its objectives in terms of what people will learn from it and how that learning will benefit the performance and development of individuals and, importantly, enhance organizational performance (the business case). Identify the key learning points related to each activity that will need to be considered when deciding on the content of any training intervention.

3 Prioritize – decide on the relative importance of the activities by reference to the business case.

4 Review the resources required (money, people and facilities) to implement the prioritized activities.

5 Establish the extent that available resources are sufficient and, if not, what additional resources may be required. In the latter case, make a realistic assessment of what is needed in accordance with priorities

6 By reference to the steps listed above, prepare a learning and development strategy and plans that incorporate the prioritized learning activities, a timetable for their implementation and the resources required.

7 Present the strategy and plans and the supporting business case to senior management for their approval.

8 Implement the strategy in order to achieve learning objectives and satisfy key learning points.

KEY LEARNING POINTS

Why the identification of learning needs is necessary

Learning activities should be planned and implemented in the light of an understanding of what should be done and why it should be done. The nature and purpose of learning programmes and events should be defined by analysing and identifying learning needs at organizational, team and individual levels.

Learning needs

Learning needs exist when:

- at organizational level it is necessary to enhance organizational capability to meet any new demands or deal with performance problems;

- at team or group level when it is evident that poor teamwork exists in the organization;

- at individual level, when different demands require new skills, to help people to develop their careers, or to overcome deficiencies in performance.

Analysis of learning needs

The analysis of learning needs establishes what needs to be done about the planning and delivery of learning programmes and events in three interconnected areas: corporate, collective and individual.

The sources of information are:

- analysis of business plans;

- analysis of business performance;

- consultation with managers and employees;

- role analysis;

- analysis of individual performance;

- gap analysis.

Stages

The stages of identifying learning needs are analysis, diagnosis and action planning.

Bibliography

Chartered Institute of Personnel and Development (CIPD) (2018) *Driving Performance and Productivity*, CIPD, London

CIPD (2020) *Identifying Learning and Development Needs*, London, CIPD

Harrison, T and Auluck, R (2014) Establishing learning needs, in *Designing, Delivering and Evaluating L&D: Essentials for practice*, eds J Stewart and P Cureton, pp 57–77, CIPD, London

Lancaster, A (2020) *Driving Performance Though Learning*, Kogan Page, London

McLelland, S (1993) Training needs assessment: an 'open-systems' application, *Journal of European Industrial Training*, **17** (1), pp 12–17

19

Planning learning events

Introduction

Learning events are formal arrangements in the shape of training courses or programmes designed to satisfy learning needs. They are usually conducted 'off-the-job', ie away from the workplace in a training centre or classroom using face-to-face teaching or direct learning. They may be supported by digital (online) techniques to provide complementary or additional remote learning. Formal events can consist of bite-sized learning modules delivered over a few hours (there is much to be said for this method of focusing the learning experience). Or they may last days or even weeks when run externally or in a corporate university. An extended development programme may incorporate a selection of relevant formal events as well as semi-formal approaches as described below.

Learning events are sometimes called learning interventions because they add to or support the natural process of learning that takes place at work. But a policy of encouraging self-directed learning could be regarded as a type of intervention because it complements or supports 'experiential learning'.

This chapter covers:

- the initial considerations to be taken into account before making the final decision on whether a learning need should be satisfied by a formal event or through some other means;

- the criteria for success when planning an event;

- defining learning objectives;

- deciding who runs the learning event;

- creating content for face-to-face learning events;

- instructional design;
- deciding on the event's programme and length;
- selecting and briefing trainers;
- planning the facilities required;
- selecting or obtaining nominations for attending the event, briefing them and planning and administering pre-programme activities or tests.

Initial considerations

An initial decision is required on whether to go ahead to plan a formal learning event involving face-to-face training in a learning centre or classroom. Face-to-face learning means that complete control is maintained over the learning process – trainers can ensure that the planned learning content is delivered and as far as possible absorbed, they can switch easily between different methods as appropriate to the needs and reactions of the learners, and they will be able to react swiftly if problems arise in the learning process. Interaction between those attending the event and the trainer will help learning to take place.

The alternative for consideration is to rely on digital learning, for example e-learning and/or the use of apps on smartphones. This would allow people to learn remotely, in their own time, wherever and wherever they choose. It provides greater flexibility and supports self-directed learning, and guidance on how to transfer learning to the workplace can readily be provided. But it does not allow for social interaction during the event, which is an important element in promoting learning. And some control is lost on how well people have learnt, although this can be monitored to a degree on a learning management system. Blending face-to-face and online learning can get the best of both worlds but it may be difficult to ensure that the right mix is used and that the two methods do complement one another.

When considering how to satisfy learning needs, the best solution may be self-directed learning rather than a formal learning event. This may involve remote learning – the provision of learning content and programmes online from sites or locations other than the learner's own organization. Learners can be advised on how to manage their own learning and on the availability of relevant remote learning material, for example, MOOCs, the Open University or Ted Talks.

If a decision is made to run a formal learning event, it is then necessary to set out criteria that will be used to evaluate the event, define learning objectives and decide who should plan and conduct the course. Having done this, the detailed planning of content and the arrangement for the event can take place.

Criteria for a successful learning event

The criteria for a successful learning event are that:

- the event is conducted efficiently and good facilities and learning aids are available;
- plans are made and action is taken to ensure that individuals transfer their learning to the workplace;
- the quality of the event is evaluated against the success criteria.

Learning objectives

Learning objectives describe how the learning needs identified in the first stage of the sequence will be satisfied and define the benefits to the individual participants and the organization that will result from the learning event. This means defining expectations on the impact that the event will make in terms of criterion and terminal behaviour. Criterion behaviour is the performance standards or changes in behaviour on-the-job to be achieved if a learning process is to be regarded as successful. Terminal behaviour is what learners will be able to do in their workplace on completing a training programme, for example: 'On completing this programme participants will be able to… ' It is essential at this stage to consider how the learning event will be evaluated and return-on-expectations is often the best way to do that.

Donald Kirkpatrick, quoted in Kirkpatrick Foundational Principles (2020), said:

> Trainers must begin with desired results and then determine what behavior is needed to accomplish them. Then trainers must determine the attitudes, knowledge, and skills that are necessary to bring about the desired behavior(s). The final challenge is to present the training program in a way that enables the participants not only to learn what they need to know but also to react favourably to the program.

The learning objectives should specify the people for whom the learning event is being designed and how they and the organization will benefit. Nominations are usually made by line managers who may need to be convinced that the experience will be worthwhile.

Deciding who runs the learning event

There is a choice between planning and running the event internally or outsourcing the whole or part of the process. The latter alternative may be adopted when the subject matter is beyond the capacity of people in the organization to deliver but it can be expensive and particular care will be needed in defining the objectives of the event and selecting and briefing the external providers.

Creating content for face-to-face learning events

Content creation puts together the information required to meet the learning needs that a learning event or some form of digital learning is intended to satisfy. The 'AGES' model which provides general guidance for creating content in both digital and face-to-face learning events was described in Chapter 13. The steps required to create content for the latter events are spelt out below.

The starting point should be a definition of the objective of the event set out as criterion and terminal behaviour. If the event is concerned with an aspect of knowledge or skill which will be dealt with in a single session, this may provide a sufficient basis for creating the content. However, if the event is covering a more complex subject area and has many subsidiary goals, more than one session may have to be planned and learning goals determined for each of these separate sessions.

The second step is to decide on the key learning points for each session. A key learning point describes the essence of what someone has to take away from the event and apply at work in the shape of knowledge, skills and behaviour.

The third step is to assemble the learning content required to get each learning point across. Material can be sourced externally from books, journals, magazines, social media posts, blogs, podcasts and reports. Or it may be appropriate to use relevant internal material in the form of policy guidelines, manuals, reports, statements of prescribed practices, the activities of communities of interest or learning communities, material such as handouts, PowerPoint slides or videos used in learning events, or in databanks where knowledge is codified and stored.

To summarize, the basic principles to be taken into account when creating content for a learning event are that it:

- meets defined learning needs;
- is based on a clear definition of the key learning points emerging from the analysis of learning needs;
- uses relevant and up-to-date information and material from internal and external sources that meet the requirements set out in the key learning points;
- will convince those at the receiving end that they are learning something that they will find helpful and therefore put into practice, making it clear how good use can be made of the learning presented by the content;
- presents the material in a form that will facilitate learning, ie it is easy to assimilate and remember;
- sequences the learning in steps that learners can easily follow – they may need to grasp one concept before they can move on to another. Beevers *et al* (2020: 109) point out that it can be helpful to think about learning as 'blocks', which build on top of each other until the desired scope and level of learning has been covered. To be most accessible, learning content should be delivered in a logical flow, allowing learners to build up through simple to more complex areas of learning.

Instructional design

Instructional design defines how a learning event should be delivered including the methods to be used in running it and the use of learning aids. It should be distinguished from content design which concentrates on what material is to be presented rather than how it is to be presented.

The Gagne approach to instructional design

The following nine conditions for effective instructional design (the ISD model) were proposed by Gagne (1977):

1 Gain the attention of learners.

2 Inform learners of learning objectives.

3 Stimulate recall of prior learning.

4 Present the content and break it down into components to avoid information overload.

5 Provide learning guidance.

6 Elicit performance.

7 Provide feedback to learners.

8 Assess the performance of learners.

9 Enhance knowledge retention and transfer to real life in the workplace.

The ISD model is more of a blueprint for effective training than a guide to instructional methods. And it has its limitations. It is largely instructor focused and places the emphasis on content rather than method. The learner plays a passive role as the receiver of information, Pouring information into people only works to a limited extent.

The process of instructional design

Instructional design starts with the overall approach to running the event. This will vary according to its nature. For example, a course for managers or team leaders may make maximum use of facilitation rather than lecturing. This could take the form of discussions involving all the course members which could involve splitting the course into small groups, ideally with no more than five or six members to take part in 'break-out' sessions to discuss particular subjects or issues or to complete a case study (these used to be called syndicates, a military staff college term). Group discussions can take place in the training room or in separate break-out rooms. Alternatively, a course devoted mainly to the development of technical or manual skills will rely more on instruction supported by digital learning such as augmented reality.

More detailed consideration can then be given to the use of learning methods and aids such as lectures (kept to a minimum), instruction, exercises (case studies, role-plays and games), visual aids such as PowerPoint slides, videos and virtual reality. A blend of these with more conventional lecturing or instruction can be a useful way of maximizing impact and learning effectiveness, particularly when the emphasis is on skills development. This is in accordance with learning theory and neuro-science which advocate the engagement of a maximum number of senses – especially visual – when designing learning. Steps can then be taken by L&D or whoever is responsible for running the learning event to create or obtain the aids.

Programming the event

Programming a formal face-to-face learning event when more than one session is required to cover the subject area means deciding on the order in which the material should be presented and the time required to deal with each of the elements of the content. The sequence of elements should be logi-cal; following the introduction, each one should be linked to its predecessor so that the cumulative learning required takes place leading to the complete fulfilment of the event's learning objectives. The objectives of each session should be defined.

The amount allowed to present the material in a single session is typically limited to no more than an hour to which can be added time for any additional exercises – case studies etc. But it may be even better to break up the day into short 'bites' each covering a major learning point.

A one-day programme during which a lot of learning material has to be covered may be limited to no more than six hours or so (eg three in the morn-ing and three in the afternoon) to avoid overload – the amount people can absorb is limited and this particularly applies to afternoon sessions, hence the need for only a light lunch. But the time taken for interactive work and exer-cises can be added to this in moderation. They are often included in afternoon sessions when receptivity to formal inputs may be limited. An estimate of the number of sessions required and the time allowed for each of them gives an approximation of the total amount of time the event could take. Adjustments may have to be made if this is too long. It may be decided that, to avoid over-load and taking up too much time on any one event, a series of short courses – a day or less – may be preferable. This spreads the load but also spreads the learning which may lose some of its impact over time.

The programme that emerges for the event following the above assessments (some iteration may be required) can be set out under the following headings:

1 The learning objectives of the event described as criterion or terminal behaviour.

2 The category of people for whom the event will be suitable.

3 The number of learners for whom the event will cater. This would only be limited to the space available if the event is simply a massive presentation. But in the typical learning event where the maximum use is made of interactive learning the number may be limited, typically to no more than 20 or so.

4 A synopsis of the main material that the event will cover.

5 The timetable of the sessions that will be included in the event. Information about each session should be provided, namely:

   o its objectives;

   o timing;

   o a summary of its contents in the form of the key learning points;

   o the methods to be used including the use of exercises such as case studies and learning aids such as videos and virtual reality environments;

   o the name of the presenter of the session, where known.

6 The location of the event.

Selecting and briefing trainers and speakers

The trainer or trainers who run the course as a whole or are responsible for individual sessions may be members of the L&D function. The briefing will clearly be unnecessary when they have been involved in planning the event. Experts from within the organization can also be used as speakers and will need to be briefed. There is a lot to be said for getting them to take part to convey the knowledge and experience of practitioners and to keep course members in touch with the reality of day-to-day work especially when the training is concerned with operational or administrative procedures, introducing new policies or practices or conveying product knowledge before a launch takes place.

Consideration will have to be given to bringing in outside experts to deal with subjects that are beyond the scope of people from inside the organization. It may be decided that the best way to satisfy a learning need is to outsource the whole event to an external provider.

Any briefing needed should cover the session's objectives, an outline of what should be presented and, if appropriate, tactful guidance on how their session should be conducted, including the use of training aids. Help can be provided in obtaining or preparing those aids.

Planning facilities

The facilities to be provided will include a room or rooms in which the event can take place. The size of the room will depend upon the numbers expected to attend but allowance will have to be made for the proposed layout of the session (alternative layouts are considered in Chapter 20). Additional rooms for 'break-out' sessions may be required. Check that the room is suitable for the event and that it has the required electrical connections and heating.

The other facilities are training aids and equipment such as projectors, presentation software, interactive smartboards, virtual or augmented reality equipment, flip charts, podcasts, video clips and polling apps (for gauging opinions and quizzes during sessions), note pads, pens or pencils and name plates and badges.

Nominations

Line managers can be invited to nominate people to take part in the event. The managers will need to be briefed on its purpose, the main areas it will cover and who is most likely to benefit from it. Alternatively, and less preferably, more senior management working with L&D can decide who should attend. It may be a good idea to give people the opportunity to apply for the event although this risks creating disappointment.

Those nominated or selected to attend should be briefed on the purpose and contents of the event and how they will be expected to benefit from it. Joining instructions will set out when and where the event will take place and any other information that might be helpful for example, a dress code.

Any pre-event literature for study by those due to attend could be distributed or recommended although this should be limited to essential material.

As far as possible learning events should stand on their own two feet and imposing 'homework' may antagonize those due to attend. Pre-event tests to establish the level of knowledge of nominees can be helpful but again, caution is required not to overburden people.

KEY LEARNING POINTS

Learning events defined

Learning events are formal arrangements in the shape of training courses or programmes designed to satisfy learning needs. They are generally conducted 'off-the-job', ie away from the workplace in a training centre or classroom using face-to-face or direct learning. They may be supported by digital (online) techniques to provide complementary or additional distance learning.

Planning learning events

1   Establish learning needs.

2   Define learning objectives including who the event is for.

3   Create content.

4   Decide on instructional method.

5   Decide on the event's programme and length and where it should take place.

6   Select and brief trainers.

7   Plan the facilities required.

8   Obtain nominations to attend the event (or select them) brief them and issue joining instructions.

9   Decide on how to ensure the transfer of learning.

10   Decide on how the event should be evaluated.

Bibliography

Beevers, K, Rea, A and Hayde, D (2020) *Learning and Development Practice in the Workplace*, Kogan Page, London

Davachi, L, Kiefer, T, Rock, D and Rock, L (2010) Learning that lasts through AGES, *NeuroLeadership Journal*, vol 3

Gagne, R.M. (1992). *Principles of instructional design*, Fort Worth, TX: Harcourt Brace.

Kirkpatrick, D (2020) *Kirkpatrick Foundational Principles*, [Online] https://kirkpatrick partners.com/Our-Philosophy/Kirkpatrick-Foundational-Principles (archived at https:// perma.cc/KVB2-TF2Q)

20

Managing learning events

Introduction

The third stage in the training sequence is to deliver the event. This chapter starts with an analysis of what makes a good learning experience in an event and continues with descriptions of its three stages, namely, setting it up, starting it and running and closing it.

Effective learning events

An effective learning event is one that has achieved its objectives – to meet defined learning needs and to ensure as far as possible that the learning is transferred to the workplace and contributes to performance improvements. The quality of the learning event itself will be measured by the relevance of its content to participants, the quality of the trainer(s) and speakers, the usefulness of the learning aids and resources and the extent to which the event was well organized. A study by Donovan and Darcy (2011: 130) used the following criteria to assess a learning event in terms of the effectiveness of the trainer.

- the trainer was well prepared;
- the trainer was enthusiastic about the subject matter;
- the trainer showed commitment to the goals of the training;
- the trainer related the training content to job needs;
- the trainer provided good feedback.

The rest of this chapter is devoted to exploring how the process of delivering a learning event can result in reactions such as those.

Setting up the event

The event plan as described in the last chapter should have ensured that all the preparations have been made. These would include the programme, the venue, arrangements for food and refreshments, training aids and equipment, badges and name plates, note pads and pens.

Layout

A decision will have been made about the layout of seating in the venue. The choice will depend on the number of people involved and the extent to which the event will involve discussions and group exercises. The alternatives are:

- theatre style with rows of seats – this may be necessary for a large event but inhibits discussion;
- cafeteria style with separate, preferably round tables, each seating up to about six people – this promotes interaction between members of groups and enables the event leader to quickly and easily switch from a presentation mode to a discussion/facilitation or joint exercise mode and back again (break-outs), but it may make it difficult for the trainer to keep in touch with individuals and some people may have to sit with their backs to the trainer;
- horseshoe style with tables laid out as illustrated in Figure 20.1.

FIGURE 20.1   Horseshoe arrangement of a training room

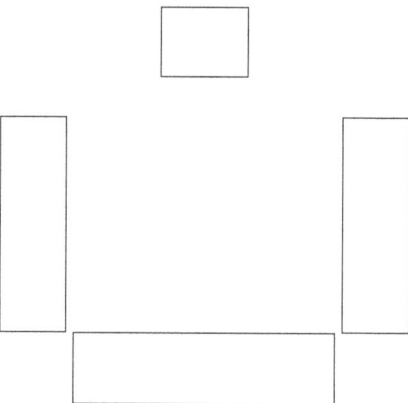

This allows for a reasonable amount of interaction between all those taking part but the line of sight for those seated at the side tables may be restricted. Cafeteria or horseshoe layouts are the most popular.

Preliminary check

The first thing to do when setting up the event is to check that the equipment is all there and working, that the room is properly heated and ventilated with adequate lighting and safety exits, that there is space for participants to move around a little (necessary in a longish session) and that the arrangements for food and refreshments are satisfactory.

Starting the event

It is crucial to get off to a good start. The trainer will be faced with a group of probably unknown people, some of whom will be glad to be there and looking forward to the experience, some full of trepidation because they do not know what is in store for them and feel that their inadequacies might be exposed and some who don't know why they are there and don't want to be there anyway. The atmosphere can be icy.

The event leader has somehow to get over all this. A welcoming message can be posted on a whiteboard. Learners should be greeted individually. The trainer should get to know their names quickly and it will help to make a note of where they are sitting with brief details of their background that will emerge during the opening session. The ice has to be broken. Participants need to understand why they are there and how they will benefit from the programme. The aims of the event should be spelt out, the contents summarized and the methods that will be used explained. It may be important to stress that interaction between the trainer and learners and the latter with each other is a key feature of the programme. Finally, the domestic arrangements have to be explained – safety considerations, tea and meal breaks, toilets, use or non-use of mobiles.

There are many ways to break the ice. The most popular is to get each participant to tell the group something about themselves – where they work, what they do, what they hope to get out of the programme. This has the advantage of getting them into action. A variation of this approach is to get adjacent participants to interview each other and present what they have learnt to the whole course. If a cafeteria layout has been adopted the process of getting the information can be shared between the whole group and one or two members will present the outcomes.

Some trainers start with a group exercise or game but this can be risky when participants do not know each other and should be used with care.

Running the event

The way in which the event is run will depend on its aims and content, the methods used, its length – from one session to a multi-session programme over a number of days – and the number and type of people attending it. However, there are some factors common to all types of events. There should be a comprehensive event plan covering aims, content and methods (presentations, discussions, exercises, case studies or role-plays, as described in Chapter 13). Speakers should have been briefed and all the learning aids tested and in place. The event leader has to ensure that the plan is followed and the planned instructional techniques are used properly.

Flexibility is necessary, switching from one approach to another if the occasion demands it. In a longer event the leader has to ensure that, as it progresses, continuity is maintained and participants are aware of how the subject matter is developing and different aspects of it are linked together. Summaries of what has been achieved so far can be made from time to time. The leader must always be aware that the purpose of the event is to get something done differently and better by the participants: the event should be 'action orientated'. At the front of the leader's mind should be consideration to how the learning can be transferred to the workplace.

Closing the event

It is essential to send participants away with action plans – what they are going to do about applying the learning when they get back to their workplace. As suggested by Beevers *et al* (2020: 166) the following questions could be asked:

- What are you going to do differently as a result of this learning?
- What specific actions do you need to take for this?
- When will you take them?

- What support will you need and from whom?
- What could stop you from being successful?
- How could you prevent this?
- How will you know that you have achieved your plan?
- What are the specific results you expect to see?

The essential points included in these plans should be noted so that as part of the evaluation process L&D can follow up with the individuals and their line managers to check out what has happened.

Participants should be asked to complete an assessment of the event – a 'happy sheet'. The questions asked can assess the level of satisfaction with:

- the extent to which the stated objectives of the event were achieved;
- the degree to which the joining instructions were helpful;
- the quality of delivery;
- the relevance of the material presented;
- the venue and the arrangements for refreshments etc.

KEY LEARNING POINTS

Setting up the event

The event planner should have ensured that all the preparations have been made.

Starting the event

It is crucial to get off to a good start. The ice has to be broken. Participants need to understand why they are there and how they will benefit from the programme. The aims of the event should be spelt out, the contents summarized and the methods that will be used explained.

Running the event

How the event is run will depend on its aims and content. But there are some factors common to all types of events:

- there should be a clear and comprehensive event plan covering aims, content and methods (instructional design). Speakers should have been thoroughly briefed and all the learning aids needed in place;

- the event leader has to ensure that the plan is followed and the learning methods used properly;
- in a longer event the leader has to ensure that as it progresses continuity is maintained
- the event should be 'action orientated'.

Closing the event

It is essential to send participants away with action plans – what they are going to do about applying the learning when they get back to their workplace. Participants should be asked to complete an assessment of the event – a 'happy sheet'.

References

Beevers, K, Rea, A and Hayden, D (2020) *Learning and Development Practice in the Workplace,* Kogan Page, London

Donovan, P and Darcy, D P (2011) Learning transfer: the views of practitioners in Ireland *International Journal of Training and Development,* **15** (2), pp 121–39

21

Transferring learning

Introduction

Learning events are there to develop transferable skills. An event will only be successful if those skills are put to good use in the place of work. Account needs to be taken of the problem of transferring learning from a formal training course. Research on the transfer of training has treated transfer as the primary outcome of training, or as Salas *et al* (2012) observed, its 'endgame'.

Training can seem to be remote from reality and the skills and knowledge acquired can appear to be irrelevant. Problems in transferring learning often occur after management or supervisory training, but the manual skills learnt in a training centre can also be difficult to transfer. Estimates of the extent of transfer range from a pessimistic 10 per cent (Georgenson, 1982) to approximately 50 per cent (Saks & Belcourt, 2006).

This chapter starts with a description of the process of transferring learning and continues with explanations of the issues involved – the transfer problem and the factors affecting it as illustrated by several research projects – how the factors should be analysed and what can be done to facilitate transfer.

The nature of the learning transfer process

The nature of the learning transfer process was defined by Holton *et al* (2000: 334) as 'the application, generalizability and maintenance of new knowledge and skills.' They referred (page 335) to the notion of a transfer-of-training climate. 'Transfer climate is seen as a mediating variable in the relationship between the organizational context and an individual's job attitudes and work behaviour. Thus, even when learning occurs in training, the transfer climate may either support or inhibit application of learning on the job.' But they observed that they preferred to use the term 'transfer system' which they defined as all the factors in the person, training and organization that influence the transfer of learning.

The transfer problem

An immense amount of research has been carried on the problem of learning transfer. The first comprehensive analysis was made by Baldwin and Ford (1988) who reviewed 63 empirical studies on the relationship between input factors and transfer. They noted that there is a transfer problem in organizations and presented a framework for examining the transfer process. This showed that three categories of training inputs (trainee characteristics, training design and work environment characteristics) predict training outputs. They defined 'positive' transfer (page 64) as 'the degree to which trainees effectively apply the knowledge, skills, and attitudes gained in a training context to the job.' They claimed that in essence, transfer is the most important of all training effectiveness criteria. They suggested two conditions for transfer: 1) the maintenance of material learned in training over time and 2) the generalization of material from the training environment to the workplace context. The model noted the training input of trainee characteristics such as the trainee's motivation and ability as a prerequisite for learning and its transfer.

Factors affecting learning transfer

Two conceptual transfer of training models have been quoted by Kontoghiorghes (2004). The first is expectancy theory which suggests that employees will be motivated to attend training programmes and try to learn from them if they believe that: a) their efforts will result in learning the new skills or information presented in the programme; b) attending the programme and learning new skills will increase their job performance; and c) doing so will help them obtain desired outcomes or prevent unwanted outcomes. The second is Baldwin and Ford's 1988 model which asserts that the effectiveness of a training intervention is contingent upon training design, trainee characteristics and work-environment.

Other results from the considerable amount of research on the transfer problem are summarized below:

- Research by Clarke (2002) established that barriers to transfer in a social services department were: 1) heavy workloads; 2) time pressures; 3) lack of reinforcement of training; and 4) an absence of feedback on performance.

- A study by Lim and Johnson (2002: 46) showed that ensuring a supportive work climate may be the single most important requirement for the successful transfer of learning. The second key factor in learning transfer is the opportunity for trainees to apply what they have learned to their jobs.

- Research by Ruona *et al* (2002) established that the reactions of people to a training course make only a small contribution to the prediction of motivation to transfer. These reactions tend to be broad, vague and are therefore not very useful measures in identifying and diagnosing the causes of transfer (or lack thereof).

- Motivation to transfer was found to be the most important predictor of training transfer when compared with other individual, organizational and training-related variables (Bates *et al*, 2007, Kauffeld *et al*, 2008).

- Research into the views of trainers about the transfer problem revealed that they erroneously believed that trainee reactions were predictive of transfer (Hutchins and Burke, 2007).

- A meta-analytic review of transfer research based on 89 empirical studies conducted by Blume *et al* (2010f) found that both trainee characteristics (eg cognitive ability, conscientiousness and motivation) and work environment factors (eg transfer climate, supervisor support) are positively related to transfer.

- Research by Donovan and Darcy (2011) on the views of practitioners on learning transfer found that the first five main factors affecting transfer in order of importance were:
  - trainer effectiveness;
  - perceived relevance;
  - job design;
  - organizational support for learning;
  - motivation to attend.

- Trainee characteristics, such as cognitive ability, motivation and self-efficacy have been shown to have moderate to high associations with successful training transfer (Grossman and Salas, 2011).

- Transfer design and perceived content validity act as a starting point for successful training transfer (Grohmann *et al*, 2014).

- Co-worker support is positively related to perceived transfer (Homklin *et al*, 2014).

- Research by Saks and Burke-Smalley (2014) found that transfer of training was positively related to firm performance and that on-the-job training was the strongest predictor of transfer of training.

Analysing the transfer problem

It was observed by Hesketh (1997: 72) following his research that: 'An important practical implication of this study is that a transfer of training needs analysis (TTNA) should be conducted in order to determine the kinds of transfer obstacles that exist in the organizational context and for a particular training program.' For this purpose, Holton *et al* (2000) developed their Learning Transfer System Inventory consisting of the following factor headings:

- *Supervisor support* – the extent to which supervisors-managers support and reinforce the use of training on the job.

- *Supervisor sanctions* – the extent to which individuals perceive negative responses from supervisors-managers when applying skills learned in training.

- *Perceived content utility* – the extent to which trainers judge training content to reflect job requirements accurately.

- *Transfer design* – the degree to which: 1) training has been designed and delivered to give trainees the ability to transfer learning to the job and 2) training instructions match job requirements.

- *Opportunity to use* – the extent to which trainees are provided with or obtain resources and tasks on the job enabling them to use training on the job.

- *Transfer effort, performance expectations* – the expectation that effort devoted to transferring learning will lead to changes in job performance.

- *Performance outcomes expectations* – the expectation that changes to job performance will lead to valued outcomes.
- *Resistance, openness to change* – the extent to which prevailing group norms are perceived by individuals to resist or discourage the use of skills and knowledge acquired in training.
- *Performance self-efficacy* – the general belief of individuals that they can change their performance when they want to.
- *Performance coaching* – formal and informal indicators from an organization about an individual's performance.

What can be done about the transfer problem?

The following suggestions, based on research, have been made on what can be done about the transfer problem:

- The more the procedural nature of the task is emphasized, the more successful the transfer (Clark and Voogel, 1985).
- The more the training content and programme reflect the workplace, the more successful the transfer (Baldwin and Ford, 1988).
- The more trainees practise in different contexts and use novelty in their practice exercises, the more successful the far transfer (Baldwin and Ford, 1988).
- The more encouragement trainees receive during training to discuss and apply the training in situations of their own choosing, the more successful the transfer (Noe, 2000).
- Research by van der Klink *et al* (2001) showed that to achieve learning transfer special efforts have to be made to encourage line managers to provide support.
- Yamnill and McLean (2001: 206) suggested that the following steps should be taken by organizations to encourage learning transfer:
  - Collaborate with key stakeholders in the organization at each step of the process to provide links to strategic goals, reinforce organizational priorities and support performance-related factors.

- Encourage managers to provide clear performance objectives so that employees know exactly what they are expected to do. Managers should provide the necessary support (resources) for high performance and establish clear rewards for performance. They should provide prompt feedback to let employees know whether their performance meets the established standards.

- Assign high priority to learners as full stakeholders in the design and implementation of training (based on research results, the relevance of knowledge, skills and attitude taught in training is of value in determining transfer). Thus, groups of learners may be responsible for identifying training objectives, assessing their learning needs, developing action plans and identifying organization-wide strategies to support full transfer to new contexts.

- Assigning work projects that relate to the training content, before the training occurs, during the training and even after the training, should promote transfer of learning. Lim and Johnson (2002: 46).

- Design training programmes with a specific transfer component or intervention that takes place after the actual programme and provides trainees with guidance and strategies on how to transfer their newly acquired knowledge and skills to the work environment (Gaudine and Saks, 2004).

- To enhance transfer of training, organizations should design training that gives trainees the ability to transfer learning, reinforces the trainee's beliefs in their ability to transfer, ensures the training content is retained over time and provides appropriate feedback regarding employee job performance following training activities (Velada *et al*, 2007).

- The views of training professionals in the US on 'best practice' in learning transfer were (starting with the most frequently reported) supervisory support activities, coaching, opportunities to perform, interactive training activities, transfer measurement and job-relevant training (Burke and Hutchins, 2008).

- Trainers can improve the transfer design of a training programme, for example, if they include transfer-related case studies that show how participants can effectively apply training contents and skills back at work (Grohmann *et al*, 2014).

- Diamantidis and Chatzoglou (2014: 165) recommended that for a training programme to be successful and achieve its goals, the firm should not expect impressive changes in employees' performance immediately after the programme's completion. Supervisors need to give time, 'space' and support to their employees, forming an encouraging job environment, in order to enable them to implement the taught/acquired knowledge and skills in their jobs. Also, managers should ensure that during the training process, their employees will have the opportunity to apply the new knowledge and skills that are taught. This can be done by solving problems and exercises that simulate the trainees' actual job conditions. This will allow trainees to learn from their mistakes in a controlled environment and when they return to their jobs they will be fully prepared to apply what they have learned and avoid their previous mistakes. Finally, trainees' peers and supervisors should be patient and not discourage them from implementing the newly acquired knowledge and skills in their job.

- 'For a formal programme to result in learning that actually enables people to do different things, training courses must require learners to take some tentative steps to try things out, to experience through trial and error, to reflect on lived experience, and to discuss and connect with others' (Hoyle, 2015: 3).

- Peer and supervisor support for learning transfer have consistently been shown to be one of the strongest predictors (of learning transfer) as they increase trainee self-efficacy and motivation to transfer (Hart *et al*, 2019).

A learning transfer model

The learning transfer model, illustrated in Figure 21.1, emphasizes the requirement to anticipate transfer problems at each stage of the process of planning and running learning events. The onus is very much on learning and development professionals to ensure that each of these stages takes place as planned. The work involved, especially in planning and follow-up, will be considerable. But this is what L&D professionals are there to do – get out into the field to understand and help to deal with any learning issues. Keeping in touch like this is the best way for them to appreciate the concerns about learning that they are there to deal with.

FIGURE 21.1   Learning transfer model

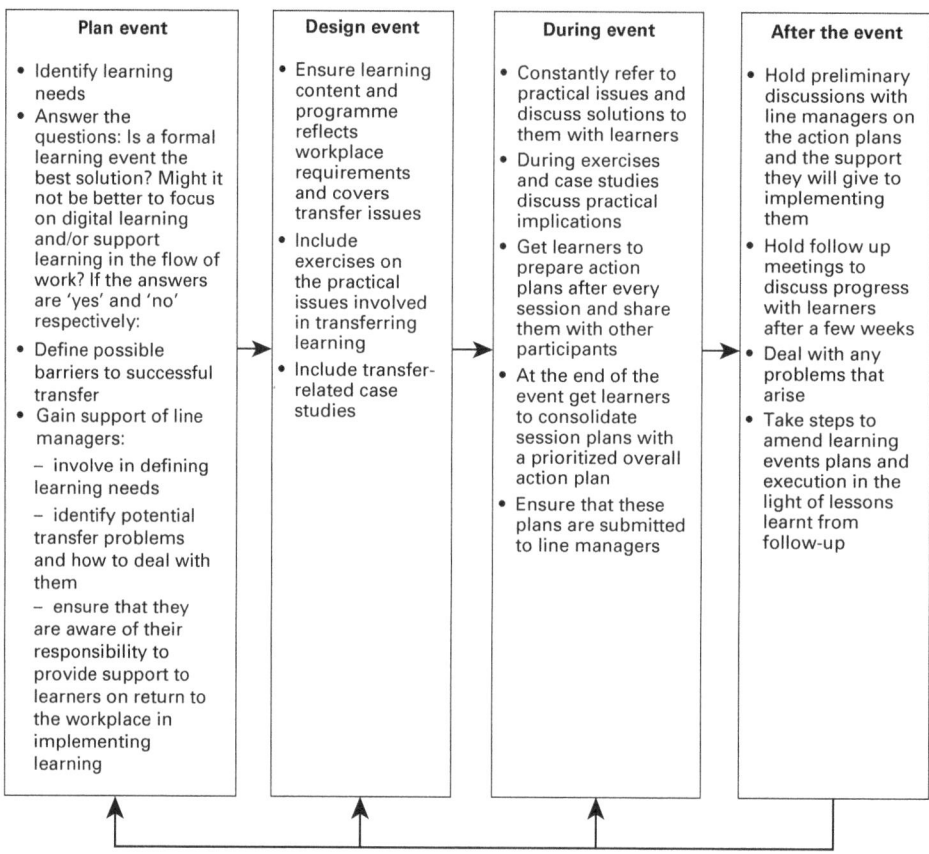

Another solution

The other solution to the transfer problem is to avoid it altogether or at least reduce it by focusing on 'learning in-the-flow of work'. This takes account of the 70:20:10 learning model which suggests that only 10 per cent of learning takes place through formal training. This 10 per cent may be crucial – learning some skills will best take place in a training course designed to meet a defined training need and taking place 'off-the-job', perhaps in a designated training centre. But the 70 per cent 'experiential learning' and the 20 per cent 'social learning' happens in the workplace and should be encouraged. It is remarkable that the literature search conducted by the writer for this chapter only found one reference to on-the-job learning as a solution to the transfer problem (Saks and Burke-Smalley, 2014).

KEY LEARNING POINTS

Transferable skills

The focus of off-the-job training in learning events should be to develop transferable skills and it will only be successful if those skills are put to good use in the place of work. Account should therefore be taken of the problem of transferring learning from a formal training course.

The nature of the learning transfer process

The nature of the learning transfer process was defined by Holton *et al* (2000: 334) as 'the application, generalizability and maintenance of new knowledge and skills'.

The transfer problem

Baldwin and Ford (1988) noted that there is a transfer problem in organizations and presented a framework for examining the transfer process.

Factors affecting learning transfer

Two conceptual transfer of training models have been proposed by Kontoghiorghes (2004). The first is expectancy theory. The second is Baldwin and Ford's 1988 model which asserts that the effectiveness of a training intervention is contingent upon training design, trainee characteristics and work environment.

Analysing the transfer problem

A transfer of training needs analysis should be conducted to determine the kinds of transfer obstacles that exist.

What can be done about the transfer problem?

It is necessary to make the training as relevant and realistic as possible, anticipating and dealing with any potential transfer difficulties. Individuals are more likely to apply learning:

- when they can put what they have learned into practice;
- do not find it too difficult;
- believe what they learnt is relevant, useful and transferable;
- are supported by line managers;
- have job autonomy;
- believe in themselves (self-efficacy);
- are committed and engaged.

References

Baldwin, T T and Ford, J K (1988) Transfer of training: A review and directions for future research, *Personnel Psychology,* **41,** pp 63–105

Bates, R, Kauffeld, S and Holton, E F III (2007) Examining the factor structure and predictive ability of the German-version of the Learning Transfer Systems Inventory, *Journal of European Industrial Training,* **31,** 195–211

Blume, B D, Ford, J K, Baldwin, T T and Huang, J L (2010) Transfer of training: A meta-analytic review, *Journal of Management,* **36,** 1065–105

Burke, L A and Hutchins, H M (2008) A study of best practices in training transfer and proposed model of transfer, *Human Resource Development Quarterly,* **19** (2), pp 107–28

Clark, R E and Voogel, A (1985) Transfer of training principles for instructional design, *Educational Technology Research and Development,* **33** (2), pp 113–20

Clarke, N (2002) Job/work environment factors influencing training transfer within a human service agency: some indicative support for Baldwin and Ford's transfer climate construct, *International Journal of Training & Development,* **6** (3), pp 146–62

Diamantidis, A D and Chatzoglou, P D (2014) Employee post-training behaviour and performance: evaluating the results of the training process, *International Journal of Training & Development,* **18** (3), pp 149–70

Donovan, P and Darcy, D P (2011) Learning transfer: the views of practitioners in Ireland *International Journal of Training & Development,* **15** (2), pp 121–39

Gaudine, A P and Saks, A M, (2004) A longitudinal quasi-experiment on the effects of post-training transfer interventions, *Human Resource Development Quarterly,* **15** (1), pp 57–76

Georgenson, D L (1982) The problem of transfer calls for partnership, *Training and Development Journal,* **36,** 75–8

Grohmann, A, Beller, J and Kauffeld, S (2014) Exploring the critical role of motivation to transfer in the training transfer process, *International Journal of Training & Development,* **18** (2), pp 84–103

Grossman, L and Salas, E (2011) The transfer of training: what really matters, *International Journal of Training & Development,* **15** (2), 103–20

Hart, S L, Steinheider, B and Hoffmeister, V E (2019) Team-based learning and training transfer: A case study of training for the implementation of enterprise resources planning software, *International Journal of Training & Development,* **23** (2), pp 135–52

Hesketh, B (1997) Whither dilemmas in training for transfer, *Applied* Psychology, **46,** pp 380–85

Holton, E F, Bates and R A Ruona, W E (2000) Development of a generalized learning transfer system inventory, *Human Resource Development Quarterly,* **11** (4), pp 333–60

Homklin, T, Takahashi, Y and Techakanont, K (2014) The influence of social and organizational support on transfer of training: evidence from Thailand, *International Journal of Training & Development,* **18** (2), pp 116–31

Hoyle, R (2015) *Informal Learning in Organizations,* Kogan Page, London

Hutchins, H M and Burke, L A (2007) Identifying trainers' knowledge of training transfer research findings - closing the gap between research and practice, *International Journal of Training & Development*, **11** (4), pp 236–64

Kauffeld, S, Bates, R, Holton, E F III and Müller, A C (2008), Das deutsche Lerntransfer-System-Inventar (GLTSI): Psychometrische Überprüfung der deutschsprachigen Version [the German version of the Learning Transfer System Inventory (GLTSI): Psychometric validation, *Zeitschrift für Personalpsychologie*, 7, 50–69

Kontoghiorghes , C (2004) Reconceptualizing the learning transfer conceptual framework: empirical validation of a new systemic model *International Journal of Training & Development*, **8** (3), pp 210–21

Lim, D H and Johnson, S D (2002) Trainee perceptions of factors that influence learning transfer, *International Journal of Training & Development*, **6** (1), pp 36–48

Noe, R N (2000) Invited reaction: development of a generalized learning transfer system inventory, *Human Resource Development Quarterly*, **11** (4), pp 361–65

Ruona, W, Leimbach, M, Holton, E and Bates, R (2002) The relationship between learner utility reactions and predicted learning transfer among trainees, *International Journal of Training and Development*, **6** (4), pp 218–28

Saks, A M and Belcourt, M (2006), An investigation of training activities and transfer of training in organisations, *Human Resource Management*, **45**, 629–48

Saks, A M and Burke-Smalley, L A (2014) Is transfer of training related to firm performance? *International Journal of Training & Development*, **18** (2), pp 104–15

Salas, E, Tannenbaum, S I, Kraiger, K and Smith-Jentsch, K A (2012), The science of training and development in organizations: What matters in practice, *Psychological Science in the Public Interest*, **13**, 74–101

van der Klink, M, Gielen, E and Nauta , C (2001) Supervisory support as a major condition to enhance transfer, *International Journal of Training & Development*, 5 (1), pp 52–63

Velada, R, Caetano, A, Michel, J W, Lyons, B D and Kavanagh, M J (2007) The effects of training design, individual characteristics and work environment on transfer of training, *International Journal of Training & Development*, **11** (4), pp 282–94

Yamnill, S and McLean, G N (2001) Theories supporting transfer of training, *Human Resource Development Quarterly*, **12** (2), pp 195–208

22

Evaluating learning events

Introduction

Learning events are evaluated to establish how well they have achieved their specified objectives and to identify any improvements that need to be made. This is the final stage of the training sequence, although evaluation is a matter for consideration in each of the earlier stages of the sequence: planning (setting objectives), delivering (continuous assessment) and transfer (checking on how well learning has been put into practice).

Learning events evaluation should be distinguished from the evaluation of the overall impact of learning and development on the organization and, by implication, the effectiveness of the L&D function as covered in Chapter 7.

The nature of learning evaluation is examined in the first part of this chapter and the second part covers methods of evaluating individual learning events and programmes.

The nature of the evaluation of learning events

The evaluation of learning events involves measuring how the learning provided by an event has impacted on skills and knowledge and therefore performance. It provides information on what needs to be improved and what still needs to be done and how to make the best use of the resources available. The CIPD (2020a: 7) pointed out that: 'Effective learning and development evaluation needs to be linked to learning needs and focused on evaluating learning outcomes, not inputs... the feedback that matters most from evaluation is the results that learning brings in terms of improved individual, unit or organizational performance.'

As suggested by the CIPD (2020b) evaluation activities comprise:

1 *Impact* – where L&D can work with the organization to show how the learning interventions have impacted on performance – these can include links to key performance indicators (financial and operational).

2 *Transfer* – where L&D can work with the organization to show how any learning undertaken on L&D events has been transferred back into the employee's role and work area – these can include performance goals and how new skills and knowledge have been used.

3 *Engagement* – where L&D can demonstrate how stakeholders are engaged with learning, this can be at an organizational level where a positive learning environment is the goal, at team levels or at an individual level.

4 It is also possible to analyse what Mattox and Van Buren (2016) call 'scrap learning'. They define this as learning which may have been absorbed on a course but is wasted because it is not applied on the job. Following up a training event with an online survey to find out from each participant what proportion has been put to use can produce a percentage 'scrap rate' which may signal that there is a serious learning transfer problem that needs to be sorted.

Methods of evaluation

A number of methods of evaluating learning events have been produced over the years as described below.

Kirkpatrick's four-level model of evaluation

The Kirkpatrick (1979, 1994) model is the best known and the most popular. Its four levels are:

LEVEL 1: REACTION
At this level, evaluation measures how those who participated in the training have reacted to it, ie an assessment of immediate customer satisfaction. Reactions may be recorded on a form (sometimes called a 'happy sheet'). Those attending the event could be asked to indicate the extent that their time was well spent, if they learned something they could apply immediately to their work and if the course provided them with new ways of thinking about their job.

Kirkpatrick suggested the following guidelines for evaluating reactions:

- determine what you want to find out;
- design a form that will quantify reactions;
- encourage written comments and suggestions;
- get 100 per cent immediate response;
- get honest responses;
- develop acceptable standards;
- measure reactions against standards and take appropriate action;
- communicate reactions as appropriate.

Research by Warr *et al* (1970) showed that there was relatively little correlation between learner reactions and subsequent measures of changed behaviour. Ruona *et al* (2002: 226) noted that: 'Despite their widespread use, participant reactions do not seem to contribute greatly to predicting transfer of learning nor do they seem to predict actual performance improvement.' As pointed out by Hutchins and Burke (2007: 257–258): 'In their evaluation of learning interventions, trainers may inaccurately reason that stopping at a reaction level (satisfaction) of measurement is sufficient… This misinterpretation alone would represent a flawed assumption in the field and may explain, in part, the widespread neglect of measurement activities in firms beyond assessing learning outcomes.' But as Tamkin *et al* (2002) claimed, despite this, organizations are still keen to get reactions to training and used with caution this can produce some information on the extent that the event has been organized successfully and why.

LEVEL 2: EVALUATE LEARNING

This level obtains information on the extent that learning objectives have been attained. It will aim to find how much knowledge was acquired, what skills were developed or improved and the extent to which attitudes have changed in the desired direction. When possible, the evaluation of learning should involve the use of tests before and after the programme – written, oral or performance tests.

LEVEL 3: EVALUATE BEHAVIOUR

This level evaluates the extent that the expected changes in behaviour have happened when people attending the programme return to their jobs. Ideally, the evaluation should take place both before and after the training. Time should be allowed for the change in behaviour to take place. The evaluation needs to assess the extent that specific learning objectives relating to changes in behaviour and the application of knowledge and skills have been achieved.

LEVEL 4: EVALUATE RESULTS IN TERMS OF IMPACT ON ORGANIZATIONAL PERFORMANCE

This is the ultimate level of evaluation and provides the basis for assessing the benefits of the training against its costs. The objective is to determine the added value of learning and development programmes – how they contribute to raising organizational performance above its previous level. The evaluation has to be based on before-and-after measures and should determine the extent that the fundamental objectives of the training have been achieved in areas such as increasing sales, raising productivity, reducing accidents or increasing customer satisfaction. Evaluating results is easier when they can be quantified. However, it can be difficult to prove the contribution to improved results made by training as distinct from other factors and, as Kirkpatrick said, evaluators should be satisfied with evidence, because proof is usually impossible to get.

The Kirkpatrick four-level model of evaluation has been criticized by Holton (1996) because that it does not specify outcomes correctly, is no more than a taxonomy, ie a classification scheme and has not been supported by research. He observed (pages 10–11) that: 'The inclusion of trainee reactions as a primary outcome, particularly when defined as happiness, is one of the greatest flaws of the four-level model. The effect has been to divert the field's attention away from the truly important HRD outcomes (for example, performance) and focus many practitioners on activities that generate high ratings.'

In practice, organizations find it difficult to advance much above level 1 although level 2 should not be too difficult. That is why there have been moves to use overall measures such as return on expectations and return on investment as described later in this chapter.

Easterby-Smith model

A four-factor model for evaluating management development and training courses was developed by Easterby-Smith (1994). The factors are:

- *Proving* – that the training worked or had measurable impact in itself.
- *Controlling* – for example, the time needed for training courses, access to costly off-the-job programmes, consistency or compliance requirements.

- *Improving* – for example, the training, trainers, course content and arrangements.
- *Reinforcing* – using evaluation efforts as a deliberate contribution to the learning process itself.

The Brinkerhoff success case method

The Brinkerhoff (2003) success case method (SCM) is concerned with the evaluation of the impact of L&D activities, particularly learning events, on performance. It starts by finding out through surveys or performance reports 'success cases' where individuals or teams have benefited from the learning. Those involved in these cases are interviewed to find out if they are really success stories and to obtain evidence confirming this. The factors that contributed to success following the learning event are then identified. An SCM evaluation also looks at 'non-success cases' to establish the reasons for failure. Following analysis, the success and non-success 'stories' are shared.

The method obtains answers to four questions:

1 How well is an organization using learning to improve performance?

2 What organizational processes/resources are in place to support performance improvement?

3 What needs to be improved?

4 What organizational barriers stand in the way of performance improvement?

SCM is not a comprehensive evaluation method but it can produce useful insights on what works and what doesn't.

Return on investment

There is pressure in every organization to produce financial justification for major expenditures. Senior management wants to know that the money invested in such things as equipment, facilities, processes, property and research and development activities produces worthwhile benefits measured in monetary terms. To do this, use is generally made of the return on investment (ROI) methodology. This is the ratio of the financial gain from an investment relative to the amount invested. The tendency has been to leave supporting activities such as learning and development out of this process, mainly because it is believed that while the costs are easily measured the financial benefits are not.

Commentators such as Kearns and Miller (1997) beg to differ. They argue that particular hard measures should be used to evaluate specific training; for example, if the training aims to improve levels of customer service then its impact should be measured by the eventual effect on customer spend, customer satisfaction and number of customers. But there are difficulties as explained in Chapter 7 which contains a full description of the technique as applied to the overall evaluation of learning and development rather than that of individual learning events.

Return on expectations

Return on expectations is an approach to the validation of learning processes and the outcomes of learning that focuses on what stakeholders anticipate will be the result of a learning experience. For individual learning events, these are defined as objectives (terminal behaviour) during the planning stage. The objectives are expressed as outcomes rather than the inputs of the training event itself. Outcomes consist of any changes in the behaviour of people at work that follow an event and the impact this has on their performance and that of the organization. These are covered by levels three and four of the Kirkpatrick model but in using that model, the concentration on level one (reactions to a learning event) and the perceived difficulty of quantifying outcomes has meant that they are largely ignored. Return on expectations as a method of evaluation has been criticized because, it is said, its judgements are qualitative. But this is not necessarily so. Anticipated results can be expressed in quantitative terms such as increases in output, higher sales, improvements in customer service levels, quicker progress to experienced worker standard (EWS), higher 360–degree feedback ratings (upward assessments of managers by their subordinates) and fewer grievances or cases of bullying or harassment.

Kirkpatrick, as reported in Kirkpatrick Foundational Principles (2020) started that:

Stakeholder expectations define the value that training professionals are responsible for delivering. Learning professionals must ask the stakeholders questions to clarify and refine their expectations on all four Kirkpatrick evaluation levels, starting with Level 4 results. This is a negotiation process in which the training professional makes sure that the expectations are satisfying to the stakeholder and realistic to achieve with the resources available.

Once stakeholder expectations are clear, learning professionals then need to convert those typically general wants into observable, measurable success outcomes by asking the question, 'What will success look like to you?' Those outcomes then become the Level 4 results – the targets to which you can sharply focus your collective efforts to accomplish return on expectations.

The following suggestions on how to use return on expectations were made by Priest (2018: 19):

1 Be clear on what exactly will be measured. Figure out the goals and direction of a business and identify the return on expectations – begin with the end in mind. When employees receive training without clarity or next steps, the seriousness of the learning will fall by the wayside

2 Sit with all the stakeholders and identify who needs training – a specific department, management or entry-level positions. And what kind of training – is it for time management, better communication or process improvement?

3 From this information, determine what behaviours need to change and what success would look like. These questions should be asked during the initial assessment, before the design phase, because they help shape the overall learning programme.

Return on expectations has much to offer because it focuses on the comparison of results with clearly defined objectives and does not rely entirely on the difficult task of assessing the financial benefits of learning events as does return on investment. It also avoids the problem of the Kirkpatrick method which in practice is mainly used to evaluate learning at level one – immediate reactions – which means that the impact of the training on behaviour and performance will not have been assessed.

Use of evaluation

The survey conducted by the CIPD (2020a: 34, 36) found that 70 per cent of the respondents' organizations evaluated the impact of their L&D initiatives in some way although at varying levels. The most commonly reported method was by participant satisfaction (28 per cent). Only 16 per cent measured the behaviour change of participants by assessing the transfer of learning into the workplace and just 12 per cent evaluated the wider impact on the business. As the CIPD commented: 'Evaluations are considerably more common in organisations where L&D is aligned with business strategy, where learning is valued by senior leaders, and where there is a clear vision for learning and development... the more embedded learning is in operational delivery, the more sophisticated and rigorous the impact measurement.'

Many organizations encounter barriers to evaluation, with lack of learner or management time and the pressure of other business priorities being the most common obstacles. Grove and Ostroff (1990) listed five reasons for ineffective training evaluations:

1 Senior management often not insisting on or requesting information on the impact of the training that was provided.

2 The lack of expertise among L&D professionals on how to carry out training evaluations.

3 A lack of clear objectives attached to training programmes so that actually knowing what to evaluate against is difficult if not impossible.

4 The limited budgets available to training departments means that resources are devoted to training provision rather than training evaluation.

5 The risks associated with evaluation may be too great, given that the evaluation data might reveal that the training had little impact.

It was emphasised by the CIPD (2020a: 8) that: 'The lack of robust evaluation and measurement of impact creates a catch-22 situation: organisations don't invest in evaluating learning and development because it isn't seen as important (they lack the time, resources or support), or too hard, and learning and development activity isn't valued because organisations can't demonstrate its impact. Without being able to measure learning impact, valuable time and resources are wasted.'

Evaluating the effectiveness of learning events is difficult and time consuming – results may be hard to measure and quantified measures such as the ROI formula are hard to use. But a learning event can still be justified by assessing the extent that any changes in behaviour that the programme was expected to produce have happened (return on expectations). This is based on the assumption that the analysis of learning needs indicated that a specified change in behaviour is likely to deliver the desired results.

Conducting learning evaluations

Learning evaluations are more likely to be effective if:

a. the purpose and aims of the evaluation have been defined;

b. an appropriate and feasible method of evaluation has been selected;

c. senior management believe that evaluation is essential;

d. clear objectives, quantified if possible, have been set for the event based upon a thorough assessment of learning needs;

e. the emphasis is on assessing the impact of the training on learners' work performance;

f. evaluation is perceived as an integral part of the whole process of planning and delivering learning events not just an afterthought;

g. members of the L&D function are committed to evaluation and have the skills and persistence (it takes time and trouble) to do it;

h. the value of evaluations is demonstrated by the results achieved following the actions taken to respond to their findings

Kirkpatrick, as reported in Kirkpatrick Foundational Principles (2020), observed that: 'It is important that the results are defined in measurable terms so that all involved can see the ultimate destination of the initiative. Clearly defined results will increase the likelihood that resources will be used most effectively and efficiently to accomplish the mission.'

The following suggestions on evaluation practice were made by Paine (2015: 130):

> We need to know who has taken the programme, what networks they belong to and what they have been saying about the programme. We need to know how they learnt and their degree of engagement with the programme. We need to know why they took this programme and the working context that led to that decision. We need to know where they learnt and their mode of learning, and we need to know the precise times when they were engaged and, if possible, the depth of engagement. Finally, we need to know how much of the programme met their needs, helped them in a specific work problem or equipped them to deal with contingencies they have yet to meet but could encounter in the future.

Paine commented (page 131) that it could be impossible to capture all this data manually but there are technologies that can provide enough of it to obtain a significant impact assessment of how well a programme worked. He gave an example of how learning analytics could be used to evaluate a leadership programme. The starting point would be an assessment by the managers and possibly the colleagues of the individuals taking the programme of what sort of behaviours will be expected as a result. Each individual could be scored on a scale of, say, 1 to 10 and an indication given of what it would be desirable for her or him to be able to do after the programme. The same questions could be asked one or two months later to produce another score that would reveal the impact the programme had achieved. So, if before the course the course the average score of the participants was 4 and after it the score had increased to 6, some hard data has been obtained on the programme's effectiveness

It was also noted by Diamantidis and Chatzoglou (2014:166) that 'it is not sufficient to measure the results of a training programme only once (after the programme's completion), but as a dynamic process that has to be performed periodically (for one year) after the completion of the programme.'

KEY LEARNING POINTS

The need to evaluate learning

It is necessary to find out if the learning and development activities of an organization are effective so that steps can be taken to measure their value and make improvements. The value of learning and development is demonstrated by assessing its impact on individual and organizational performance.

Learning evaluation defined

Learning evaluation is about measuring the results of learning and development (L&D) activities in terms of their impact on individual and organizational performance and assessing the effectiveness of L&D activities.

Evaluating individual learning events

Individual learning events can be evaluated by one or more of the following methodologies:

- Kirkpatrick's four-level model;
- the Easterby-Smith model;
- the Brinkerhoff success case method;
- return on expectations;
- return on investment.

Of these, the Kirkpatrick system is the most used although often not beyond the first level. Return on expectations has much to offer.

The overall evaluation of the L&D contribution

An attempt should be made to measure the value of the L&D contribution, assess the effectiveness of L&D activities and determine the extent that L&D processes are aligned with the organization's strategic priorities. Evaluation can be conducted by:

- return on expectations;
- internal surveys;
- external benchmarking.

Bibliography

Beevers, K, Rea, A and Hayden, D (2020) *Learning and Development Practice in the Workplace*, Kogan Page, London

Brinkerhoff, R O (2003) The Success Case Method: Find out quickly what's working and what's not, Barrett-Koehler, Oaklands, C A

Chartered Institute of Personnel and Development (CIPD) (2020a) *Learning and Skills at Work 2020*, CIPD, London

CIPD Development (2020b) *Evaluating Learning and Development*, London CIPD

Diamantidis, A D and Chatzoglou, P D (2014) Employee post-training behaviour and performance: Evaluating the results of the training process, *International Journal of Training & Development*, **18** (3), pp 149–70

Easterby-Smith, M (1994) *Evaluating Management Development and Training*, Gower, Aldershot

Grove, D A and Ostroff, C (1990) Training programme evaluation in *Developing Human Resources*, eds K N Wexley and J R Hinrichs , Bureau of National Affairs, Washington, DC

Holton, E F (1996) The flawed four-level evaluation model, *Human Resource Development Quarterly*, **7** (1), pp 5–21

Hutchins, H M and Burke, L A (2007) Identifying trainers' knowledge of training transfer research findings – closing the gap between research and practice, *International Journal of Training & Development*, **11** (4), pp 236–64

Kearns, P and Miller, T (1997) Measuring the impact of training and development on the bottom line, *FT Management Briefings*, Pitman, London

Kirkpatrick, D L (1979) Techniques for evaluating training programmes, *Training and Development Journal*, **3** (6), pp 37–50

Kirkpatrick, D L (1994) *Evaluating Training Programmes*, Berret-Koehler, Oakland CA,

Kirkpatrick, D L (2020) *Kirkpatrick Foundational Principles* (2020) [Online] https://kirkpatrickpartners.com/Our-Philosophy/Kirkpatrick-Foundational-Principles (archived at https://perma.cc/SV8B-MM7L)

Mattox, J R and Van Buren, M (2016) *Learning Analytics*, Kogan Page, London

Paine, N (2015) *The Learning Challenge*, Kogan Page, London

Priest, N (2018) Evaluation at first sight, *Training Journal*, November, pp 18–20

Ruona, W, Leimbach, M, Holton, E and Bates, R (2002) The relationship between learner utility reactions and predicted learning transfer among trainees, *International Journal of Training and Development*, **6** (4), pp 218–28

Tamkin, P, Yarnall, J and Kerrin, M (2002) Kirkpatrick and Beyond: A review of training evaluation, Report 392, Institute for Employment Studies, Brighton

Warr, P, Bird, M and Rackham, N (1970) *Evaluation of Management Training: A Practical framework with cases, for evaluating training needs and results*, Gower, Aldershot

PART SIX

Aspects of learning and development

23

Leadership and management development

Introduction

Organizations must take deliberate and positive action to ensure that they have the effective leaders and managers they need. They cannot leave it to chance. Peter Drucker (1955: 158) made the point that: 'The prosperity if not the survival of any business depends on the performance of its managers of tomorrow'. And according to Pfeffer and Sutton (2006), research has shown that the most stressful aspect of people's jobs is their immediate manager.

The chapter starts with a review of the basis of leadership and management development. This leads to a discussion of the nature of leadership and management followed by a description of what leadership and management development activities cover and an examination of how they differ. The conclusion is reached that while they are closely associated and indeed may be conducted jointly, they are sufficiently different to justify being examined separately. The chapter ends with an analysis of the roles in management development of the organization, managers themselves and L&D professionals.

The basis of leadership and management development

Leadership and management development programmes aim to ensure that organizations have managers with the leadership and managerial qualities they need now and in the future. They are concerned with unlocking potential and form a vital ingredient in talent management. A blended learning approach is used which combines activities such as formal education and training, planned experience, self-directed learning, coaching, mentoring, action learning and outdoor learning.

The value of a leadership and management development programme depends on the extent that it:

- is linked to organizational goals and context so that it is relevant to the requirements of the organization as well as those of individuals;
- is based on an understanding of the learning needs of existing and potential managers;
- helps those taking part to develop the skills they need for success;
- is supported by appropriate HR policies to do with recruitment and selection, talent management, succession planning and reward;
- has the full commitment of those involved – senior management and the line managers themselves.

The nature of leadership and management

To plan and implement leadership and management development programmes it is necessary to understand the nature of leadership and management and the differences between them. There has been much debate on how leadership differs from management. The problem is that leadership involves management and management involves leadership so that it may be difficult to separate the two. There is some consensus on the essential nature of both and the skills involved, as set out below, but there is more disagreement on which is the most important.

Leadership

Leadership means inspiring people to do their best to achieve a desired result. It involves developing and communicating a vision for the future, motivating people and securing their engagement. As defined by Dixon (1994: 214): 'Leadership is no more than exercising such an influence upon others that they tend to act in concert towards achieving a goal which they might not have achieved so readily had they been left to their own devices.' Leadership skills include the ability to:

- inspire others;
- persuade others willingly to behave differently;

- clarify what needs to be done and why;

- communicate a sense of purpose to the team;

- understand, as established by research conducted by Tamkin *et al* (2010), that leaders cannot create performance themselves but are conduits for performance through their influence on others;

- get the team into action so that the task is achieved.

Management

Managers are doers. They deal with events as they occur. But they must also be concerned with where they are going. This requires strategic thinking, especially at higher levels. As strategic thinkers, managers develop a sense of purpose and frameworks for defining intentions and future directions. They are engaged in the process of strategic management.

The traditional model of what managers do is that it is a logical and systematic process of planning, organizing, motivating and controlling. But this is misleading. Managers often carry out their work on a day-to-day basis in conditions of variety, turbulence and unpredictability. Managers may have to be professionals in ambiguity, with the ability to cope with conflicting and unclear requirements.

What are the differences?

Are leadership and management the same or different? Some commentators regard leadership as synonymous with management; others see them as distinct but closely linked and equally necessary activities and yet others consider management to be a subset of leadership. Bennis (1989) viewed managers as those who promote efficiency, follow the rules and accept the status quo, while leaders focus on challenging the rules and promoting effectiveness. Kotter (1991) saw managers as being the ones who plan, budget, organize and control, while leaders set direction, manage change and motivate people. Hersey and Blanchard (1998) claimed that management merely consists of leadership applied to business situations; or in other words, management forms a subset of the broader process of leadership. It can be argued that leadership is about managing people while management is about managing all the available resources, including people. It has been said that 'managers aim to do things right while leaders aim to do the right things'. It has also been said that 'good leaders are required to inspire teams to achieve rather than simply to control and co-ordinate their activities.'

But as Birkinshaw (2010: 23) commented: 'By dichotomizing the work of executives in this way, Kotter, Bennis and others squeezed out the essence of what managers do and basically left them with the boring work that 'leaders' don't want.' His view was that: 'To put it simply, we all need to be both leaders and managers' (page 23). Burgoyne (2010: 42) observed that: 'Both [management and leadership] are needed and need to work closely together, often through the same person or team.' Earlier, Mintzberg (2004: 22) summed it all up (as he often did) when he wrote: 'Let's stop the dysfunctional separation of leadership from management. We all know that managers who don't lead are boring, dispiriting. Well, leaders who don't manage are distant, disconnected.'

Leadership and management development compared

In some quarters the term 'leadership development' has replaced 'management development', perhaps because the importance of ensuring that people have leadership qualities has been recognized, while it is believed that they can be safely left to acquire management skills in other ways such as experience. However, they are not the same although they are closely associated.

The difference between them is that leadership development tends to be concerned with nurturing the softer skills of leadership through various educational processes, including formal learning events and programmes and coaching. In contrast, management development relies more on ensuring that managers acquire the ability to do their jobs by managing a whole range of resources, including people. Because they have to work on a day-to-day basis under the influence of 'VUCA' (volatility, uncertainty, complexity and ambiguity) their development largely takes place by gaining the right sequence of experience although this may be supplemented by self-directed learning and courses on management skills and techniques. Further guidance can be provided by coaching and mentors.

Leadership development

Leadership development is the process of developing leadership skills and preparing people for leadership roles and situations beyond their current experience. Burgoyne (2010: 42) observed that: 'Leadership development in the widest sense involves the acquisition, development and utilization of leadership capability or the potential for it.' It is sometimes said that leaders are born not made. This is a rather discouraging statement for those who are not leaders by birthright, should any such leaders exist. It may be true to the extent that some exceptional people seem to be visionaries, have built-in charisma and a natural ability to impose their personality on others. However, even they probably have to develop and hone these qualities when confronted with a situation demanding leadership. As noted by Burgoyne (page 43): 'The will to lead is largely innate but the ability to do it well is largely learnt.' Ordinary mortals need not despair: they too can build on their natural capacities and develop their leadership abilities.

Yukl (2006) proposed the following conditions for successful leadership development:

- clear learning objectives;
- clear, meaningful content;
- appropriate sequencing of content;
- appropriate mix of training methods;
- opportunity for active practice;
- relevant, timely feedback;
- high trainee confidence;
- appropriate follow-up activities.

Leadership development programmes may focus on the acquisition and use of 'soft skills' – those needed to relate to people successfully – rather than the 'hard skills' that are concerned with management techniques and practices such as budgeting, computer technology, market research, product development and project management. The following are some examples of soft skills:

- leadership;
- teamwork – working effectively with others;
- emotional intelligence – sensitivity to what other people are feeling and the use of social skills in handling relationships;
- communication – spoken and written communication and listening;
- providing performance feedback;
- coaching;
- managing conflict;

- handling people problems and challenging conversations;
- problem solving;
- mindfulness.

Soft skills are developed in the flow of work but they are too important to allow this process to happen by chance. They can be taught in formal training courses although where possible – and affordable – individual coaching is better. Perhaps the best approach is self-directed learning but it is still necessary to provide some guidance on where it should go – the aspects of leadership that are important and the sources of information on what is involved in applying them. Individuals should be encouraged to reflect on their experience, reach conclusions on any lessons it has taught on what skills they need to develop and decide what to do about it. The role of L&D professionals is to act as guides and curators. They may also create online learning content (e-learning). Performance management reviews can identify the need to improve the use of a soft skill.

Leadership development is not all about subjecting leaders to development programmes. The organization has to play its part in ensuring that leaders are provided with the support and the working conditions they need to carry out their role properly. As Fiedler (1967: 276) emphasized: 'If we wish to increase organizational and group effectiveness we must learn not only to train leaders more effectively but also to build an organizational environment in which the leaders can perform well.'

CASE STUDY

Leadership development at Cargill

Cargill is an international provider of food, agricultural and risk management products and services. Those in Cargill's different talent pools, such as the 'Next Generation Leaders' and 'Emerging Leaders' undertake both formal and informal development. In Cargill's high-performance Leadership Academy, entrants learn about the fundamentals of leadership and management in the company and work through a number of accelerated leadership modules, gaining the knowledge to enable them to lead Cargill businesses. All of these courses are interspersed with more challenging projects and work assignments. Cargill corporate leaders also take part in the Leadership Academy, where they learn transformational leadership skills and the essentials of coaching and mentoring in formal programmes and informal learning activities, all of which form an important part of their leadership development.

CASE STUDY
Leadership development at Diageo

At Diageo, the international beverages company, a series of development strategies, particularly for leadership, have been based on Diageo's five values, which were created as the common heartbeat of all the component businesses. The values – 'Be the best', 'Passionate about consumers', 'Proud of what we do', 'Freedom to succeed' and 'Valuing each other' – have become central to Diageo's success, alongside a comprehensive performance management framework. Conversations about performance are now on a 'partnership' basis, where managers, with their employees, are expected to discuss the latter's aspirations and how their growth needs can be satisfied by the business.

The company's first leadership development programme, 1998's 'Building Diageo talent', was designed to help link strategy and organizational performance with individual performance. This had many components, including coaching and benchmarking for leadership development for 4,000 managers. Over the past six years, the company's leadership training has evolved to focus more on building 'a core Diageo mindset'. The senior team has prioritized developing a 'total talent strategy' and HR processes have been thoroughly embedded in management thinking worldwide.

CASE STUDY
Leadership development at HML

At HML (a financial services company) the leadership development programme for middle and senior managers consisted of the following elements:

- orientation event – introduction and contracting;
- action learning sets (sets of six people, three sets in one programme group);
- four modules: profit, client, effectiveness, engagement;
- big event – transformational residential learning;
- self-directed modules;
- individual 360-degree feedback – benchmark scores;
- accreditation and celebration event.

Leadership development – the views of Pierre Nanterme CEO of Accenture the global professional services firm with 330,000 employees

The following answer was given by Pierre Nanterme to the question: 'You served as Accenture's chief leadership officer at one point. What's your philosophy on the best way to train employees to be better leaders?'

I learned a lot through that role, which frankly I had to figure out a bit, because it was quite new. My background is around economics and finance; yet of course, in professional services, talent is key. And for many of our clients, whatever the industry, they all are coming to me saying their No. 1 challenge is getting the right talent. So first, I figured out that leadership and talent is the name of the game. Second, it's all about how you motivate people, how you're making sure they're going to stretch their own boundaries.

It's about selecting, hiring the best people, but that's not enough. Performance management is extraordinarily important to get people to their very best. Do you feel good in your role? If yes, that's the perfect time for you to experiment with something new, to get out of your comfort zone. This willingness to learn is probably the most important thing for leaders of today and tomorrow.

Management development

Management development is concerned with improving the performance of managers in their present roles and preparing them to take on greater responsibilities in the future. It was defined by Peters (2010: 28), as: 'A complex process by which individuals learn to perform effectively in a management role.' A systematic approach to management development is necessary to meet the needs of organizations for the talented managers they require and because the increasingly onerous demands made on line managers mean that they have to possess a wider range of developed skills than ever before.

The object of management development is to find ways in which the organization can produce, mainly from within, a supply of managers better equipped for their jobs at all levels. The principal method of doing this is to ensure that managers gain the right sequence and variety of experience, in good time, which will equip them for whatever level of responsibility they have the ability to reach in the their career. This experience can be supplemented – but never replaced – by courses carefully timed and designed to meet particular needs. Management development policies and programmes involve the use of formal, semi-formal and informal approaches.

Formal approaches to management development

Formal approaches to management development consist of learning events that are planned and provided by the organization. These should be based on the identification of development needs. The methods of defining learning needs described in Chapter 18 can be used to determine collective needs. For individuals, performance management reviews are an important means of producing personal development plans and learning contracts as described in Chapter 5. This can be done more systematically at development centres. These consist of a concentrated (usually one or two days) programme of exercises, tests and interviews designed to identify managers' development needs and to provide counselling on their careers. Competency frameworks can be used as a means of identifying and expressing development needs and pointing the way to self-managed learning programmes or the provision of learning opportunities by the organization.

Formal learning events can usefully help managers to learn about organizational policies and procedures such as budgeting or performance management. They can also provide onboarding (induction) training for newly recruited managers and compliance training in health and safety etc. Especially in the latter case, online learning may be better than a face-to-face training course. Formal events also have a part to play in developing soft skills because of the opportunities they provide for simulations and practice. But in all cases, attention must be paid to ensuring that the learning is transferred.

The content of training programmes and events is determined by established learning needs. But the significance of the line manager's contribution to the implementation of people management practices suggests that a choice from the following areas could be included:

- assessing potential;
- coaching and instructing;
- conducting challenging conversations.
- handling absenteeism;
- handling discipline;
- job design;
- managing onboarding;
- performance management;

- providing feedback;
- selection interviewing;

These are best made available in bite-sized learning modules using digital techniques as well as more formal classroom training. The self-direction of learning through these modules should be encouraged and L&D should take the responsibility of keeping managers informed on sources of learning materials either provided by the firm or available elsewhere (curating).

The following checklist on planning and delivering management training events was produced by the CIPD (2017):

1 Integrate the programme with the organization's business strategy.

2 Set multiple aligned goals for participants.

3 Keep senior management support.

4 Encourage participants to seek opportunities to apply new learning.

5 Consider a range of post-training activities.

6 Ensure the programme's goals and actions are integrated with the organization's performance management system.

7 Maintain opportunities for participants to practise and get feedback on their learning.

8 Enhance learning by using action learning sets.

9 Make participants accountable for applying their learning.

10 Create opportunities for participants to teach others.

11 Use after-event reviews and conduct follow-up with participants.

12 Use a mentor or colleague to hold participants accountable for applying learning.

An extended development programme may incorporate a selection of relevant formal events as well as semi-formal approaches as described below.

Semi-formal approaches to management development

Management development processes that do not involve formal training events or online learning may provide a better alternative because they can be tailored to meet learning needs, make use of experiential learning and encourage self-development. Semi-formal approaches consist of planned experience, self-directed learning, individual coaching and mentoring, action and outdoor learning, team building (group dynamics) and interactive skills development.

Planned experience

Planned experience gives individuals extra opportunities to learn that would be unavailable if they remain in one job. It can be provided by job rotation (moving from one job to another), taking part in project teams or task groups, or secondment within or outside the organization. It can be organized by a learning and development professional in conjunction with the individual and his or her manager. Secondments can work well as long as they provide relevant experience from which the individual can learn. The learning that is expected to take place should be defined in advance (the L&D professional can help to do this) and agreed with the manager of the internal department or an authority in the external organization where the secondment is taking place. The L&D professional can follow up to check that everything has gone according to plan.

Structured self-development

Structured self-development is the process of drawing up a self-directed learning programme with, if necessary, the help of a learning and development professional adviser, setting it out in a personal development plan and agreeing it as a learning contract with the individual's manager and/or the adviser.

Coaching and mentoring

An individual approach to learning can be achieved through coaching or mentoring. Coaching is a personal and usually one-to-one approach to help people develop their skills and levels of competence. Mentoring is the process of using specially selected and trained individuals (mentors) to provide guidance, pragmatic advice and continuing support that will help the person or persons allocated to them to learn and develop.

Action learning

Action learning is a method originated by Revans (1989) of helping managers to develop their talents by exposing them to real problems or issues facing the organization on the principle that managers learn best by doing rather than being taught. An 'action learning set' of five or six managers is brought together to investigate and solve the problem. They are required to analyse the problem, formulate recommendations and then instead of being satisfied with a report, take action. The project has to be managed by the group like any other project: deciding on objectives, planning resources, initiating action and monitoring progress. A 'set adviser' (an external consultant or a member of the L&D function) sits in with group regularly to clarify the process and help its members to learn about the management issues that have emerged from what they are doing and from each other. The programme involves change embedded in the web of relationships called 'the client system'. The web comprises three separate networks: the power network, the information network and the motivational network (this is what Revans means by 'who can, who knows and who cares'). The adviser's role is to point out the dynamics of this system as the work of diagnosis and implementation proceeds.

Team-building

Team building is the development of the effectiveness of teams through training and indoor or outdoor exercises or games. The aim is to develop well-functioning teams with the following characteristics:

- team members work well together;
- team members listen to each other;
- the atmosphere tends to be informal, comfortable and relaxed;
- team members are multi-skilled as required to get the task done;
- many decisions are reached by consensus;
- action is taken by means of assignments that are clear and accepted;
- team leaders provide effective leadership but do not dominate their teams – the issue is not who controls but how to get the work done.

Team-building activities were originated by Kurt Lewin (1947) as 'group dynamics' the aim of which was to improve the ways in which people work in groups by increasing self-understanding and awareness of social processes and by enhancing interactive skills. They consist of a minimum amount of instruction on the principles of good teamwork and the maximum amount of practice, analysis and discussion. Team-building programmes usually include exercises – groups of people undertake a task or project and then with the help of a facilitator analyse how they performed as a team and reach conclusions on how they could do better. Use may be made of interactive skills training or outdoor learning (see below) or gamification (see Chapter 13),

Interactive skills training

The aim of interactive skills training is to increase the ability of individuals to work well with others. It is based on the assumption that limitations on managerial effectiveness do not necessarily occur within each job boundary but on the interface between jobs. There are no preconceived rules on how people should interact. The way it happens depends on the situation and the people in it. This is what the training helps people to analyse.

The training takes place through groups and enables people to practise interactive skills – this is the only way that such skills can be developed. A facilitator uses behaviour analysis techniques to provide feedback on performance and encourage participants to work out for themselves the significance of what they have learnt and how they can apply this learning. The processes that can be used include transactional analysis (an approach to understanding how people behave and express themselves through transactions with others), behaviour modelling (the use of positive reinforcement and corrective feedback to change behaviour) and neurolinguistic programming or NLP (teaching people to programme their reactions to others and develop strategies for interacting with them).

Outdoor learning

Outdoor learning gets individuals or groups of people to carry out tests or projects involving physical activities such as mountain walking, rock climbing, caving and canoeing. The activities will probably be new to most participants. The rationale of outdoor learning is that the tests are paradigms of the sort of challenges people meet at work but their unfamiliar nature helps them to learn more about how well they work under pressure, alone or with others. A facilitator is there to help participants learn from their experiences.

Informal approaches to management development

Informal approaches to management development make use of the learning experiences managers encounter during their everyday work. Managers are learning every time they are confronted with an unusual problem, an unfamiliar task or a move to a different job. They then have to evolve new ways of dealing with the situation. They will learn if they reflect on what they did in order to determine how and why it contributed to success or failure. This retrospective or reflective learning will be effective if managers can apply it successfully in the future.

Managers also learn from their managers. This may include how not to do things as well as what to do. Again, they will learn more if they have the capacity to reflect on what they have learnt and apply it to their own circumstances.

Experiential and reflective learning is potentially the most powerful form of learning. It comes naturally to some managers. They seem to absorb, unconsciously and by some process of osmosis, the lessons from their experience, although in fact, they have probably developed a capacity for almost instantaneous analysis, which they store in their mental databank to retrieve when necessary.

But many managers either find it difficult to do this sort of analysis or do not recognize the need. This is where informal methods can be used to encourage and help managers to learn more effectively. These comprise:

- emphasizing self-assessment and the identification of development needs by getting managers to assess their own performance against agreed objectives and analyse the factors that contributed to effective or less effective performance – this can be provided through performance management;

- getting managers to produce their own personal development plans – self-directed learning programmes;

- encouraging managers to discuss their problems and opportunities with their manager, colleagues or mentors to establish for themselves what they need to learn or be able to do.

The role of the organization

The traditional view is that the organization need not concern itself with management development. The natural process of selection and the pressure of competition will ensure the survival of the fittest. Managers are born not made. Cream rises to the top (but then so does scum). Management development has also been seen as a formal process using management inventories, multicoloured replacement charts, 'Cook's tours' around different departments for newly recruited graduates, detailed job rotation programmes, elaborate points schemes to appraise personal characteristics and lots of formal courses operating on the 'sheep-dip' principle (ie everyone undergoes them).

The true role of the organization in management development lies somewhere between these two extremes. On the one hand, it is not enough, in conditions of rapid growth (when they exist) and change, to leave everything to chance – to trial and error. On the other hand, elaborate management development programmes cannot successfully be imposed on the organization. A mix of formal, semi-formal and informal methods is required that has to fit the organization's context and specific requirements.

The success of any management development programme depends upon the degree that there is commitment to it at all levels. It is not a separate activity to be handed over to a professional and forgotten or ignored. The development of members of their team must be recognized as a natural and essential part of any manager's job. But the lead must come from the top.

The role of the individual

The ability to manage is eventually something individuals develop for themselves while carrying out their normal duties. But they will do this much better if they are given encouragement, guidance and opportunities by their organization and their managers.

As Drucker perceptively wrote many years ago (1955: 162): 'Development is always self-development. Nothing could be more absurd than for the enterprise to assume responsibility for the development of a man (sic). The responsibility rests with the individual, his abilities, his efforts.' This point and the following point are still valid despite the sole use of the male pronoun.

'Every manager in a business has the opportunity to encourage individual self-development or to stifle it, to direct it or to misdirect it. He (sic) should be specifically assigned the responsibility for helping all men working with him to focus, direct and apply their self-development efforts productively.

And every company can provide systematic development challenges to its managers'. Douglas McGregor (1960: 192) made a similar point when he wrote:

> Managers are grown – they are neither born nor made: The individual will grow into what he (sic) is capable of becoming, providing we can create the proper conditions for that growth.
>
> The ability to manage is eventually something individuals mainly develop for themselves while carrying out their normal duties. But they will do this much better if they are given encouragement, guidance and opportunities by their organization and their managers.

The role of learning and development professionals

L&D professionals play an important part in management development. They interpret the needs of the business and advise on how management development as a business-led activity can play its part in meeting these needs. They encourage managers to carry out their developmental activities, provide guidance as required, curate learning material and act as coaches and mentors. They also, of course, conduct or manage formal learning events and programmes, but their most important role is to help in developing a climate in which managers can grow.

KEY LEARNING POINTS

Leadership and management development defined

Leadership and management development programmes ensure that managers have the leadership and managerial qualities required to achieve success.

Leadership

Leadership means inspiring people to do their best to achieve a desired result. It involves developing and communicating a vision for the future, motivating people and securing their engagement.

Management

Defined as deciding what to do and then getting it done through the effective use of resources.

Leadership development compared with management development

Leadership development tends to be concerned with nurturing the softer skills of leadership through various educational processes, including formal learning events and programmes and coaching.

Management development relies more on ensuring that managers have the right sequence of experience, which may be supplemented by self-directed learning and courses on management techniques.

Leadership development

Leadership development programmes prepare people for leadership roles and situations beyond their current experience.

Management development

Management development is concerned with improving the performance of managers in their present roles, preparing them to take on greater responsibilities in the future and also developing their leadership skills.

Formal approaches to management development consist of learning events and digital learning programmes.

Semi-formal approaches consist of planned experience, structured self-development, coaching and mentoring, action learning and team-building.

Informal approaches make use of the learning experiences that managers encounter during the course of their everyday work.

Responsibility for management development

Individual managers are largely responsible for their own development but need guidance, support and encouragement from their own managers and L&D professionals.

References

Bennis, W G (1989) *On Becoming a Leader*, Addison Wesley, New York

Birkinshaw, J (2010) An experiment in reinvention, *People Management*, 15 July, pp 22–24

Burgoyne, J (2010) Crafting a leadership and management development strategy, in *Gower Handbook of Leadership and Management Development*, eds J Gold, R Thorpe and A Mumford, Gower, Farnham, pp 42–55

CIPD (2017) *Developing managers to manage sustainable employee engagement, health and well-being*, CIPD, London

Dixon, N F (1994) *On the Psychology of Military Incompetence*, Pimlico, London

Drucker, P (1955) *The Practice of Management*, Heinemann, Oxford

Fiedler, F E (1967) *A Theory of Leadership Effectiveness*, McGraw-Hill, New York

Hersey, P and Blanchard, K H (1998) *Management of Organizational Behaviour*, Prentice-Hall, Englewood Cliffs, NJ

Kotter, J P (1991) Power, dependence and effective management, in *Managing People and Organizations*, ed J Gabarro, Harvard Business School Publications, Boston, MA

Lewin, K (1947) Frontiers in group dynamics, *Human Relations*, **1** (1), pp 5–42

McGregor, D (1960) *The Human Side of Enterprise,* McGraw-Hill, New York

Mintzberg, H (2004) Enough leadership, *Harvard Business Review,* November, p 22

Peters, K (2010) National and international developments in leadership and management development, in *Gower Handbook of Leadership and Management Development,* eds J Gold, R Thorpe and A Mumford, Gower, Farnham, pp 23–38

Pfeffer, J and Sutton R I (2006) *Hard Facts, Dangerous Half-Truths & Total Nonsense*, Harvard Business School Press, Boston

Revans, R W (1989) *Action Learning, London*, Blond and Briggs

Tamkin, P, Pearson, G, Hirsh, W and Constable, S (2010) *Exceeding Expectation: The principles of outstanding leadership*, The Work Foundation, London

Yukl, G (2006) *Leadership in Organizations*, 6th edn, Prentice-Hall, Upper Saddle River, NJ

24

Sales training

Introduction

Sales training aims to equip sales representatives with the knowledge, skills, attitudes and habits required to meet or exceed their sales targets. Because it is essential to develop these attributes, few organizations with a sales force neglect this form of training even if they only pay lip service to others. This chapter starts with a description of the content of sales training and continues with an examination of the methods that can be used.

The content of sales training

Sales training has been described by Matthews and Schenk (2018) as a process of 'sales enablement' which aims to equip sales people with the knowledge and skills, understanding of customers and working environment they need.

Knowledge

Sales representatives need to know the products or services they sell – not just what they are, their specifications – but the benefits they provide for those who use them. Any special characteristics need to be highlighted, particularly those that make the product or service unique and/or mean that it is superior to any provided by the competition. Representatives are trained to promote these benefits and not to dwell on the nature of the product itself. As Matthews and Schenk (2018: 5): commented: 'Buyers are not so much interested in what a product, service or solution *is* as what it *does*. They want to know how it will solve their challenges or reach a business goal. That requires a very different selling approach that translates capabilities into business value. This need cannot be met by adding a little bit of customer-centric color to an otherwise product-centric approach.'

They will also need to know about the company, its customers and its competitors. And they have to be familiar with sales administration procedures.

Skills

The skills needed by sales representatives vary according to the product. Persuading corner shops to buy tinned soup is different to negotiating the sale of 50 passenger jets with an airline. But there are some basic skills all representatives use, albeit in different ways. These are prospecting (looking for likely sales), making the approach, describing the product and its benefits (in formal presentations or informally in a retail outlet), handling objections, closing the sale and handling complaints.

In addition, representatives need analytical ability. They should know how to analyse their product or service into its technical characteristics and, most importantly, its selling points — its properties. They also need to know how to analyse their customers from the viewpoint of their buying habits and the features of the product that are most likely to appeal to them. And they must be able to analyse themselves - their own strengths and weaknesses. Sales representatives have to be helped in their initial and continuing training (it never stops) to gain the confidence and self-belief (self-efficacy) they need and to be equipped with the motivation to go out and sell – a task that requires courage, determination and persistence.

Customers

The importance of customer service needs to be emphasized. Representatives have to learn to understand, indeed tolerate, potential and existing customers and need to appreciate the levels of service they are expected to provide.

Working arrangements

Representatives need to know about the work habits they are expected to adopt: organizing time, planning activities, following up leads, maintaining records and submitting reports.

Methods of sales training

It is essential to base sales training, especially in the case of formal or online training, on a thorough analysis of learning needs covering knowledge, skills and abilities. These should be established by detailed analysis of the role of sales representatives and the context in which they operate. The context will include the company, the product or service to be sold, the market, competitors, customers, the allocation to sales territories, the management and supervision they will receive, and how sales are administered.

Sales training can be provided in classrooms, online, by sales supervisors or managers (coaching), by 'buddying' or through working alongside colleagues (social or collaborative learning). It will be most effective if a combination of some if not all these methods is used. It should be continuous; there can never be a time in a sales representative's career when she or he would not benefit from some form of training or development.

Classroom training

Classroom training is still widely used, especially for new starters (induction or onboarding training), to lay the foundations for or develop the skills that will be used and to impart product knowledge and understanding of the company, its markets and its customers. Many firms have their own sales trainers but widespread use is made of the multitude of sales training providers that are available.

Classroom training should rely mainly on an interactive approach with the emphasis on facilitated discussions, simulations, games and practice in exercising skills. The issue of transferring learning will need to be addressed (see Chapter 21). But businesses are relying more on learning methods that are better suited to the needs of sales representatives working on their own out in the field. In this context they will benefit from informal, bite-sized or micro-learning content that can be accessed on-demand, wherever and whenever it might be needed. However, as Matthews and Schenk (2018: 95) point out: 'Most salespeople tend to be people-orientated, and there is a benefit of getting them together to interact and learn from each other.' And classroom training provides opportunities for them to practise skills in role plays and simulations.

Online learning

Digital methods as described in Chapter 16 are increasingly being used for sales training. Online learning through smartphones or mobiles can provide 'learning on the move' – bite-sized learning on demand which can be self-paced. It can replace classroom training but it also supplements it, for example, by making available pre-event introductory material or material for applying and developing the learning after the event.

Self-paced digital content can be put into the everyday workflow so that learning can be delivered at the at the point of need. Sales representatives can then have the learning resources from which they can benefit built into the systems they use to perform their jobs. Experienced representatives can record videos presenting good practice and including tips and tricks or 'win' stories. These can be converted into formal learning content and made available for future reference,

Virtual learning environments and webinars can be set up to cater for online collective and interactive learning. Virtual and augmented reality technology can be used in training events to help sales people learn interactive skills. By allowing the learner to practise, repeat, and correct the targeted skills, greater confidence in the new skill can be gained and the learning is more likely to be transferred.

The continuous training role of sales management

Sales managers have a key part to play in training their sales staff. It begins with onboarding – ensuring that newly appointed representatives understand their role and how they are expected to carry it out, and arranging for them to learn from an experienced representative (shadowing). It then becomes a continuous process. Every time a target is set and results are reviewed presents an opportunity to identify a learning need and to provide one-to-one coaching. Sales managers can analyse sales 'wins and losses' to identify what can be learned from them, convey the outcome to their team and share it with other managers to build up a body of learning material that can become part of online learning content. They need to be trained themselves on their responsibilities for developing their staff and the skills they have to use (providing feedback, reviewing performance, identifying learning needs and coaching).

KEY LEARNING POINTS

Sales training defined

Sales training aims to equip sales representatives with the knowledge, skills, attitudes and habits required to meet or exceed their sales targets

The aim of sales training

Sales training aims to equip sales people with the knowledge and skills, understanding of customers and working environment they need.

The content of sales training

Sales training can be provided in classrooms, online, by sales supervisors or managers (coaching), by 'buddying' or through working alongside colleagues (social or collaborative learning).

   It will be most effective if a combination of some if not all of these methods is used. It should be continuous; there can never be a time in a sales representative's career when he or she would not benefit from some form of training or development.

Reference

Matthews, B and Schenk, T (2018) *Sales Enablement,* Wiley, Hoboken, NJ

25

Apprenticeships

Introduction

Apprenticeships exist to meet the skills needs of employers and to give young people the opportunity to embark on a worthwhile career. This chapter starts with a description of the nature of apprenticeships and then describes how they should function as defined in the standards developed in the UK in recent years.

Apprenticeships defined

Apprenticeships are paid jobs with an accompanying skills development programme provided by on-and off-the-job training. They take between one and four years to complete (the minimum length is 12 months) and in the UK are available in 1,500 occupations across more than 170 industries. Successful apprentices can receive a nationally recognized qualification on completing their contract.

Apprenticeships are built upon an agreed partnership between the employer and the individual apprentice. The employer undertakes to provide the education and training, relevant experience from which the apprentice will learn and the end-point assessment. The apprentice is expected to learn and work diligently to complete the apprenticeship.

Apprenticeships should be distinguished from traineeships. The latter last up to six months although, like apprenticeships they provide training, education and work experience.

How apprenticeships function

The training of apprentices in the UK is regulated by the Education and Skills Funding Agency (a government organization). It is made available either wholly or partly in-house by the employer or delivered on behalf of the employer by a registered training provider, college or university. This training teaches the apprentice the knowledge, skills and behaviours set out in the apprenticeship standard so they can achieve occupational competence. The regulations cover education and training arrangements and the application of apprenticeship standards. Quality indicators for apprenticeships have been set by the Institute for Apprenticeships and Technical Education (an employer-led body sponsored by the Department of Education.

Training and qualifications

On-the-job training is provided by employers but apprentices must spend at least 20 per cent of their working hours completing off-the-job training. It can be flexible and does not have to mean one day out of the workplace every week. Most employers contract training providers to deliver education and off-the-job training. The training provider has a key role to play in providing off-the-job training, assessing progress towards achieving their qualifications and supporting apprentices generally during their apprenticeship. They work very closely with the employer to ensure that the apprentice receives:

- an induction programme on starting;
- a detailed training plan (including on-the-job training)
- regular progress reviews
- opportunities to put into practice off-the-job learning so that they can achieve their qualifications/requirements of the apprenticeship
- mentoring and general support throughout the apprenticeship.

The frequency with which training takes place can vary, for example one day a week, part of a working day, or blocks of time. Some apprenticeships begin with a period of training to get the apprentice work-ready. The apprentice may also need to study for mathematics and English qualifications but this is not counted as part of the 20 per cent minimum off-the-job training requirement. The employer must allow the apprentice time to study for this within their normal working hours.

The main qualification levels in England, Wales and Northern Ireland are:

- Level 2 Intermediate – equivalent to GCSE
- Level 3 Advanced – equivalent to A level or NVQ 3
- Levels 4, 5 Higher – equivalent to foundation degree, Higher National Certificate or NVQ 4 (4), or Higher National Diploma (5)
- Levels 6 and 7 Degree – equivalent to bachelor's or master's degree

Apprenticeship standards

Apprenticeship standards were introduced in response to the recommendations of the Richard Report (2012), which stated that apprenticeship outcomes should be 'meaningful and relevant for employers'. Standards for different types of apprenticeships are developed by 'trailblazer' groups that represent groups of employers and sector organizations, and will always include an end-point assessment.

The standards require an employer to conclude an apprenticeship agreement with their apprentices. This gives details of what the employer undertakes to do for the apprentice, including how long they will be employed, the training they will receive, their working conditions and the qualifications they are working towards. The employer must also agree an 'apprenticeship commitment statement' with their apprentice and the training provider which includes the planned content and schedule for training, what is expected and offered by the employer, the training organization and the apprentice and how to resolve queries or complaints.

The standards set out the requirements for 'End-point Assessment' – a demanding independent assessment at the end of the apprenticeship, carried out by a registered apprenticeship assessment organization. They may also provide for certification by the Institute for Apprenticeships & Technical Education which has produced the quality indicators set out below.

Quality indicators

The Institute for Apprenticeships & Technical Education measures the cumulative entry to and achievement of apprenticeships by occupation, level and age group compared to the mix in the labour market. It records the number of employers recruiting and training apprentices by size and sector and monitors standards development and implementation by level in relation to occupational maps. The retention of apprentices is measured up to sign-off for end point assessment and the ratio of entry to success (including grades) in that assessment. The Institute also records where the apprentice goes on to be employed (with the training employer or with a different employer).

Specifically, the Institute specifies the following apprenticeship quality indicators:

- A challenging and stretching training and learning programme developed and delivered with the active involvement of the employer(s), which uses a range of effective on- and off-the-job training methods as well as work itself.

- A motivating and supportive workplace with coaching and mentoring support for the apprentice and continuous assessment of progress.

- An extended period of on- and off-the-job training (at least twelve months duration with a minimum of 20% of the time in off-the-job training) which develops not only the knowledge and skills required but also the additional transferable skills which allow an apprentice to deal with new employers, situations, problems and equipment.

CASE STUDY

BT Fleet Solutions apprenticeships

Background

BT Fleet Solutions is a subsidiary of BT Group with over 120,000 vehicles on their books. The service and maintenance of this fleet is carried out in 64 garages. These workshops are the setting for their apprenticeship scheme, which supports and trains young people to become qualified motor technicians with a job guarantee and career path, both within BT Fleet and the wider BT Group for the future.

SOURCE CIPD, 2018

The Apprenticeship Levy Scheme

The Apprenticeship Levy Scheme was established by the government in 2017 to encourage the extended use of apprenticeships to provide the skilled people the country needs. Under the scheme, all employers with a wage bill greater than £3m pay 0.5 per cent of their payroll into a central fund. In return they receive vouchers, which can be used to fund apprenticeships.

But research by the CIPD (2017) revealed that only 9 per cent of organizations planned to use the levy to create new apprenticeships, while 18 per cent said they would use the funding to enhance existing apprenticeship training programmes.

Reform of the apprenticeship system

The CIPD (2020) made the following recommendations on the reform of apprenticeships based on its research:

- Remove any narrow or overlapping apprenticeship standards.
- Put more consistent and explicit focus in apprenticeship standards on the development of broader transferable 'essential' skills alongside technical skills.
- Support greater collaboration through strengthened sectoral and local skills partnerships.
- Ensure a greater share of apprenticeship opportunities are for the under-25s by requiring employers to co-invest in over-25 apprentices' training.

KEY LEARNING POINTS

Apprenticeships defined

Apprenticeships are in paid jobs with an accompanying skills development programme provided by on- and off-the-job training and planned experience. They take between one and four years to complete (the minimum length is 12 months).

Apprenticeships are built upon an agreed partnership between the employer and the individual apprentice. The employer undertakes to provide the education and training, relevant experience from which the apprentice will learn and the end-point assessment. The apprentice is expected to learn and work diligently to complete the apprenticeship.

Training

On-the-job training is provided by employers but apprentices must spend at least 20 per cent of their working hours completing off-the-job training.

Most employers contract training providers to deliver education and off-the-job training. The training provider has a key role to play in providing off-the-job training, assessing progress towards achieving their qualifications and supporting apprentices generally during their apprenticeship. They work very closely with the employer.

References

Chartered Institute of Personnel and Development (CIPD) (2017) *The Apprenticeship Levy,* CIPD, London

CIPD (2018) *Apprenticeship Case Studies,* CIPD, London

CIPD (2020) *Making Apprenticeships Future-fit,* CIPD, London

Richard, D (2012) *Richard Review of Apprenticeships*, Department for Business, Innovation and Skills, London

PART SEVEN

Conclusion

26

Learning and development trends and issues

In recent years, learning and development has shifted towards a more learner-centric perspective. It is less concerned with how to plan, run and evaluate training courses and impose them on employees. Instead, the major preoccupation is understanding how people learn and knowing what the best environment is in which they *will* learn. These considerations dictate their role to L&D professionals. The focus is primarily on workplace learning – including the concept of 'learning in-the-flow of work' – and on self-directed learning in which learners manage their own learning with the support of their line managers and the help of L&D professionals. But increased attention is also being paid to remote learning, especially following the COVID-19 pandemic.

Trends

The CIPD (2019) listed the following shifts in L&D policy and practice:

1 Focus on business needs not L&D priorities.

2 L&D outputs informed by metrics not guesses.

3 Learning underpinned by science not good ideas.

4 L&D shifting to a curator-concierge approach not just creator.

5 User-choice and co-creation, not prescription learning.

6 Social learning, not just formal.

7 Just-in-time and in-the-flow learning, not delayed.

8 Bite-sized learning, not just feasts.

9 Digital-mobile learning not just face-to-face.

10 Measuring learning value not volume.

Issues

The major issues facing L&D are the needs to:

- Ensure that L&D policy and practice supports the achievement of the organization's strategic objectives.

- Shift away from a focus on running formal training courses to the promotion of workplace learning and the provision of help and guidance to line managers in carrying out their responsibilities for learning and development in their departments. This is by no means straightforward. Everyone recognizes a training course when they see one. The subtleties of workplace learning and the problems of getting line managers involved and ensuring they have the skills required are less obvious. Considerable powers of influence and persuasion are required on the part of L&D specialists.

- Encourage and support self-directed learning. Again, a less obvious requirement than the delivery of learning events but nevertheless important.

- Extend the use of digital learning. This means possessing expertise in selecting and developing the technology and fitting it into a blended learning programme.

- Responding to the challenges following the COVID-19 pandemic, especially the shift to home working.

The issues associated with the pandemic were summed up well by Elizabeth Crowley, Senior Policy Adviser, CIPD (2020: 2) who wrote:

> These are certainly challenging times, but they also potentially offer us the opportunity to do things differently. Already we are seeing many organisations leveraging the technologies needed to work and learn any time, any place, to support learning in the flow of work. Now is the time to harness this trend further and ensure that we do as much as we can now to support individuals and organisations to prepare for the future.
>
> Digital solutions will of course not replace other forms of development, but the increasing quality of online learning coupled with scalability, accessibility, and the ability to personalise this type of learning highlights its potential to play a far stronger future role in supporting workplace and adult skills development.

References

Chartered Institute of Personnel and Development (2019) *Learning and Development Evolving Practice*, CIPD, London

Crowley, E (2020) *Learning and Skills at Work 2020*, CIPD, London

AUTHOR INDEX

SUBJECT INDEX

EU Representative (GPSR)

Authorised Rep Compliance Ltd, Ground Floor, 71 Lower Baggot Street, Dublin, D02 P593, Ireland

www.arccompliance.com

www.ingramcontent.com/pod-product-compliance
Ingram Content Group UK Ltd.
Pitfield, Milton Keynes, MK11 3LW, UK
UKHW061543081025
463716UK00006B/42